Tact and the
Pedagogical Relation

PAEDAGOGICA

Norm Friesen and Karsten Kenklies
General Editors

Vol. 1

The Paedagogica series is part of the Peter Lang Education list.
Every volume is peer reviewed and meets
the highest quality standards for content and production.

PETER LANG
New York • Berlin • Brussels • Lausanne • Oxford

Tact and the Pedagogical Relation

Introductory Readings

Edited by Norm Friesen

PETER LANG
New York • Berlin • Brussels • Lausanne • Oxford

Library of Congress Cataloging-in-Publication Data

Names: Friesen, Norm, editor.
Title: Tact and the pedagogical relation: introductory readings / edited by Norm Friesen.
Description: New York: Peter Lang, 2022.
Series: Paedagogica; Vol. 1 | ISSN 2771-6481 (print) | ISSN 2771-649X (online)
Includes bibliographical references and index.
Identifiers: LCCN 2021053756 (print) | LCCN 2021053757 (ebook)
ISBN 978-1-4331-9094-0 (hardback) | ISBN 978-1-4331-9098-8 (paperback)
ISBN 978-1-4331-9095-7 (ebook pdf) | ISBN 978-1-4331-9096-4 (epub)
Subjects: LCSH: Teachers—Psychology. | Teaching—Psychological aspects. | Teacher-student relationships.
Classification: LCC LB2840 .T34 2022 (print) | LCC LB2840 (ebook) | DDC 370.15—dc23/eng/20220124
LC record available at https://lccn.loc.gov/2021053756
LC ebook record available at https://lccn.loc.gov/2021053757
DOI 10.3726/b19251

Bibliographic information published by **Die Deutsche Nationalbibliothek**.
Die Deutsche Nationalbibliothek lists this publication in the "Deutsche Nationalbibliografie"; detailed bibliographic data are available on the Internet at http://dnb.d-nb.de/.

© 2022 Peter Lang Publishing, Inc., New York
80 Broad Street, 5th floor, New York, NY 10004
www.peterlang.com

All rights reserved.
Reprint or reproduction, even partially, in all forms such as microfilm, xerography, microfiche, microcard, and offset strictly prohibited.

This book is dedicated to my students.

"the study of pedagogy ... can only begin with the description of the educator in... relationship to the one being educated."

Wilhelm Dilthey, 1888.

Table of Contents

Acknowledgements   xi
Illustrations   xiii
Editor's Introduction   1

Prefigurations
Chapter One: J.H. Pestalozzi: Letter to a Friend on His Work at Stans   15
Chapter Two: J.F. Herbart: Introductory Lecture to Students in Pedagogy   25
Chapter Three: F.D.E. Schleiermacher: Outlines of the Art of Education—
    Introductory Lecture—Selections   39

Definitions
Chapter Four: H. Nohl: Thoughts on the Educational Practice of the
    Individual with Special Reference to the Findings of Freud and Adler   61
Chapter Five: H. Nohl: The Pedagogical Relation and the Formative Community 75
Chapter Six: J. Muth: Pedagogical Tact: Study of a Contemporary Form of
    Educational and Instructional Engagement (Selections)   85

Reconfigurations

Chapter Seven: E. Fink: The Questionableness of the Modern Educator 117
Chapter Eight: O.F. Bollnow: Risk and Failure in Education 137
Chapter Nine: W. Lippitz: Otherness and "Alienness" in Pedagogical Contexts 153
Chapter Ten: J. Zirfas: Pedagogical Tact: Ten Theses 175

Index 197

Acknowledgements

For his advice and for the time and effort of his students, I would first like to thank Dr. Prof. Malte Brinkmann of the Institute of Educational Studies of the Humboldt University of Berlin. During my visits to Berlin, he and I were able to discuss various options and strategies for selecting and organizing the texts included in this collection. Also, in the demanding task translating some of the texts included here, Malte Brinkmann made available the time and skills of his graduate students. In this regard, I would especially like to thank Johannes Türstig for his invaluable assistance with Chapter Seven, *The Questionableness of the Modern Educator*. I would also like to thank Sophia Zedlitz for her initial translation of both texts by Herman Nohl included here (Chapters Four and Five). Although this collection benefitted greatly from this assistance and the advice of Malte Brinkmann, the final decisions, both in editing and translating this collection, remain my own.

I would also like to thank Dr. Prof. Wilfried Lippitz and Jörg Zirfas for their generosity in granting permission for their work to be translated and republished, and for responding to my questions as translator. I would like to thank Wilfried Lippitz in particular for his guidance and support particularly in my initial explorations in questions of phenomenology and pedagogy as they are understood in the German context. Similarly, I would like to thank Dr. Karsten Kenklies for his assistance not only in co-translating the excerpt from Schleiermacher's lecture

(Chapter Three), but also for his patient support with my work and my developing understandings in continental pedagogy.

Last but certainly not least, thanks are also due to the German Academic Exchange Service (DAAD) for their generous assistance through their "Research Stays for University Academics" program, which supported a one-month visit in May 2014 to the Humboldt University in Berlin. It was during this time that the translation work for this volume was initiated.

Illustrations

Figure 6.1: The Didactic Triangle. (Footnote 40, p. 129; Diagram created by Editor.). 108

Figure 9.1: A Feast (Convivium) from Comenius' 1658 *Orbis Sensualium Pictus* Image (Courtesy of Archive.org). 161

Editor's Introduction

"To speak of pedagogy is to speak of everything at once."

- Jean Paul[1]

In an age of ever-increasing specialization and professionalization, this book makes the case that pedagogy is not just about teaching techniques but is instead a deeply personal and interpersonal endeavor. Pedagogy is regarded in this text both as a mode of thought and of action, relevant to the classroom, but also beyond its walls.

This collection provides readers with a series of original and in some cases canonical texts that engage with two key themes in pedagogy: "pedagogical tact" and the "pedagogical relation." The first refers to educators' attunement to the children or young people in their care, and the second to the educator's professional and *personal* relationship with a young person, for the sake of that person. Although both of these notions were originally articulated and developed in German-speaking Europe, they are receiving increasing attention in English-language articles and books by scholars such as Gert Biesta, Andrea English, Rebecca Horlacher, Max van Manen, and others.[2]

It is consequently surprising that both canonical and more recent German texts that discuss the themes of the pedagogical relation and pedagogical tact have long been unavailable or difficult to access in English: For some of the earliest texts that prefigure these two themes, this is largely due to dated and inaccurate translations that have long been out of print. The absence of more recent texts can be ascribed to a general lack of translation or "bilingual" work over the past 100 years in the field of education in general (Biesta, 2011). Thinking alone of the influence of Vygotsky or Freire (both in translation) one can only conclude that there are dozens if not hundreds more sources and oeuvres with compatible potential that remain inaccessible and unknown to the English-speaking world.

Given that the origin of the texts brought together here spans over 200 years, their nature and characteristics are quite varied. The first is a passionate letter to a friend; the ones immediately following are lectures to students or practitioners. Still later texts are excerpted from books or handbooks,[3] while the most recent are all taken from journal articles or chapters in German-language books. This introduction provides a brief overview of these varied texts and their interrelationship. Following the organization of this book's table of contents, this overview begins with texts that *prefigure* the pedagogical relation and pedagogical tact, moving through ones that give these terms fuller *definition*, and ending with their contemporary *reconfiguration*. This initial overview is then followed by further discussion of the meaning of pedagogy as it appears both in this introduction and in the texts brought together in this volume. It concludes with a consideration of the implications of this meaning for other terms and references in this collection.

Pedagogical Tact and the Pedagogical Relation

The phrase pedagogical tact was coined by J.F. Herbart in an introductory lecture to his students from 1802. Meanwhile, the pedagogical relation was named as such by Herman Nohl over 100 years later—despite the fact that the themes central to this relation can be traced at least as far back as the earliest texts included here. The subject of pedagogical tact has remained a topic of lively interest to this day—both in English and in German. However, the phrase "pedagogical relation" fell into disfavor in the German-speaking world only a few decades after being given definition by Nohl. Of course, this does not mean that the question of the actual relationship between educators and young people was no longer of interest. But the question of this relationship can be said to have been recast and reformulated—turned into the more abstract question of the relation of the self with the other, and of the encounter of what is called "ownness" with that which is "alien."

Nevertheless, favorable references to Nohl and his conception of the "pedagogical relation" have started reappearing in German scholarship in the last few years. Perhaps surprisingly, this has occurred in connection with the educational researcher John Hattie, whose meta-analyses of educational outcomes show "that the attainment of a quality student-teacher relation" is a critical factor in "student success." In particular, Hattie's findings also emphasize the importance of "the 'teacher and their passions' very directly, bringing Nohl's concept," as one author notes, "once again into play."[4]

Prefigurations

To begin with the first section in this collection, one significant theme that prefigures and later underlies both tact and the pedagogical relation is the educator's concern with the experience, feelings and "inner life" of the child: "First of all, I had to wake and give life to their inner selves," Pestalozzi says of the children in his care in his letter from Stans in Chapter One (p. 21). Pestalozzi sought to awaken this inner vitality through the "simple circumstances of domestic life"—ones that he felt were intrinsically pedagogical in and of themselves. Taking care of the children's everyday "common needs" Pestalozzi argues, helped to bring "out their natural intelligence, form their judgment, and… arouse [in them] capabilities which… cannot become active and useful till they are set free" (p. 19).

Only three years after Pestalozzi's letter, Herbart (Chapter Two) gives explicit definition to "pedagogical tact" in a lecture to an audience of male student teachers at the University of Göttingen. Tact, Herbart explains, is

> a mode of action that is dependent on… [the teacher's] feeling but that only remotely relies on certainty of belief. This is a mode of action that gives vent to feeling and expresses how one has been affected from the outside. It shows one's emotional state rather than the results of one's thinking. (p. 32)

Herbart's advice here, however, is not merely for teachers to surrender to their feelings. His approach is instead closely related to theory, and he sees tact precisely as the mediation of the generalities of theory with the specificities of practice. For theory—with its generalizations, rules and expectations—is what Herbart sees as having a special role in "attuning" teachers in their work. Herbart says that the teacher can use theory to "prepare his head as well as his heart to correctly receive, perceive, feel, and judge the phenomena awaiting him and the situation in which he will be placed" (p. 33).

Schleiermacher (Chapter Three) can be said to give Herbart's understanding of theory and practice a name—specifically, the "dignity of practice:" "Originally, it was parents who educated," Schleiermacher observes, and "they did *not* do so following a 'theory.'" It would therefore "be incorrect to say that practice gains its character and specificity only through theory." Instead, Schleiermacher concludes, theory comes afterwards, and "only makes practice more conscious" (pp. 44, 48; emphasis added). Theory for Schleiermacher—as for Herbart—is thus not so much a set of direct instructions, solutions or prescriptions, but a way of helping teachers get the right "feel" for and "awareness of" what they are doing.

Schleiermacher also laid the foundations for the idea of the pedagogical relation by coming up with a counterintuitive definition for education as a whole. Namely, that education is ultimately not about learning outcomes, students' grades or teachers' curricula, but about the *relation* between the older generation and the younger—and the responsibility of the former for the latter. What is most important for Schleiermacher is the question of the "pedagogical influence" in this relation: How the older generation—collectively and individually, consciously and unconsciously—seeks to shape and affect change in the younger. Schleiermacher's general definition of education and his concern with this influence served as the basis for Herman Nohl's definition of the pedagogical relation almost 100 years later.

Definitions

Herman Nohl (Chapters Four and Five) defines the pedagogical relation not as one between whole generational groups as Schleiermacher suggests, but between individual "representatives" of these generations—one older individual and one younger. In his canonical definition of the pedagogical relation, Nohl states that "the basis of education is the passionate relation between a mature person and one who is becoming, specifically for the sake the latter, so that he comes to his life and form" (p. 79). Again, what is paramount for Nohl is the developing inner, emotional life of "the one who is becoming" in this relationship. The perspective of this type of pedagogy, Nohl emphasizes, "is unconditionally that of the one being educated," of the child or young person (p. 65). In taking this perspective, Nohl is also able to connect the pedagogical relation with pedagogical tact—specifically by seeing in the pedagogical relation a kind of distance that gives space for the child's "becoming:" The characteristics of this relation, Nohl says, "give the educator a singular *distance* to... his student. In its most refined expression this distance is called *pedagogical tact*" (pp. 80–81).

Despite the canonical nature of his texts, Nohl's legacy was tarnished by the inclusion of references to Nazi ideology in some of his writings from the 1930s. (For example, he speaks of a "search" for the elements—both "spiritual" and "biological"—for the development the German people as a "*Volk.*"[5]). As mentioned, the phrase "pedagogical relation" has consequently all but disappeared from German pedagogical writing. But the actual phenomenon of interpersonal connection between educator and youth that Nohl identified has remained of central importance.

Jacob Muth defines "pedagogical tact" in his book of the same name (excerpted in Chapter Six) in terms of "two essential defining moments:" *reserve* and *sensitivity*. Reserve, Muth says, "is manifest in tact through its non-influence, its non-interference; it is an omission rather than an overt act" (p. 92). Muth echoes Nohl in remarking that in "the final analysis, reserve allows the other to be and to become—to become that which they are called or given, without abandoning them" (p. 92). Sensitivity, on the other hand, again reflects the importance of the feelings and inner life of the child or young person. Muth defines it as "a feeling for the 'you'…for one's fellow human being" (p. 92). Using the (then) new vocabulary of the self and the other, Muth also defines sensitivity as a feeling "for the singularity and singular rights of the other; it is a respect for the ultimate inaccessibility of the other" (p. 92).

Reconfigurations

Eugen Fink's *The Questionableness of the Modern Educator* is the first chapter in this volume that critically examines the common presuppositions underlying tact and the pedagogical relation as explored thus far. Fink's philosophical background as well as the events of the Second World War mean that not just the educator, but the nature of the human being as a whole is radically thrown into question. Through this questioning, Fink comes to see education as a deeply personal and even existential task, one that is unavoidably "part of the substance of being human" (p. 121). Fink grants education the status of something like an existential humanizing force; he describes it as "the means towards human-self relation that is most necessary to life" (p. 134). And this means for Fink that "the educator occupies" nothing less than "the most essential function in humanity" (p. 121).

Otto Friedrich Bollnow (Chapter Eight) follows Fink in questioning the legitimacy or adequacy of the contemporary educator. Bollnow was a student of Herman Nohl, but like Fink, Bollnow studied existentialist philosophy that emphasized both radical freedom and individuality, and that—like Muth—used the language of "self" and "other:" The "educator must take into account the freedom of the *other*" Bollnow writes, adding that this freedom is one that "is fundamentally beyond all pre-calculation" (p. 140). "To recognize the freedom of the other," Bollnow continues, "means also to affirm the fundamental uncertainty, risk and audacity of education" (p. 140). Education—and by extension also the pedagogical relation—is risky, audacious, and even prone to failure because the relation between the adult "self" and the younger "other" is not just a professional and transactional one. It is one that constantly requires the exercise of the teacher's trust and their entry into situations of risk. "The need to extend one's trust in these ways is something particular to educators. It is also necessarily their fate to be deceived and to fail in their trust" (p. 148).

The understanding of "the other" in the pedagogical relationship—and for the question of tact—is further developed by Wilfried Lippitz (Chapter Nine). Lippitz' focus is not so much on the other or otherness as it is on "the alien" and "alienness." Unlike "the other," the alien is not another person with whom we might meet and speak with eye-to-eye. The alien is instead an aspect of otherness or alterity which simply does not possess this symmetry. It is something we experience in terms of an immediate emotional response, for example, to a child's or young person's unexpected words or action—something that might reveal an utterly unknown aspect of their inner life. The child in this case may still be "the other," but what they might say or do is "alien." The alien is also something that is experienced in our relation to the world around us—for example, in foreign languages and cultures, or in professions or situations that are unfamiliar to us, in which we are not feeling at home. Lippitz examines the history of European pedagogical thought and everyday pedagogical engagement to understand how "that which is alien" has been treated within it. Across time, Lippitz concludes, we have consistently attempted to disguise, repress, exclude or even systematically eliminate the alien as it has appeared in the child. This has happened through our psychology, our philosophy and our everyday pragmatic activity. The tradition in which pedagogical tact and the pedagogical relation were initially developed, in other words, can be seen to have assumed that the inner life of the child or young person is much more within reach for adults than it actually is.[6] Recent art, philosophy and also contemporary events—for example, school shootings—suggest that this inner life is moving ever further from reach. We can no longer unproblematically say with Muth, for example, that the teacher or adult "experiences the experience of the child in his own being" and allows it to become the basis for his action (p. 92). Nonetheless, Lippitz sees this alienness not as a reason for inaction, but rather as "open[ing] up the actual possibility" of "pedagogy" itself (p. 172).

Jörg Zirfas' "Pedagogical Tact: Ten Theses" closes this volume by returning to an explicit discussion of tact and of pedagogical relations. Like Lippitz, Zirfas presents the reader with a historical reconstruction—in this case, of the notion of tact itself. In doing so, he revisits names and themes from previous chapters in this book, including Herbart, Schleiermacher, Nohl, and Muth. In particular, Zirfas builds on and expands Herbart's notion of tact, stressing its proximity to feeling while also acknowledging its symbiotic relation to theory.

The ninth of Zirfas' "Ten Theses" on tact simply states: "The determining moments of pedagogical tact are principles of relation…connected to the pedagogical relationship of the educator to the one being educated" (p. 189). And it is not surprising that in listing the characteristics of this relationship, Zirfas' account resonates with those of Muth and Nohl before him. Echoing Nohl's wish to take a perspective that "is unconditionally that of the one being educated" (Chapter Four, p. 65), Zirfas underscores the significance of "compassion, taking on others' perspectives… think[ing] from others' perspectives" and "expect[ing] and tak[ing] into account expectations of others" (p. 189). Zirfas also emphasizes "restraint" in "the pedagogical relationship of the educator to the one being educated," pointing out the importance of "limiting oneself for the sake of the other" and of "striking a balance between proximity and distance" in one's relation with a young person (p. 189).

In making points like these, Zirfas effectively brings this collection of translated texts on tact and the pedagogical relation full circle: Back to the question of awakening, fostering and giving space for the "other," for the inner life of the child or young person. Indeed, Zirfas closes his text by describing pedagogical tact as nothing less than a "response to the riddle of the other"—a "resonance with the openness, dynamics, variability and unfathomability of the other" (p. 192).

Pedagogy, Education and Educators

The word "pedagogy" as used above and also in the texts collected here is understood rather differently from what is typical in English. Whereas the "pedagogical" is generally taken to refer either to instructional methods (e.g., constructivist pedagogy) or a political program (e.g., critical pedagogy; see Friesen, 2021), the meaning of pedagogy (*Pädagogik; pedagogía*), in much of Europe, is considerably broader. This is particularly clear in Schleiermacher's lecture (Chapter Three) and remains consistent throughout the chapters in this book. Pedagogy and also education are not about a program or method, nor are they just about what happens in institutions like a school or college. Instead, pedagogy (and with it education) is primarily about the *influence* of *one* person or group on *another*.[7] As Schleiermacher makes clear, it is specifically about the intention and influence of an *older person or generation* in relation to a *younger one*.

Educational and pedagogical efforts, then, are not just undertaken by professional educators in places like classrooms or lecture halls. Instead, pedagogy is relevant wherever a pedagogical intention or influence is in play. Examples of this influence could range from advertisements and public service announcements on

TV, to outings and other activities. But the influence of the older on the younger that is constitutive of pedagogy does not have to be quite so obvious or overt. Traces of this influence can be found in things like the playground designs, in arrangements for learning to ride a bike or even in a young child's carriers and toys. After all, through aspects of their design, each of these entities influences the child or young person in specific ways: how they play, how they learn to move and balance, or (with a baby carrier) where the young child's attention is focused. Going even further, things not necessarily purpose-built for children can also be seen as pedagogical. Traffic signs, digital interfaces, even sidewalks all educate: they get us to stop and go, to tap, swipe and scroll, or simply to walk here and not there. They subtly influence our gestures, habits, interactions and expectations. Pestalozzi, for example, sees the "simple circumstances of domestic life" (p. 19) as being intrinsically educative or pedagogical (Chapter One). Nohl (Chapter Five) marvels at how "a formative or educative moment subsists in every life context, in every conversation" (p. 76). Fink (Chapter Seven) pronounces:

> Human existence always subsists in the element of teaching, everyone is a teacher of life to another, everyone can serve as a good or a bad example to another. That which is educational is part of the substance of being human, not simply a random side-effect. (p. 121)

Children are educated everywhere, and through the widest range of circumstances—and this process sometimes influences them in ways desirable for some (e.g., advertisers) but perhaps not for others (e.g., parents).

One implication is clear: By simply reflecting on how the child and young people are influenced and shaped in any of the ways mentioned above, one engages a mode of thought that can itself be characterized as pedagogical. Does the playground or toy encourage play that is safe and stimulating, or, perhaps, activity that is also cooperative in nature? Is baby more comfortable or better oriented facing me or looking out onto the world? Such pedagogical thinking, moreover, is almost unavoidably ethical in nature and relational in substance. That which can be seen as pedagogical—those things which are relevant to the influence of adults on the young—is not difficult to find, both in our own thoughts and in the everyday world around us.

Understood in this way, pedagogy can ultimately be said to present a perspective on life as a whole—a perspective which asks after the meaning and value of different aspects of our "ways of life" for those growing up, for the new generation (e.g., see: Mollenhauer, 2014, pp. 1–11). In addition, the study of and participation in these modes of action and thought can be seen as constituting a "pedagogical" discipline in and of itself. Indeed, in raising the question of the relation of pedagogical practice (or art) and pedagogical theory (or science), both Herbart and Schleiermacher in this volume are addressing one of the concerns of this discipline that remains fundamental to this day: the idea that each child is unique and that pedagogical practice can never be fully reduced to a science—to a rigorous set of theories positing universal rules and principles.

The understanding of pedagogy that is implied in pedagogical tact and the pedagogical relation is expansive. Although *some* texts in this collection are indeed concerned with teachers, students and the classroom (primarily in Chapters Two, Six and Eight—by Herbart, Nohl and Bollnow), this should clearly *not* be taken to mean that tact and the pedagogical relation only arise in schools or in explicitly educational settings. Pedagogical tact and the pedagogical relation are relevant in interpersonal contexts whenever a broadly pedagogical intention or type of influence is at play. Although pedagogical tact or the pedagogical relation are themselves not directly embodied in something like a baby carrier or playground design, these designs can certainly be made responsive and conducive to pedagogical tact and the pedagogical relation.

The meaning given to pedagogy in this collection also affects the use of other terms, including references to "teachers" and "students." If education happens both inside and outside of the classroom, and if things like traffic signs or digital interfaces can be said to be pedagogical, then the use of the terms "teacher" and "student" are insufficient in discussing both pedagogy and education. Instead, alternative words and phrases like "educator," "adult," and perhaps awkwardly, "the one being educated" become more appropriate. Adult or educator, in this sense, do not just refer to teachers or instructional personnel, but rather, to anyone who takes up a pedagogical way of thinking, acting or relating to a child or young person. A person fulfilling such a pedagogical role can of course be a parent; but such a role can in principle be fulfilled by any adult, even a stranger, for whom the welfare of a young person or a child—even just briefly—becomes an issue. Apprehension for a homeless teenager or a child wandering alone in public are expressions of concern that can be seen as specifically educational or pedagogical. Expanding the meaning of "educator" also means that the word "student" needs to be replaced by reference to "children and young people" or simply, "youth" or "the young."

The texts collected in this volume, in other words, not only enrich the theoretical and historical sources and background available for discussions of tact and the pedagogical relation, they also point to what (for English readers) is likely a new and different way of understanding education and pedagogy, of approaching teaching and learning themselves. They illustrate how a special pedagogical way of thinking of education originated a couple of hundred years ago, and how it remains current in Germany and other parts of Europe today. They also show how this intrinsically ethical and relational way of thinking can enrich and expand our own ways of thinking and talking about—as well as practicing—pedagogy and education today.

Notes

1. As quoted in: Gudjons, H. (2003). *Pädagogisches Grundwissen 8th ed.* Klinkhardt, p. 26.
2. For further examples, see items in the reference list, including: Biesta (2012); Bingham and Sidorkin (2004); Friesen (2017, 2018, 2020); Griffiths, et al. (2015); Saevi (2011); Smith (1998); Spiecker (1984).
3. Note that throughout this book, phrases or sentences not included are indicated through plain ellipses "…" Ellipses in brackets "[…]" indicate the omission of paragraphs or larger units of text.
4. Mattes, E. (2020). Aktualität der Geisteswissenschaftlichen Pädagogik. *Vierteljahrsschrift für Wissenschaftliche Pädagogik 96*, 220. See also: Felten, M. (2020). *Unterricht ist Beziehungssache.* Reclam, pp. 13–36; Terhart, E. (2014). *Die Hattie-Studie in der Diskussion: Probleme sichtbar machen.* Klett/Kallmeyer, p. 23.
5. Nohl, H. (1988). *Die pädagogische Bewegung in Deutschland und ihre Theorie.* Vittorio Klostermann, p. 286.
6. Note that Herbart's original conception of tact represents an exception to this. Herbart talked not about knowledge of the child's inner life, but about the teacher "guessing" on the basis of their informed feelings.
7. See, for example, the definition of education offered by Zirfas in Chapter Ten: "The term 'education'… designates those practices that provide the conditions for enabling people to develop towards a certain desired action and disposition. Such practices, it should be noted, may be more personal, intentional and direct or they may be more broadly and socially functional and indirect. Education is an influence or intervention for the purpose of promoting development. The goal of education in the modern age is the independence of the individual in all practices of human life (economic, political, social, aesthetic, etc.)" (p. 178).

References

Biesta, G. (2012). No education without hesitation. *Philosophy of Education.* http://ojs.ed.uiuc.edu/index.php/pes/article/view/3594/1215

Bingham, C., & Sidorkin, A. (2004). *No education without relation.* Peter Lang.

Biesta, G. (2011). Wanted, dead or alive, educationalists: On the need for academic bilingualism in education. In Aubry, C, Geiss, M, Magyar-Haas, V. (Eds.), *Positionierungen. Zum Verhältnis von Wissenschaft, Pädagogik und Politik* [Positionings: On the Relationship between Research, Education, and Politics]. Beltz.

Böhm, W., & Seichter, S. (2018). *Wörterbuch der Pädagogik.* Ferdinand Schöningh.

Friesen, N. (2017). The pedagogical relation past and present: Experience, subjectivity and failure. *Journal of Curriculum Studies, 49*(6), 743–756. https://doi.org/10.1080/00220272.2017.1320427

Friesen, N. (2020). "Education as a *Geisteswissenschaft*:" An introduction to human science pedagogy. *Journal of Curriculum Studies, 52*(3), 307–322. https://doi.org/10.1080/00220272.2019.1705917

Friesen, N. (2021). The necessity of translation in education: Theory and practice. In: Jornitz, S., & Willmers, A. (Eds.), *Transatlantic discourse in education research*. (pp. 337–351). Buderich.

Friesen, N., & Osguthorpe, R. (2018). Tact and the pedagogical triangle: The authenticity of teachers in relation. *Teaching and Teacher Education, 70*, 255–264. https://doi.org/10.1016/j.tate.2017.11.023

Griffiths, M., Hoveid, M. H., Todd, S., & Winter, C. (2015). *Re-imagining relationships in education: Ethics, politics and practices*. Wiley.

Mollenhauer, K. (2014). *Forgotten connections: On culture and upbringing*. Routledge.

Saevi, T. (2011). Lived relationality as fulcrum for pedagogical–ethical practice. *Studies in Philosophy and Education, 30*(5), 455–461. https://doi.org/10.1007/s11217-011-9244-9

Smith, S. J. (1998). *Risk and our pedagogical relation to children: On the playground and beyond*. SUNY Press.

Spiecker, B. (1984). The pedagogical relation. *Oxford Review of Education, 10*(2), 203–209.

PREFIGURATIONS

CHAPTER ONE

J.H. Pestalozzi: Letter to a Friend on His Work at Stans

Editor's Introduction

Johann Friedrich Pestalozzi (1746–1827) was the most famous reformer and educator of his time—in fact, probably of any time. He was translated into English (and other languages); people went on pilgrimages to visit him; they saw him as "the Columbus of intellectual human education," and even as a latter-day Christ figure.[1] But what did he do, and why is he forgotten today (at least in the English-speaking world)?

First of all, Pestalozzi invented what is today known as "phonics" in reading education, a way of teaching reading by making children aware of the connection between letters and sound. Second, he was famous for what he called his "method:" for engaging children interactively by working with their concrete everyday-life sensory experiences.[2] Third, he was likely the first in education to embrace education for the "whole child"—recognizing that as long as children are hungry or uncared for, they cannot grow either mentally or morally. Fourth and finally, Pestalozzi was very early in realizing the importance of personal relationships and of feelings and dispositions in education overall—especially the significance of the stability of the child's inner life and feeling. Although Pestalozzi did not explicitly reference tact or the pedagogical relation in his writing, one can say their later articulation owes much to his ideas.

Despite these remarkable achievements, Pestalozzi wrote in a manner that was neither "scientific" nor "professional." Instead, some of his most valuable ideas were communicated in a highly personal form, as in the "Letter to a Friend on his Work in Stans" translated here. Also, like Rousseau—who influenced Pestalozzi greatly—Pestalozzi embedded his ideas in fictionalized accounts of how children could be brought up (e.g. see Rousseau's *Emile; or, on Education* (1762/1979) or Pestalozzi's own *How Gertrude teaches her Children*, 1898). Together with the fact that the history of educational reform is often seen as beginning only with John Dewey (1859–1952), these are the most likely reasons for Pestalozzi's current neglect.

Pestalozzi's work in setting up and running an orphanage in Stans allowed him not only to put many of his educational innovations into practice, but also to test them in the most extreme conditions. These conditions arose through destructive aftermath of Napoleon's invasion of Switzerland, which in the case of Stans, left many children orphaned or alone. As mentioned, Pestalozzi knew he needed to care for the whole child: "Giving school lessons without encompassing the whole self… leads, I believe, to an artificial reduction of our humanity" (p. 19). But Pestalozzi was not interested in freeing children from abject hunger and poverty just so that they could become better learners. He saw the organized provision for their everyday needs as having profound pedagogical significance in itself. As Klaus Mollenhauer (2014) later noted, this was especially important when the world itself was effectively out of order:

> When the circumstances of everyday life no longer have any inherent pedagogical value, then the basis for responsible upbringing had to be found [by Pestalozzi] in the minutest but indispensable moments of all pedagogical relationships between adult and child. [For Pestalozzi] this relationship … is concerned with concrete social arrangements—with a "household" (p. 52).

When the world is profoundly dis-ordered, then an order that educates in the most basic way can to be constructed around the basic elements of life like eating, sleeping, and work. Caring for and educating the child become a single process. But what is perhaps most important is not this process itself, as Mollenhauer points out, but the *pedagogical relationships* that arise between the adult and children within it. Education first occurs in concrete interrelationship—with a teacher, parent or other adult—and precisely through "minutest but indispensable moments" (p. 52).

What is most important in the pedagogical relation—both for Pestalozzi and later for Herman Nohl and Jakob Muth (Chapters Four, Five and Six)—is not the child's learning but their *subjectivity*. Pestalozzi repeatedly emphasizes that he "sought" above all "to wake and give life to their inner selves"—to "establish" and "secure" them "in their inner being." It is this inner security that Pestalozzi sees as the foundation for all subsequent development, including for what he calls "the versatile and secure development of human wisdom" (p. 23).

Pestalozzi further describes how he will accomplish this awakening and enlivening of children's inner selves when he writes, "I determined that there should not be a minute in the day when my children should not be aware from my face and my lips that my heart was theirs, that their happiness was my happiness, and their pleasures my pleasures" (p. 19). Pestalozzi thus takes as his task to cultivate the child's inner life through empathy, but also to also amplify and give it concrete expression "from my face and my lips." Tact, a term derived from the Latin word "touch" (as in "tactile") is certainly not far away from what Pestalozzi is articulating here. Although the phrase "pedagogical tact" was only defined a few years later by Herbart (Chapter Two), Pestalozzi clearly anticipates it through many characterizations of his close interrelationship with the children in his care. In already speaking, for example, of the children "being aware from my face and my lips that my heart was theirs," he grants primacy to what the children know and feel, rather than to what he himself does. This pattern is consistent across many other examples from this letter, e.g.:

- "I knew no other order, method, or art, except ones that resulted naturally from my *children's faith in* my love for them, nor did I care to know any other" (p. 22; emphasis added).
- "They were not in the world nor in Stans; *they only knew* that they were with me and I with them" (p. 20; emphasis added).

If pedagogical tact is ultimately defined as the "educational response to the riddle of the other" (Zirfas, see: Chapter Ten), then Pestalozzi's constant concern for his children's faith and knowledge, their awareness and security certainly presents an indispensable precursor to its subsequent, more explicit articulation.

Sources/Recommended Reading

Mollenhauer, K. (2014). *Forgotten connections: On culture and upbringing.* Routledge.
Pestalozzi, J. H. (1898). *How Gertrude teaches her children.* C.W. Bardeen. https://archive.org/details/howgertrudeteach00pest/page/n6/mode/2up
Rousseau, J.-J. (1762/1979). *Emile; or on Education.* W.W. Norton.
Seel, N. (2011). Herbart, J.F. N. Seel (Ed.), *Encyclopedia of the Sciences of Learning* (pp. 1419–1421). Springer.

Takaya, K. (2003). The method of Anschauung: From Johann H. Pestalozzi to Herbert Spencer. *The Journal of Educational Thought*, 37(1), 77–99.

Troehler, D. (2013). *Pestalozzi and the educationalization of the world*. Palgrave.

Letter to a Friend on His Work at Stans (1799)
J.H. Pestalozzi[3]

It was my intention to find near Zurich or in Aargau[4] a place where I should be able to join local conditions together with hard work, agriculture and other means of education. In this way, I would be able to both develop an establishment and help it achieve its inherent purpose. But the misfortune of Unterwalden (September, 1798) left me no choice regarding a location.[5] The government saw it as urgent to restore this area and asked me to attempt to realize my plans in a place where almost everything that could have made it a success was absent.

I went there gladly. I felt that the innocence of the countryside would make up for what it otherwise lacked, and that people's distress would make them grateful. My eagerness to realize at last the great dream of my life would have led me to work on the very highest peaks of the Alps, without fire or water.

For a building, the government gave me a new structure in the Ursuline convent at Stans; but when I arrived it was still uncompleted, and not in any way ready for an orphanage or for a large number of children. The building itself first had to be made useable. The government gave the necessary orders, and Rengger[6] moved the work forward with much effort, zeal and action. I never wanted for money for the necessary facilities.

However, everything else was lacking, and the children crowded in before the kitchen, the rooms or the beds could be in order for them.

Because of a lack of beds, I initially had to send some of the poor children home at night. They generally came back the next day covered with vermin. Most of these children were in a condition that showed the results of an extreme regression of human nature. Many of them had a chronic skin-disease, which almost prevented their walking, or sores on their heads, or rags full of vermin; many were almost skeletons, with haggard, care-worn faces, and shrinking looks; some were brazen, accustomed to begging, hypocrisy, and all sorts of deceit; still others were broken by misfortune, patient, suspicious, timid, and entirely devoid of affection. [...] Out of every 10 children there was hardly one who knew their ABCs; any further knowledge, of course, was out of the question.

This complete ignorance troubled me least, for I trusted in the natural powers that God bestows on even the poorest and most neglected children. I had observed for a long time that behind their coarseness, shyness, and apparent incapacity, there are hidden the finest faculties, the most precious powers—even among the poor creatures who surrounded me at Stans. Marked natural abilities soon began to show themselves. I knew how useful the common needs of life are in teaching children the relations of things. These same common needs also could bring out their natural intelligence, form their judgment, and arouse capabilities which, buried as they were beneath the coarser elements of their nature, cannot become active and useful till they are set free. It was my goal to encourage these capabilities and bring them to bear on the pure and simple circumstances of domestic life.

[...]

No man on God's earth appeared to approve of my aims for the instruction and guidance of the children. I also hardly knew of anyone who could have. The more learned and educated those with whom I may have conversed would be, the less they could have understood me and the less able they were to grasp in theory my starting points. The nature of their views on the arrangements, the requirements of the undertaking, etc., were completely different from my own. Above all, they resisted the idea and possibility of the implementation of my ideas which involved no artificial resources—just the nature that surrounded the children, the daily needs and the energetic activity of the children themselves as a means of education. And thus, it was this thought on which I based the entire execution of my undertaking. It was also the middle point on which a multitude of other aims converged, and simultaneously developed.

[...]

I had but one goal: I wanted to prove that the advantages possessed by education at home must be imitated by public education—that the imitation by public education of aspects of homelife has value for humankind. Giving school lessons without encompassing the whole self, and without this being grounded on the full life of domestic interrelationships—all of this leads, I believe, to an artificial reduction of our humanity. Every good human education requires the eyes of the mother, which daily and hourly notice any change in the soul of the child, by reading it on his or her mouth and face. It essentially requires that the force of the educator be that of the father, which enlivens the entire scope of domestic interrelationships.

Such was the foundation upon which I built. I determined that there should not be a minute in the day when my children should not be aware from my face and my lips that my heart was theirs, that their happiness was my happiness, and their pleasures my pleasures.

Humans easily accept what is good, and the child easily listens to it; but it is not for you, master and educator, that he wants it, but for himself. The good to which you would lead him must not depend on your arbitrary humor or passion; it must be a good which is good in itself and good by the very nature of things—that which the child can recognize as good. He must feel the necessity of your will in things which concern his comfort before he can be expected to obey it. Anything that endears the child is what he wants. He also wants anything that brings him honor, that excites grand expectations. Everything that stimulates his powers, that makes him say "I can do it" is also what the child wants. But this will is not produced by words, but by the general concern of the child and by the feelings and powers that are stirred up in him by this general concern. Words alone cannot give us a knowledge of things; they are only useful for giving expression to what we have in our mind.

Above all, I wanted and had to win the trust and devotion of the children. I was sure that if I succeeded in doing this, all the rest would follow by itself. Think for a moment, though, of the prejudices of the people, and even of the children, and you will understand the difficulties with which I had to contend.

And yet, however painful this lack of help and support was, it was valuable for the success of my undertaking: It forced me to be always everything for my children. I alone was with them from morning till night. It was my hand that supplied all that was good for them, for both body and soul. All needful help, consolation, and instruction they received direct from me. Their hands were in mine, my eyes were fixed on theirs. We wept and smiled together. They were not in the world nor in Stans; they only knew that they were with me and I with them. We shared our food and drink. I had neither family, friends, nor servants; nothing but them. I was with them when they slept, both in sickness and health. I was the last to go to bed and the first to get up. In the bedroom I prayed with them, and, at their own request, taught them till they fell asleep.
[...]

The institution grew and grew; by 1799 I had 80 children. Most had good, and others excellent, abilities. For most of them learning was something entirely new. As soon as they found that they could learn, their enthusiasm was unflagging. In a few weeks children who had never before opened a book and could hardly repeat the Lord's Prayer or *Ave Maria*, would learn the whole day long, almost incessantly. Even after supper, when I would say to them, "Children, will you go to bed, or learn something?" they would generally answer, especially in the first month or two, "Learn something!" It is true that afterwards, when they had to get up very early, it was not quite the same. But this initial enthusiasm gave everything its direction and gave to the children's learning a level of success that far exceeded my own expectations.
[...]

It was not possible to initially force on them—through opposition or by preaching rules and regulations—an external order or organization. This would have repelled them from me and turned their existing spirit and energy directly against my purposes. First of all, I had to wake and give life to their inner selves, and to a moral and governable disposition. Afterwards, in external things, I might then be sure of their ready attention, activity, and obedience. I had, in short, to follow the precept of Christ, "Cleanse first that which is within, that the outside may be clean also."[7] If the truth of this precept was ever evident, it was made self-evident here.

My one aim was to awaken a feeling of brotherhood among the children through their first feelings of commonality and the first stirrings of their new powers. It was also to merge the building into the spirit of a single large household, and on this basis of this coalescing—and the atmosphere to which it gives rise—to share and give life to a regulated and moral disposition.

My actions were all based on this principle: First, to broaden your children's sympathies, and to make love and charity known to them by satisfying their daily needs, their sensations, their experience and their actions, thus establishing and securing them in their inner being. Then, make them familiar with those abilities so that goodwill is both secured and exercised among them. Finally, in these difficult times, do not hesitate to touch on questions of Good and Evil, and the words associated with them. Link these with ordinary household habits and surroundings, so that they are all entirely founded on them. In this way, the children may be reminded of their own feelings, and supplied with a moral and communal understanding of their lives and interrelationships. Even though you might have to spend whole nights in trying to express in two words what others say in 20, never regret the loss of sleep.

I gave my children very few explanations; I taught them neither morality nor religion. But sometimes, when they were perfectly quiet, I used to say to them, "Don't you think that you are better and more reasonable when you are like this than when you are making noise?" When they clung round my neck and called me their father, I used to say, "My children, would it be right to deceive your father? After kissing me like this, would you like to do anything behind my back that would disturb me?" When our talk turned to the misery of the country, and they were feeling glad at the thought of their own happier situation, I would say, "How good God is to have given man a compassionate heart!" Sometimes, too, I asked them if they did not see a great difference between authorities who care for the poor and teach them to earn a livelihood, and others who would leave them to their misery, or to beg for food and charity in their idleness and vice.

[...]

All of elementary moral education is based on three elements: (1) To obtain a moral state through pure emotions. (2) To engage in moral behavior by overcoming oneself and practicing what is right and good, and (3) To arrive at a moral view by reflecting on the legal and moral conditions in which the child find themselves, by virtue of their existence and surroundings.
[...]

I have generally found that great, noble, and high thoughts are indispensable for developing wisdom and firmness of character. Instruction in these matters must be complete in the sense that it must take account of all our aptitudes and all our circumstances; it also must be conducted in a psychological spirit, that is to say, simply, lovingly, energetically, and calmly.[8] Then, by its very nature, this learning produces a benevolent mood, one receptive to truth and justice. This is one in which hundreds of propositions derived from great truths will come to mind and become firmly grounded there—even if one cannot express these initial truths in words.
[...]

I believe that the initial development of thought in the child is very much disturbed by a wordy system of teaching, one which is adapted neither to his faculties nor to the circumstances of his life. According to my experience, success depends upon whether what is taught to children shows itself as intuitively true, through being closely connected with their own personal observation and experience. [...]

I knew no other order, method, or art, except ones that resulted naturally from my children's faith in my love for them, nor did I care to know any other. As a general rule I attributed little importance to the study of words, even when explanations of the ideas they represented were given.

I tried to connect study with manual labor, the school with the workshop, and to combine them into one. But I was not really able to do this because of a lack of staff, material, and tools. Just a short time before the establishment was closed, a few children had begun to spin; and I saw clearly that, before labor and learning could be combined, the two had to be grounded separately.

But in the work of the children I cared less about immediate gain than about physical training which, by developing their strength and skill, was bound to supply them later with a livelihood. In the same way I saw what is called their "learning" as an exercise of their faculties, and I felt it important to exercise attention, observation, and memory first. In this way they could strengthen these faculties before calling into play the art of judging and reasoning. This is because judging and reasoning can, through dangerous rhetorical tricks, become mere superficiality, presumption and deception. I see this as being far more dangerous for human happiness and human destiny than great ignorance. What is important is what is secured by firm observant knowledge of one's immediate surroundings, and by a pure and simple but developed sense of strength. I believe that the most beneficial knowledge generally starts from this point of view and is found in its purest form in those with the least scholarly background.

These exercises not only gave my children an ever-increasing power of attention and discernment, but also did a great deal for their general mental and moral development. They also produced a general feeling of balance in which I saw as the foundation for the versatile and secure development of human wisdom.

Notes

1. Troehler, 2013, pp. 79, 80.
2. Friesen, N. (2017). *The textbook and the lecture: Education in the age of new media*. Johns Hopkins University Press, pp. 94–109.
3. Translated by N. Friesen.
4. Zurich is a city in north-central Switzerland; Aargau is a Swiss province or canton that is immediately to its west. Pestalozzi ended up working not far away, in a canton south of Zurich.
5. Unterwalden was the province or canton in Switzerland in which the town of Stans was located. The "event" of September 1798 took the form of the violent repression of a similarly violent counterrevolutionary uprising in Stans. Earlier that year, Stans and the rest of Switzerland had been invaded by Napoleon, leading to much conflict within the country between those who took up Napoleon's modern, republican cause, and those who rebelled against it.
6. Rengger was Minister of the Interior in the government in Switzerland that had been set up after the invasion of Napoleon.
7. In Matthew 23:26, Jesus of Nazareth says: "first clean the inside of the cup and of the dish, so that the outside of it may become clean also."
8. "Psychology" for Pestalozzi refers to that which corresponds to his understanding of human nature, which was not informed by what we today know as the psychological sciences.

CHAPTER TWO

J.F. Herbart: Introductory Lecture to Students in Pedagogy

Editor's Introduction

Johann Friedrich Herbart (1786–1841) was a philosopher and an early psychologist who succeeded Immanuel Kant as Chair in Philosophy and Education in Königsberg. Together with Schleiermacher (Chapter Three), Herbart is considered one of the founders of pedagogy as a domain of academic study. Herbart was also a follower of Pestalozzi (Chapter One), having met the famous educator during a stay in Switzerland in his 20s. In fact, the King of Prussia appointed Herbart to his Königsberg Chair with the specific hope that Herbart might improve "our education system following the principles of Pestalozzi."[1] Like Pestalozzi, Herbart was passionate about experiment and reform in education. Herbart saw the practical matter of the instruction of future educators as one of his prime responsibilities.

At the same time, Herbart was also an academic, a philosopher and a theorist. He developed a theoretical system of pedagogy (i.e. a "pedagogics") in works, for example, like a *General Pedagogics: Its Principles deduced from its Aim (1806/1908)*. Herbart and his followers ("the Herbartians") are particularly well-known for their insights into planning and sequencing lessons, anticipating, for example, Robert Gagné's "nine events of instruction."[2] Being both a reformer and a theorist, Herbart sought to bring the practical and the theoretical together in his work.

Such a (re-)integration of theory and practice is his primary task in the lecture translated here, an "Introductory Lecture to Students in Pedagogy."

It is *pedagogical tact* that Herbart saw as above all bringing theory and practice together. In fact, it is in the introductory lecture published here that he first introduced this phrase to educational discourse.

Herbart begins his lecture by emphasizing that educational theory can boast of only very minor achievements—ones that are so tentative that he even declines to characterize "education" as a discipline at this point. Also, according to the way that Herbart understands education—namely as something that produces intellectually curious, moral, and autonomous people—he would likely also see today's theories as having a long way to go.[3] This, then, explains the rather long list of things that Herbart initially says he *won't* do in his lecture: He *won't* provide a tribute to education; he *won't* offer a history or even a summary. Instead, he asks his readers to follow him first in making a very basic distinction: Education, for Herbart, is both what he calls a practical "art" and a theoretical "science." And Herbart's main point of emphasis in this lecture is on the *art*, on "the sum of skills and abilities which are combined to arrive at a given purpose" (p. 30).

Herbart sees the art of education as relating to the formal science or theory of education in a number of possible ways or "modes."[4] Each mode can be seen to correspond to different stages in a teacher's early pedagogical development, beginning with modes that ignore theory altogether and rely only on practice—first simply on one's own practice, and later on possibilities for practice presented by one's colleagues. The third mode for Herbart involves trying to translate theory directly and immediately to practice. He admits, though, that because of the complexity of so many teaching situations, such a "deliberate and thoroughgoing application of scientific propositions" could only be carried out by a "supernatural being"—an entity much more capable than humans (p. 32). What is ultimately needed in interconnecting theory and practice, Herbart concludes, is something much more swift, agile and responsive, a certain "aptitude, quickness and dexterity," "a quick judgment and decision that is not habitual and eternally uniform" (p. 32). This is what Herbart calls *pedagogical tact*. And this is the fourth and—in Herbart's view—the most professional way for the teacher to bring theory and practice into interrelation in the classroom. Herbart continues:

> Based on continuous practice, there inevitably develops in humans a mode of action that is dependent on feeling but that only remotely relies on certainty of belief. This is a mode of action that gives vent to feeling and expresses how one has been affected from the outside. It shows one's emotional state rather than the results of one's thinking. [It consists of a] tact [that] is unable to boast, as a fully developed theory

should, that while remaining deliberately consistent with the rule, it can at the same time answer the true requirements of the individual case. (p. 32)

Tact, Herbart is saying, is the response of the educator to the individual child or student—and that it is more a question of how we *feel* than how we *think*. It is a question of "attunement" of "a particular pedagogical disposition" as Herbart himself emphasizes (p. 35). Despite this fact, though, Herbart sees a clear role for theory in teachers' tactful action. This is one, however, that is humbler and more tentative than the role currently played by psychological or managerial theory in today's teacher preparation. Theory doesn't tell us directly what we should and shouldn't do. Instead, the purpose of theory is to cultivate precisely the attunement or disposition that is needed for tactful action: "But even in action," Herbart explains, one learns the tactful art of pedagogical practice "only if one has earlier thoughtfully learned the science" (p. 33). One must first make this educational theory "one's own, attun[e] oneself through it, and... make sense of future experiences through it" (p. 33). The value of education as a "science," in other words, is not about memorizing specific developmental stages or cognitive schemes. Its purpose is much more humble in theory and ambitious in practice—namely, to foster the development of a kind of awareness, reflection and a way of being as a teacher precisely to be tactful, to "know what to do when you don't know what to do."[5] The teacher, Herbart concludes, "must prepare his head as well as his heart to correctly receive, perceive, feel, and judge the phenomena awaiting him and the situation in which he will be placed" (pp. 33).

Traces of Pestalozzi's thought can be found precisely in moments like these in Herbart's text—in references to a teacher's "heart" and his or her concern with their own students' experiences of education. However, Herbart's tendency towards things academic and theoretical certainly kept him away from Pestalozzi's very concrete discussion of dealing with the children placed in his care, and from Pestalozzi's effusive expressions. Unlike Pestalozzi's letter, Herbart's text opens up ways of speaking about tact in pedagogy that are indispensable for discussions of "know-how," "reflective practice" and "phronesis" today.[6] It is little wonder, then, that aspects of Herbart's account of pedagogical tact are again taken up not only by Herman Nohl (Chapter Five), but are also indispensable for Jakob Muth's understanding of tact specifically as a response to what is accidental, "unintended" and "unplannable" (Chapter Six). Finally, we should also not be surprised that it makes a significant reappearance in Zirfas' historical overview of pedagogical tact as something that has evolved over centuries (Chapter Eleven), and that it remains a part of discourses in English and German to this day.[7]

Sources/Recommended Reading

Hilgenherger, N. (1993). Johann Friedrich Herbart. *Prospects: The Quarterly Review of Comparative Education* (UNESCO: International Bureau of Education), *XXIII*(3/4), 649–664. http://www.ibe.unesco.org/sites/default/files/herbarte.pdf

Kenklies, K. (2012). Educational theory as topological rhetoric: The concepts of pedagogy of Johann Friedrich Herbart and Friedrich Schleiermacher. *Studies in Philosophy and Education*, 31, 265–273. 10.1007/s11217-012-9287-6

Seel, N. (2011). Herbart, J. F. *Encyclopedia of the Sciences of Learning*. Springer.

J.F. Herbart, Introductory Lecture to Students in Pedagogy[8]

Gentlemen: At the beginning of these lectures, you might first expect a definition of my subject and then a tribute, a history, or a synopsis of the science of pedagogy.[9]

But a definition can only be the result of this entire inquiry—and can only be provided after what is essential is *separated* from what is not. Such a definition will not become apparent to someone who is aware neither of how this separation takes place, nor of what is being excluded in the first place. A definition in this case will come more as a surprise than as a support to one's thinking. Instead of a definition, I emphasize here the main characteristics of the crude idea invoked in the word "education." And I do so in order to connect with the threads of a further investigation.

But this lecture is not a tribute! The figurative "crown" that this would represent would likely oppress rather than glorify the brow of my modest science.

It might also be appropriate to begin my account of this science with praise if its doctrine were stated precisely and unambiguously—and its benefits proven beyond a doubt in everyday experience. This would be a science that had already reached the age of its manhood. But the art of educating the young is itself still a youthful art.[10] It undertakes experiments, develops its powers, and hopes for great accomplishments in the future. But it must confess that its experiments have taught it not so much what to do as what *not* to do; it is constantly wary of the power of accidents, which it would rather run away from than stay and fight against. Education as a science is still expecting that its general principles will eventually take the form of the statements and objections of philosophy—but without knowing if these principles will unsettle more than they instruct. For such a science, any tribute would have to refer more to hopes for its future than to any actual accomplishments. It is exactly these hopes and their justification or unjustifiability that my lectures bring to light. I will gradually develop the idea of a great art and demonstrate the feasibility of carrying the idea into effect. And the degree that I will do this, I am sure, is the same degree that your respect for pedagogy will become confidence, even admiration.

I will also not provide you with a history. What does the history of a science contain? It would certainly contain the experiments and attempts that enabled it to become a science. But who can estimate the value of such attempts and judge their results as either a progression or regression? Many are also certain to have missed the best and shortest way for these attempts to reach their goal. Therefore, as a rule, the history of an art does not become comprehensible and interesting until its main ideas are mastered. Only then can one judge the history of its various attempts. Only then, in the case of mistaken attempts, one can discriminate and assess correct intentions and assign the proper measure to what was missed either through excess or weakness. One can also appropriately separate what is true and important from what is insignificant, erroneous, or even dangerous.

Instead of a history of pedagogy, a clear view of the current condition of the art of education is needed. I recommend two ways of doing this. First, think back to your own youth, and recall both how you and others were educated. When you do this, you will likely not be able to avoid thinking of your teachers and educators either positively or negatively. You are not yet old enough to view this impartially as a part of your history—for it to become instructive experience. This is particularly the case if you believe that you have suffered from profound mistakes in your education—ones which can warp or hold you back beyond recovery. In these cases, it is difficult not to feel thankless and unjustly treated. But it is easy to forget how much the prevailing spirit of the time might be to blame, and how much your education might have risen above it. It is also easy to forget the many obstacles your education had to contend with, and how much worse off one might be without it.

But this is not really what we are discussing here. Instead, it is our purpose to recognize failings as failings, regardless of how they might have arisen from circumstances. We must work to free ourselves completely from force of habit. This is a force that a father is inclined to visit upon his son, just as his own father directed it upon him. If possible, we must even step beyond the limits of our present age—especially as far as its authority might blind us to reason. We must orient ourselves to education's pure ideal one the one hand, and on the other to current means for realizing this ideal. We have to do this so that we at least do not fall short of the best that is possible, at least insofar as it can be planned. We must therefore:

- become acquainted with the pedagogical means at hand, particularly with those already prepared for pedagogical use;
- avoid the aberrations in our present age which readily distract us and receive the noisiest warnings from today's pedagogues;
- orient ourselves through the nearest and correspondingly the most obvious experience of what education is like.

For all of these reasons, we must be careful in how we regard the present. It is also for these reasons that I have asked you to place yourselves in the time of your youth. [...]

Here, I will also *not* provide a summary of my pedagogy. For would you easily understand me if I were to speak of *instruction that is at the same time education*? Or if I were to introduce a broad division of the method of this instruction into *synthetic and analytic* elements, or even speak of an *aesthetic presentation of the world* as the ideal of education? In my theses I have reluctantly declared mathematics and poetry to be the main forces in education. And I will not risk describing how all pedagogy can be seen to take place between the extremes of the formation of the imagination on the one hand and one's character on the other.[11] These kinds of paradoxes do little for the right attunement which would best prepare the mind for our investigation here.

I instead hope to help with this preparation by briefly explaining the way I will deal with my subject. First, we must distinguish between *pedagogy as a science* and the *art of education*. What is the content of a science? It is an orderly combination of propositions, logically constituting a whole, in which (where possible) results are derived from these propositions, and propositions, in turn, derived from principles. What is an art? It is the sum of skills and abilities which are combined to arrive at a given purpose. Science, therefore, requires philosophic thinking—the determination of propositions from their logical grounds. Art, on the other hand, requires consistent *action* in keeping with the propositions of science. When art is exercised to meet the needs of the moment, it must not become lost in speculation; instead, it needs to be directed against a thousand contrary circumstances.

Furthermore, we also need to distinguish between an expert educator's art from the isolated application of an art. The first consists in knowing how to deal with all types of mind and all stages of growth. The second may be successful accidentally, or by virtue of sympathy or parental love.

Which of these three spheres[12] is of concern to us? Obviously, we cannot deal with moments of actual practice; we also cannot refer to numerous exercises and experiments (which are the only way that the art of education can be learned). Our concern is with the sphere of science.

Now, let us look at the relation between theory and practice.

Theory claims to be universal, and in this sense stretches over a vast expanse. One touches only on a very tiny part of this expanse in one's individual practice. As result of this simultaneous universality and indeterminacy, theory passes over all details, over all circumstances that surround the practical teacher at any given moment. It also passes over all the individual measures, reflections, and efforts through which the teacher responds to these circumstances. In learning about science, we therefore learn both too much and too little for practice. This is the reason why practical workers dislike mixing a rigid, thoroughly investigated theory with their art. They would much rather balance such a theory with the weight of their experiences and observations. Alternatively, it is also demonstrably clear that mere practice produces unquestioned habit and extremely limited and entirely indecisive experience.

I believe that we need to learn from theory how to question through experiment and observation before we can find definite answers. Nowhere is this truer than in pedagogical practice. In it the activity of the educator is constant. Even against his will, he acts well or badly, or neglects to do that which might have been done. And he is just as constantly faced with the reaction, the result of his activity. But these results do not show him what would have happened had his action been different or what proceeding with greater power or wisdom might have achieved. They also do not indicate what might have happened if he had other pedagogical tools—even ones he has not dreamt of—available. These are all things that escape the teacher. The teacher simply does not experience these things; instead, he experiences only his own self, his own relation to others, the failure of his own plans. He does not discover his basic failings, but only the success of his method—without being able to compare it to one that is better and might have produced superior results more quickly. Thus it actually happens that a grey-haired school teacher or even one or more generations of teachers—following similar or identical paths—have no idea of what a beginner might experience in his first hour of teaching (whether this experience arises through a carefully calculated experiment or simple blind luck).

Every nation has its own domain of concern, and every age certainly has its own limitations. It is within these that the pedagogue as well other individuals—and all their ideas, inventions, experiments and resulting experiences—are enclosed. Other ages experience something else simply because they do something else. It is always true that any sphere of experience without an a priori principle not only has no right to speak of absolute completeness, but that it cannot even approximately state the extent of its correspondence to such completeness.[13] It is for this reason that a person without philosophy so easily imagines himself to have made far-reaching reforms in education when he has only trivially improved the way of doing things. Nowhere is philosophical discretion and awareness provided by general ideas as needed as it is here, where daily action and impressions of individual experience so powerfully limit one's vision.

But for every theorist who puts his theory into practice in particular cases—and who does not proceed with pedantic slowness (like a little boy with his sums in arithmetic)—a link intermediate between theory and practice involuntarily inserts itself. By this I mean a certain tact, a quick judgment and decision that is not habitual and eternally uniform. But this tact is unable to boast, as a fully developed theory *should*, that while remaining deliberately consistent with the rule, it can at the same time answer the true requirements of the individual case. Such a deliberate and complete application of scientific propositions would require a supernatural being. Based on continuous practice, there inevitably develops in humans a mode of action that is dependent on feeling but that only remotely relies on certainty of belief. This is a mode of action that gives vent to feeling and expresses how one has been affected from the outside. It shows one's emotional state rather than the results of one's thinking. But you will say: "What kind of educator depends on his whims and gives himself over to the pleasure or displeasure caused by his students?" But I ask in return: "What sort of educator would praise his students without feeling, or rebuke them only by the book? Who would reason and calculate about what to do while the boys do one foolish thing after another—rendering one incapable of countering their impulsive energy only with nothing else other than swift, manly willpower?" This question and counter-question must be weighed. But I return to our assertion that tact inevitably occupies the place that theory leaves vacant, and so becomes the immediate director of our practice. It would of course be nice if this director of our practice faithfully followed theory—whose fundamental correctness we take here on faith. The crucial question of whether someone will be a good or bad educator depends only on this: How does tact form itself in the educator to be faithful (or not) to the laws articulated by pedagogic science in its universality?

Let us reflect further on the influences on and the effective causes of the way in which this tact becomes ingrained. It is only formed through practice and the effect of our practical experience on our feelings. This effect will be different and have different results based on how we and others are *attuned*. We both can and should act through reflection, on the basis of this attunement. The success or failure of our pedagogical work depends on the correctness and weight of this reflection. It depends on the interest and moral willingness with which we give ourselves up to it. It further depends on whether and how, before and during the activity of education, our mode of sensing will order and regulate the tact upon which our success (or failure) relies. In other words, by reflection, reasoning, inquiry—in short, by science—the educator must prepare *not* his future action in individual cases as much as *himself*, his disposition. He must prepare his head as well as his heart to correctly receive, perceive, feel, and judge the phenomena awaiting him and the situation in which he will be placed. If he has, in anticipation, indulged in extensive plans, the practical circumstances will mock him. But if he has equipped himself with theoretical principles, his experience will become clear to him, and will teach him what to do in every situation. If he does not know how to distinguish the significant from the insignificant, he will fail to attend to what is vitally necessary and wear himself out on trivialities. If he confuses the lack of education among his students with mental deficiency or their crudeness with ill will, then they will constantly startle and bewilder him. If on the contrary, he knows the essential points on which his work depends and the characteristics of potential Good and Evil among his students, he will know how to grant to himself and to his students all the freedom needed for general cheerfulness—without neglecting his obligations, without losing his discipline and without giving way to foolishness and vice.

There is then—and this is my conclusion—a preparation for the art of education by way of science, a preparation of both one's understanding and one's heart before beginning one's duties. In other words, there is a way in which the experience that we can obtain only by engaging in our work itself becomes instructive to us. Only in *action* do we learn the art; only in this way do we acquire tact, aptitude, quickness and dexterity. But even in action, one learns this art only if one has earlier thoughtfully learned the science, made it one's own, attuned oneself through it, and one is able to make sense of future experiences through it.

One must therefore not expect from one's preparation that one will become a complete master of the art of education. One should also not expect this art to provide specific instructions for one's procedures. One must trust one's own powers of invention to hit upon the single thing that needs to be done at any given moment. One should expect to be instructed by one's failures. And one should expect do this in pedagogy much more than in a thousand other occupations because in pedagogy what is important is not every tiny action, but rather, the educator's general technique. Finally, one must also not expect one's memory to provide the innumerable details which are to form the basis for action.

But on the other hand, one should fill oneself with those observations which are relevant to the dignity and the importance of the main ways that education can help. Let there constantly hover before the mind of the educator the image of a pure, young soul—one which, under the influence of moderate happiness and tender love, under encouragement of the spirit and many a challenge to future action develops powerfully with ever-accelerating progress. The educator may initially abandon himself to his imagination, to adorn this image beautifully. But the educator should also engage in highly critical reflection. This will show the educator that this image is arbitrary and fictional without connection and consistency—and what, on the other hand, is the requirement of reason, the essential quality of the ideal. Having now imagined a boy—not one that he would like to educate, but one truly worthy of an excellent education—let him frame in thought a teacher suitable for this boy. This would be one that is not so much a companion of every step, as Rousseau imagines; nor would it be the warden or slave chained to the boy who eliminates freedom for both. This teacher would instead be a wise guide from afar, who, through well-timed, penetrating words and powerful actions knows how to make sure of the student and then calmly leave him to his development through play and contention with his mates. This guide also leaves the student to his own striving for action and honor, and his own dislike of examples of vice through which the world, according to our desire, either seduces or warns us.

We must seek to unlock and understand the words and actions of such a guide from afar. The amount of time which an educator will gladly dedicate will not suffice for education. This makes education itself impossible. The educator who fully dedicates all of his hours, his best years—as is so often expected of him—must then also neglect himself, and the relation between educator and the one being educated becomes a ceaseless and unnatural strain, consuming what can be called the "formative force" itself.[14] Young people would then have an overseer, not an educator. Our science must teach us an art which above all offers continued development to the educator. This art must also act with such focus and intensity, with such accuracy and sureness, that it need not assist at every moment, and that it spurns the majority of hazards and turns the most important interventions of chance *to* its advantage. Instead, it must use these interventions of fate *for* its work. For fate, circumstances and the "education" provided by the outside world—about which pedagogues so loudly complain—do not always affect the student negatively, and almost never influence him negatively in every respect. Education itself, once it has gained a certain degree of power, is very often able to turn those influences in into own purposes. As a whole the world and nature do much more for the student than education, on average, can see itself as doing.

I believe I have now described the intention of the science that is my concern here. I am not sure if I have fully attained my goal, but I trust that I have brought you closer to it than you might otherwise have come.

I only need to add something on the peculiar nature of this science to develop my suggestions for making the best use of this series of lectures.

You already know: I am attempting to develop and bring to life within you a particular pedagogical disposition, one that is the result of certain beliefs about the nature of humans and their educatability.[15] It is these ideas that I will produce, justify, construct, combine and amalgamate so that this disposition develops from them, and so that, as a result, the pedagogical tact that I have described develops as well. But to produce, justify and construct ideas is a philosophic activity of the highest, but also most difficult, kind. It is all the more difficult here because I cannot presuppose the purely philosophical basis from which I should work, especially not psychology and ethics.[16]

I will try to make the results of my speculation comprehensible to you without presenting this speculation itself as follows: I will turn to your knowledge of human nature and especially to your powers of self-observation, in which the conclusions of proper speculation must appear—if only as relatively obscure, raw and indeterminate. But I ask for your patience as I navigate various obstructions and given that my main ideas are only gradually assembled from their component parts. Everything will depend on the clarity and certainty, on the force with which the results take root in you and show themselves to be effective. In this respect a lot will also depend on how thoroughly you have mastered those sciences and exercises which are recognized as the most important resources for education. Among them I include especially Greek literature and mathematics.

When lectures deal with philosophy, the normal practice of taking notes puts one at a disadvantage. A correct understanding and complete insight is most important right from the beginning. For those of you who had the intention to see my lectures as deeply interconnected, I would advise you only to write down those things that I articulate slowly and repeatedly for this precise purpose. I think I will begin at this point tomorrow. Also, for those of you who would like to engage in further conversation about what I have presented, you can find me on Saturday in my apartment in the home of the reverend Mr. Krietsch.

From the Second Lecture

[…] There are ways of instructing moral character just as there are for of pedagogical tact. And for both these, there is science, which is ethics and pedagogy. If they know their purpose, both will work with their conceptions *not* to produce many individual rules, but rather, to develop general convictions in their students' minds. They will work in every way to strengthen, ground and to promote the living intensity of those convictions which are capable of providing the true direction of future acquisition of tact.

Notes

1. As quoted in Hilgenberger, 1993, p. 650.
2. Gagné, R. M. (1985). *The conditions of learning and theory of instruction.* Holt, Rinehart and Winston.
3. This is particularly likely given the emphasis he places in his lecture on "step[ping] beyond the limit of our present" (p. 29).
4. See: Kenklies 2012, p. 270.
5. This is an adaptation of the subtitle of M. van Manen's (2015) *Pedagogical tact.* Left Coast Press.
6. E.g., see: Schön, D.A. (1987). *Educating the reflective practitioner.* Jossey-Bass; Jope, G. (2018). Becoming ethically responsive in initial teacher education. *Research in Education, 100*(1), 65–82. https://doi.org/10.1177/0034523718762149
7. E.g., see: Burghardt, D., & Zirfas, J. (2019). *Der pädagogische Takt. Eine erziehungswissenschaftliche Problemformel.* Beltz-Juventa; Sipman, G., Thölke, J., Martens, R., & McKenney, S. The role of intuition in pedagogical tact: Educator views. *British Educational Research Journal 45*(6), 1186–1202. doi:10.1002/berj.3557
8. Translated by N. Friesen.
9. Science is usually taken in English to refer only to the natural sciences. In German, it refers to *any* area of study that is pursued systematically and with rigor. Particularly around Herbart's time, science referred (as Herbart himself here writes) to a field of study involving an "orderly combination of propositions, logically constituting a whole, in which (where possible) results are derived from these propositions, and propositions, in turn, are derived from principles" (p. 30). Herbart also sees science as something that practitioners can engage in—namely through "reflection, reasoning, inquiry" (p. 33)—to prepare themselves for teaching.
10. Art here refers *not* to an aesthetic pursuit, but τέχνη or techne, a practical knowing and doing that is variable and context-dependent, and that involves craft and technique.
11. Here and just above, Herbart is here referring to other aspects of his own pedagogical theory, some of which are outlined in texts available in English, in particular: Herbart, J. F. (1906). *The science of education: Its general principles deduced from its aim and the aesthetic revelation of the world.* Heath & Co. https://archive.org/details/scienceofeducati00herbuoft/
12. Herbart is referring to the possibilities he has mentioned above: (1) pedagogy as a science, (2) education and instruction as professional practice (e.g., by one experienced in teaching), and (3) education as a non-professional matter, one that instead arises by chance (e.g., as may be undertaken by parents). Herbart goes on to consider each of these three possibilities in greater depth but in reverse order.
13. Herbart here is speaking of imagined "scientific" principles for action and practice that would hold regardless of specific circumstances. Of course, ethics and philosophy have since not produced such absolute principles.
14. Herbart's original words are *bildende Kraft*, which refers to the potential that we as adults have to help children become themselves more fully.
15. Herbart's original term here is *Bildsamkeit*, a term that has been frequently translated as "plasticity." It refers to the idea that children and human beings in general are intrinsically malleable

and open to education. At the same time, it also suggests that children also bring something of their individuality or of their own to education.
16　Herbart hoped to find absolute, "philosophical" certainties in psychology and ethics to serve as a foundation for his theory. Unsurprisingly, he did not discover these. Much of this uncertainty still remains with us today (see footnote 13).

CHAPTER THREE

F.D.E. Schleiermacher: Outlines of the Art of Education—Introductory Lecture—Selections

Editor's Introduction

Friedrich Daniel Ernst Schleiermacher (1768–1834) is known in the English-speaking world as a liberal Protestant theologian and the founder of modern hermeneutics (the art and science of interpretation). But Schleiermacher accomplished a great deal more: He was the co-founder of the first modern research university (in Berlin with Wilhelm von Humboldt, whose last name the university subsequentially adopted). And together with J.F. Herbart (Chapter Two) Schleiermacher is seen in Germany and Northern Europe as having effectively founded pedagogy as a domain of academic study.

Schleiermacher's life, like his work, is full of opposition and contradiction. The young Schleiermacher was a chaplain, but one who rejected orthodox Christianity; he was also a tutor (at the home of a wealthy count), but later also rejected this type of education (e.g., see p. 45). Schleiermacher was deeply influenced by Enlightenment thinkers like Kant but came to be a beloved member of a circle of Romantic writers and artists in Berlin[1] who rebelled against many Enlightenment principles. In fact, this Romantic rebellion holds the key to understanding the relevance of Schleiermacher's lecture to the themes of tact and the pedagogical relation. Romanticism was a broad cultural movement that opposed the logic, reason and adult "maturity"[2] so privileged by the Enlightenment; instead, it emphasized emotion, childhood, as well as the importance of "life" itself.

The influence of Romanticism is evident in Schleiermacher's lecture, for example, in his answer to the question: "Is one permitted to sacrifice one moment of life [for the child] as a mere means to the end of another moment of life?" (p. 8). Here, what is paramount for Schleiermacher is the *life* and *feelings* of the child. Schleiermacher is particularly concerned with the fact that pedagogy frequently requires the sacrifice of moments in the child's *present* for the sake of much more abstract *future* benefits. This is today exemplified by sayings like "no pain, no gain," or "it's for your own good." Schleiermacher ultimately answers his own question by saying that such a sacrifice should *not* be permitted. And Schleiermacher works out ways that the child can best be prepared for the future without their enjoyment of the present being limited and sacrificed. In doing so, Schleiermacher's attention remains with the concrete realities of life—namely with how the child's games and play can be deeply enjoyable and absorbing while still preparing them for the future.

After his initial time in Berlin with his Romantic friends, Schleiermacher took up a professorial position in nearby Halle and later returned to Berlin to work at the university he helped found there. In both positions, Schleiermacher lectured widely on subjects ranging from theology, history and ethics to hermeneutics. And he did so, unfortunately, often without taking the time "to give written form to most of his ideas" (Schmidt, 1972, p. 451). As a result, many of his lectures, including the one discussed here, are a combination of Schleiermacher's own lecture notes, along with those made by his students, published posthumously. This is the reason for the many editorial additions and comments added in square brackets throughout.

Schleiermacher remained in Berlin until his death at 65, which was followed by an enormous public funeral. The King of Prussia, Fredrick William II, rode "in the first 100 carriages of the procession," being followed by an estimated 20,000 members of the public.[3]

The contradictions and oppositions in Schleiermacher's life are somewhat different from those evident in his thought and writing: These more conceptual opposites are deliberate, and are a part of a technique, a kind of dialectic that Schleiermacher used to structure and move his thinking forward. Schleiermacher purposefully chose not to follow any one single line of argumentation in working towards his often-powerful conclusions. Instead, as the example of his treatment of the opposition of present and future moments in the life of the child shows (pp. 50–56), Schleiermacher moves between opposed pairs of possibilities to sometimes arrive at a conclusion, and at others, he simply turns to a different pair of opposites. A relatively simple example of his work with oppositions is provided by the first section of Schleiermacher's lecture titled: "Common View. Technique of

Domestic Tutor and School Teacher," where Schleiermacher considers exactly who it is that he is addressing: "One must assume we are all familiar with what is called 'education,'" he begins, but "if we ask *for whom* this familiar knowledge is turned into a theory and what this theory should be about it is as follows" (p. 44; emphasis added). Here, Schleiermacher is not only noting that we lack a way of formally defining the familiar phenomenon of education,[4] he also opens a path to considering two opposed possibilities for education: The technique of the domestic tutor on the one hand (about which Schleiermacher, of course, speaks from experience) and the technique of the schoolteacher on the other. Briefly, Schleiermacher concludes that the work of the tutor is too particularized for the development of theory, and that the work of the teacher is similarly too bound to its subject matter. By moving from tutor to teacher, Schleiermacher arrives at a conclusion, namely that "we are concerned here neither with the technique of the tutor nor of the teacher." He then asks: "[So] What is the starting point for this lecture?" (p. 46).

This new question forms the basis for the next section in his lecture ("Foundation of a Scientific Inquiry"). Here, Schleiermacher considers a further pair of opposites, namely that between the older generation and the younger:

> Humankind is made up of individual beings who live through a certain cycle of existence on this earth before leaving it. And this happens in a way that those who are in this cycle at the same time can be divided into an older and younger generation... (p. 46)

Unlike the question of the tutor vs. the schoolteacher, the opposition of the younger and older generations is a very fruitful one for Schleiermacher. In fact, it turns out to be nothing less than the foundation for everything that Schleiermacher goes on to discuss in his lecture: "This relationship between the older and the younger, and the obligations of the one to the other," he concludes, "form the basis on which we will build everything that lies in the scope of our theory" (p. 46).

One of the key elements of Schleiermacher's theory that arises from this foundation is the idea that the way that the older generation works to realize its obligations to the younger is through a general kind of "influence:" The "older generation exerts an influence upon the younger," Schleiermacher says; and without it, he adds, "every generation would have to start from scratch... [to] achieve that which was already accomplished before" (p. 48). This broad notion of influence—which can be seen as being exercised in anything from TV shows through specialized disciplinary knowledge to a parent's loving touch—is fundamental to the understanding of pedagogy that is developed (and also put into question) not only in Schleiermacher's lecture, but in *all* of the texts collected in this book: Pedagogy, for all of these authors, is to be found everywhere that the older generation influences the younger—especially in the conscious and overt exercise of such influence. This means that pedagogy as a discipline can be defined specifically as a study of the ways and contexts in which this influence can be exercised and understood. It also means that pedagogy as a discipline is expected to outline a practical perspective that is taken up by every educator, parent or adult who engages with children. As Schleiermacher puts it, "every pedagogical influence is a materialization [*Ausfüllung*] of a moment in the life of the subject to be educated" (p. 50).

These two founding ideas—namely that education is about (i) the relationship of the older generation with the younger; and (ii) that it is particularly concerned with the influence exercised by the older—for subsequent educational thinking in north and central Europe can hardly be overestimated. It is certainly indispensable to Herman Nohl's formulation of the "pedagogical relation" itself (Chapters Four and Five). Nohl, after all, sees this relation as one arising between "a mature person and one who is becoming" (p. 79). The pedagogical relation, to put this slightly differently, can be seen precisely as the "relationship between the older and the younger, and the obligations of the one to the other" (p. 46), as Schleiermacher says but with one difference: It understands this relation *individual* rather than *collective* terms.

After dealing with this opposition, Schleiermacher goes on to consider yet another pair of opposites—namely, of theory and practice. The relation between theory and practice was discussed in some depth by Herbart in his lecture on pedagogical tact (Chapter Two). It has also been considered by scholars ranging from John Dewey (1904) to Donald Schön (1984) and beyond. It is generally one in which theory is seen as valuable but insufficient for dealing with all the details and difficulties that are presented by everyday pedagogical (and other) practice. As Schleiermacher himself notes, the "entirely general statements" typical of theory simply "do not help" in actual moments of practice: "This is in part because there are just too many exceptions and because they have nothing to say about the most difficult [question]—namely [the] application [of such general statements]" (p. 44). For Herbart on the other hand, who takes the "fundamental correctness [of theory] on faith" (p. 32), this insufficiency of theory is to be addressed through tact. For Schön's "reflective practitioner" (for example), it is dealt with through individual reflection-in-action, and for others, it is a question of practice having as much "fidelity" to theory as possible (e.g., Kalafat et al., 2007).

However, Schleiermacher deals with this question in a way that is quite different: He doesn't try to "save" theory in the face of the complexity and variability of practice; he begins instead with practice itself, granting it a value (a "dignity") that is far greater than what can be ascribed to theory. For example, he notes: "Originally, it was parents who educated, and as is commonly acknowledged, they did not do so following a 'theory'" (p. 44). Later, he concludes: "Therefore, it would be incorrect to say that practice gains its character and specificity only through theory. The dignity of practice exists independently from theory. Theory only makes practice more conscious" (pp. 48).

It is through this important insight that Schleiermacher can be seen to add something to Herbart's articulation of tact and to make his own essential contribution to future understandings of both tact and the pedagogical relation (e.g., see: Muth, Chapter Six, Lippitz, Chapter Nine and Zirfas, Chapter Eleven). Although Schleiermacher does not address the question of tact directly in the text included here, in granting practice its own primacy and dignity, he suggests that practice itself should tell us what our theory should be about. We should not take "the fundamental correctness" of theory "on faith," as Herbart urges. The challenge for pedagogical practice in this sense becomes not about implementing any one technique or idea for instruction. Instead, it becomes a kind of negotiation with singularity and uniqueness presented both by the child and the situation itself. And it is exactly this singular moment of adult responsibility that forms the starting point for Herman Nohl's initial formal definitions of the pedagogical relation, and the understanding of tact that develops from it (Chapters Four and Five).

Sources/Recommended Reading

Dewey, J. (1904). The relation of theory to practice in education. In C. A. McMurry (Ed.), *The third yearbook of the national society for the scientific study of education. Part I* (pp. 9–30). The University of Chicago Press. https://archive.org/details/r00elationoftheorynatirich

Friesen, N. (2020). "Education as a *Geisteswissenschaft*:" An introduction to Human Science Pedagogy. *Journal of Curriculum Studies, 52*(3), 307–322. doi.org/10.1080/00220272.2019.1705917

Kalafat, J., Illback, R. J., & Sanders, D. Jr. (2007). The relationship between implementation fidelity and educational outcomes in a school-based family support program: Development of a model for evaluating multidimensional full-service programs. *Evaluation and Program Planning, 30*(2), 136–148.

Kenklies, K. (2012) Educational theory as topological rhetoric: The concepts of pedagogy of Johann Friedrich Herbart and Friedrich Schleiermacher. *Studies in Philosophy and Education, 31*, 265–273. 10.1007/s11217-012-9287-6

OED. (2003). *Oxford English Dictionary* (3rd ed.). Oxford University Press.

Schmidt, G. R. (1972). Friedrich Schleiermacher, a classical thinker on education. *Educational Theory, 22*(4), 450–459.

Schön, D. A. (1984). *The reflective practitioner: How professionals think in action*. Basic Books.

Vail, T. (2013). *Schleiermacher: A guide for the perplexed*. Bloomsbury.

Outlines of the Art of Education: Introductory Lecture from 1826[5]

Common View. Technique of Domestic Tutor and School Teacher

One must assume we are all familiar with what is commonly called "education." But if we ask for whom this familiar knowledge is turned into a theory and what this theory should be about [we would say] it is as follows: Originally, it was parents who educated, and as is commonly acknowledged, they did not do so following a "theory."[6] However, parents do not only educate [their children]; and their "educational" activities are neither separated nor stand out from the other aspects of their lives. But now, one associates "general educational guidance"[7] with those who help parents with education, with persons whose calling it is to work together with parents on matters of domestic education for a limited period of time. [One also associates this guidance] with those who dedicate their entire professional life to taking on a specific part [of children's] education in a public institution. In both of these cases, a theory of education and upbringing appears to be fruitful, even necessary. The practices of both [tutor and teacher] are opposed to one another. What is important for the private tutor, undertaking education in the narrow meaning of cultivating moral sense, of children's minds and souls in general,[8] seems overshadowed in the context of the teacher. What is important for the teacher is instruction, or the transmission of skills and information—something that is only of secondary importance for the tutor. However, it is for both that a set of instructions, a technique, is sought in general guidance for education.

But whatever can be achieved in this regard does not seem aligned with what is usually presented in academic lectures. For in general guidance [for education], one can proceed only from relationships that are entirely by chance. At least as far as the tutor's vocation goes, it has long been said that the education he provides is a necessary evil, and not anything particularly purposeful or good. When the tutor and the parents meet initially, numerous conflicts and collisions are sure to arise. As a result, much of the guidance for the tutor's work consists of something one might—through reference to "pastoral prudence"—call "tutorial prudence." This guidance either seeks to align the tutor with the parents, or to give him a kind of independence from them. But these are things for which it is very difficult to provide advice. One can only formulate entirely general statements that do not help. This is in part because there are just too many exceptions and because they have nothing to say about the most difficult [question]—namely [the] application [of such general statements].

Therefore, one can ask if it would not be much better if such [artificial, tutored] relationships did not actually come into being. Do not relations arise naturally in every family that could, just on their own, provide the necessary [educational] foundations for children? Through such foundations the child can be prepared in the family—in both a moral and intellectual sense—for instruction in public institutions. The fact that this does not happen is due to both domestic and public limitations. There is no way to develop a theory particularly for such situations because of these deficiencies. However, as long as the necessary evil of the household tutor remains, learning to teach will naturally be based on the general guidance that arises from experience.[9] And this necessary evil is all the worse the more the young tutor has no way to make up for his lack of experience. The means of assistance, however, that are in this case readily available—in the form of collections of experiences and rules derived from them—do not appear from a distance at all rigorous or scientific.[10]

But when it comes to advice and guidance for work in public educational settings—where instruction is the principle activity—we cannot necessarily say that one is dealing with something that is based only on chance. It is difficult to think of a highly developed commonwealth, such as our states, without public institutions for the instruction of the youth. Rather, both [state and education] seem to belong together. But we consider on the one hand what is expected of school [by the state] because the school mirrors the type of commonwealth [that the state is]. And given this commonwealth is a nation governed by laws, this means that education, too, is so governed. This further means that any theory of education would appear to belong to the political realm [rather than being an autonomous field of inquiry]. After all, Plato introduces laws for education in the context of his book about the state, [*The Republic*].

But on the other hand, the principle activity [in public educational institutions] is instruction, which is much less dependent on the laws of the state. And the theory of instruction is so closely wedded to the arts and sciences [or the school subjects that it addresses] that it cannot be separated from them. Every science and art has its own method that arises much more directly from the content itself than from the relation of teacher and learner. [Therefore] didactics, [or the] method of instruction, is hardly autonomous as it is a supplement to the sciences and arts which are being taught. Life itself confirms this, where it is regulated reasonably. Because for those whose instruction in the sciences and arts has been taken to the point where they can consider teaching it to others, there are institutes (seminaries) that teach [instructional] methods in a way that practice can follow directly from technique. And this [close connection of practice and technique] is the only way, since learning to teach ψιλῷ λόγῳ (just by words) is worthless.

Foundation of a Scientific Inquiry

If we are concerned here neither with the technique of the tutor nor of the teacher, the question arises: What is the starting point for this lecture?

Humankind is made up of individual beings who live through a certain cycle of existence on this earth before leaving it. And this happens in a way that those who are in this cycle at the same time can be divided into an older and younger generation, with the older being the first to leave this earth. However, when we look at humankind in terms of the large masses that we call peoples [or nations], it is clear that over generations, things do not remain the same. Instead, there is a rise and fall in every aspect [of the welfare of nations] that is important to us. However, in looking at the life of a people, we cannot tell exactly whether the first half leads to a high point and the second half to a low point, or whether we are confusing the two altogether. Regardless, it is clear that any such increase and decrease are based upon human activity. This activity is more complete and perfect the more it is governed by an idea of what should happen—the more it has an exemplar to guide its action—the more it is an art.[11]

A significant part of the activity of the older generation extends toward the younger, and it is less complete or perfect, the less aware the older generation is about what it is doing and why it is doing it. Therefore, there has to be a theory that is based on the relation of the older generation and the younger, one that proceeds from the question: What does the older generation actually want with the younger? To what extent does the action [of the older] correspond to the [given] goal, the result to the [original] action? This relationship between the older and the younger, and the obligations of the one to the other, form the basis on which we will build everything that lies in the scope of our theory.

The Dignity of Pedagogy Presented in Formal Terms; Seen in Itself as a Theory of an Art[12]

So that this [theory] does not seem unjustified, we have to go back to the beginning. We started by saying that the activity of the older generation toward the young [i.e. education] would have to possess the characteristics of an art. If this presupposition is correct, then there obviously has to be a theory of education as art—since every art demands its own [theory]. At the same time, there are human activities which have little to do with art. So the question is: Is education really an art? Humans are beings that carry in themselves the sufficient ground for their development from their start to their completion. This is already in the idea of life, especially of life of the spirit [*Geist*] and intellect. Where there is no such internal ground, there is no change in the subject, or only change of a mechanistic nature. However, this does not mean that the changes of a living being must not be shaped or modified through external influence.[13] Indeed, this is the essence of the idea of community—or to take it to a higher level, the idea of the world. The idea of community here is nothing other than the idea of the species. If the sum of all individual beings constitutes the species, then the development of the individual being will be determined through their common nature which make them a species, as well as through the mutual influence [of individual beings]. Without this there is no humankind, no human species. One can think of the relationship between the principle of internal development and external influence in many different ways. Either [internal development or external influence can be seen] as minimal or maximal. The more one minimizes the importance of external influences, the less reason there is to view it [i.e. external influencing] as an art, and to develop a theory about it. But where does this leave us? Is the influence of the older generation on the younger so minimal that it is simply not worthwhile to regard it as an art? This is the first and preliminary question. Apparently, there are two ways to answer it: The first is historical and the second *a priori*, purely conceptual. However, if we want to begin with the correct starting points, the second option would lead us too far back. So we will opt for the historical path, and will find the answer in experience. In historical experience, we find societies at very early stages of development in which the older generation exerts an influence upon the younger without producing any theory [to account for it]. Let us look at two peoples who are very close to us [Europeans]; the first in religious or spiritual matters and the other in philosophical and scientific terms: The first, the Jewish nation, out of which Christianity evolved, and the [second, the] Greek, upon whose culture ours has been built. At its height, the Jewish nation was an [entity] grounded within itself and had reached an appreciable level of development.[14] This society had only very limited public institutions for education; most education apparently took place in the realm of the family. There is no doubt that this education followed a specific paradigm, but we cannot speak of a theory of education in this case. But with the Greeks, we can be very precise about the origin of such a theory. Education was primarily a task that was undertaken within a community; it was much more public, and more closely connected to laws of the state. However, there is no trace of a theory predating Plato. The elements of such a theory, however, were of course available much earlier in the form of very general maxims and proverbs. But these only prepare the ground for theory.

These peoples [the Jews and the Greeks] placed great emphasis on external influences; and even though their theory developed later, their education did not lack the characteristics of an art. And it is true for every domain that can be called an art in the narrow sense of the word that practice always precedes theory. Therefore, it would be incorrect to say that practice gains its character and specificity only through theory. The dignity of practice exists independently from theory. Theory only makes practice more conscious.

We now try to find something more general and formalized in these specific historical observations. It is impossible to think of the individual, especially from the beginning of [his] life, in complete isolation from others. This is a general fact of experience. At the beginning of life, external influences greatly exceed any internal developmental force. However, if an individual were [already] developed to a certain extent through external influences, we could well imagine him being able to forge his own existence independent from society. However, we cannot suppose that he would flourish intellectually as he would in society. We have to infer from this that those who live within human society will develop much more fully than those who are isolated, even if the isolated individual had more original developmental force within him. Drawing on our conception of the human race, it seems clear that the difference between individuals is never so great that someone deprived of external influence would develop to the same level as one who lives in society. Those scenarios that offer examples of very young children who have been removed from society show that intellectual development is strongly and unfavorably affected. Even though we should not generalize from these isolated instances, and more study is needed, we can still assume the following [in the case of the isolation of the young]: Not only would every younger generation lag behind the older, if not for the significant influence of the older, but also every generation would have to start from scratch, and achieve that which was already accomplished before. [In addition,] we could not talk about any kind of development in humankind. In a sense every individual starts life "afresh;" but what matters is how soon he can take part in the advancement of human activity on earth. The more quickly this can occur, the more the forces for the development of the human spirit are aroused. This is already part and parcel of the general moral undertaking. The influence exercised on the younger generation is a part of this moral undertaking. [It is] thus a purely ethical matter.

The more importance we ascribe to this accelerating influence (although it is admittedly not always accelerating in effect), the more important it is in reality, and the more the older generation has already been developed, the less we can leave question of this influence to mere chance. Consequently, we can now see the relation of the theory of education to ethics more clearly, and that it is a theory of an art that is derived from ethics.

Considered in Relation to Politics

One point offers itself here as a parallel. If we ask how long the older generation continues to exercise influence on the younger, we realize that in general, there is no clear limit. But there will always be a co-existence of the two temporally separated generations, [a co-existence] in which the older does not simply influence the younger, but in which both work together toward one goal. To the same degree that this shared activity increases, the influencing of the older generation on the younger decreases. And in the end [this one-way influence] ceases to exist. That is when education itself stops. In any case, every large mass of people forms a common social and cultural [*geistige*] existence. When this develops to a certain point, a living whole comes into being—the state. This continues to exist simply through human activity, since it is only a complex of such activity. As long as the state remains the same [as a political entity] and does not exclude [the possibility of] its eventual perfection, its social and cultural [*geistige*] activity will intensify. Then, the [complex of human] action must also remain the same in its kind, itself rising toward perfection. Communal life in the state is so significant that from a certain perspective, it includes all moral activity. And even if we cannot share this particular perspective, we must admit that it is necessary to have a theory that reveals how the goal [toward which communal life strives] is to be reached—so that the state might continue through generational changes, and its enterprise flourish. This theory will explain how the desired continuation and rise of the state in its entirety can be reached—notwithstanding intervening generational changes. This [theory] is [called] politics. Both the theory of politics and the theory of pedagogy are inextricably intertwined; both constitute fields of ethical inquiry and need to be treated in the same way. Politics will not reach its goal unless pedagogy is an integral part of it or [unless pedagogy] stands next to it as an equally developed field. To the degree that communal life in the state is disrupted in practice and misconstrued in theory, the less the influence of the older generation on the younger can be accounted for. Here we have the starting point for our inquiry into our object [for this lecture]. Pedagogy is a science [*Wissenschaft*] that is at once closely connected to ethics, and also derived from it as an applied field, and [it is one] that is coordinated with politics.

The fact that there are two views on the relationship between the fields of pedagogy and politics arises from the difference between our Christian era and the earlier heathen [i.e. Greek and Roman] one. Our Christian era knows a collective life [not only] in the state but also in the church. One cannot be subordinated to the other; both [church and state] must co-exist. There are many Christian states in which the church is not the one or only [church, and in these cases,] the church is not the state; at the same time, there are other states in which the church is the *one* church, but in which the state is not the same as the church.[15] Notwithstanding its separation into different churches, the church remains an undivided whole, and it is therefore in some respects the same in all Christian states. The divisions within the church do not mirror the separation of the states just as the different states cannot be traced back to the[ir] conception of the church. Since we cannot deny either one—church or state—we must acknowledge both. It is part of our moral duty to sustain the life of the church from one generation to the next just as we do so for [the life of] the state. Our theory has to relate to both to the same degree.

If we have now established [the grounds for] the dignity of pedagogy, we [can] say: On account of the great importance of the influence of the older generation on the younger, we are in need of a theory in order to gauge rules for practice. [Such a] theory is connected to ethical considerations as much as the activity exercised by the older generation [on the younger] is itself connected with general ethical activity. If this is the case, then we have defined the task for our inquiry—but only in very general, formal terms. So far, we only know that there is an influence of the earlier generation on the later, and that for this [influence] we need a theory of an art. [...]

Is One Allowed to Sacrifice One Moment for Another?

Both goals of education [to develop individuality and community] may coincide or [they] may not. [Nevertheless,] every pedagogical influence is a materialization [*Ausfüllung*] of a moment in the life of the subject to be educated. [At the same time,] this [pedagogical] influence calculates its direction regarding the future, and its value consists in what emerges out of it in the future. On the one hand, this is easily comprehended, since there is no awareness of the state and church in the child at the point where those influences begin. The child therefore cannot desire such a practice that relates only to state, church and so on. However, the child surely desires in every moment some kind of specific activity in life. In all purely pedagogical moments, though, something is generated that the child does not desire, meaning that every predominantly pedagogical moment would be an inhibiting one. The unmediated consciousness [of the child] is entirely abrogated.

The same is the case in relation to the development of the individual nature. Even though individuality isn't completely absent in any given moment, we still need to differentiate between behavior that is an expression of the personal individuality of the child, and a practice that encourages something to appear that has not yet come into appearance. Also in this relation, the [young] child lives entirely in the present, not for the future, and they therefore cannot participate in this purpose, and cannot have an interest in it for the development of their own individual character.

We therefore must deal with a contradiction regarding these two directions. In both cases, the activity of education appears at every single moment in opposition to what the person to be educated can desire. Every pedagogical influence presents itself as the sacrifice of a present moment for a future one; and it raises the question whether we are justified in making this sacrifice. From the start, common sense [*das allgemeine Gefühl*] refutes this. The clearer it is perceived that the children despise and oppose the education they receive, the more everyone holds this education to be harsh, and disapproves of it. It does not matter whether this opposition becomes more or less apparent. The problem remains.

If we consider the matter more theoretically, then it is transformed into an ethical question: Is one permitted to sacrifice one moment of life as a mere means to the end of another moment of life?

All of our life activity manifests consistent opposition to such a practice [of sacrifice]. For example, the act of nourishment, thought of as an act [of sheer animal ingestion] that fills one moment in time—and nothing else—appears incongruous with human dignity. If one actually sensually enjoys the taste of food and drink, then it is better than being defined by mere ingestion—although only in comparison to that which is animalistic. Such an act must not exclusively occupy one moment in time; we associate it with conversation and make those moments of ingestion into something that is at the same time social, and this humanizes the process. This example can stand in the place of all others; we only need to consider its diametric opposite.

We can, however, emphasize a more immediate aspect. Seen in terms of his or her appearance, the human being is governed by constant change, as is everything that is becoming in time [*alles Zeitliche und Werdende*]. Strictly speaking, the human is not at any given moment the same as he was in a previous one. Also, the internal activity which becomes apparent is governed by constant change. If we now consider two moments quite separate in time, namely one from childhood, and another from later in life in which self-conscious activity is most distinctively manifest, then everyone would admit that the two moments are indeed quite different. If we isolate one of these two moments, then we are confronted with a specific [kind of] human existence. However, this is as such still part of the whole, and is therefore to be supported in our common life through cooperation. In the relationship of the whole to the individual, there is a specific ethical obligation to support every moment in life as such. The more completely the essence of a person is manifest in every moment of life because of this affiliation with a greater, common realm of human life, the more complete life itself becomes.

However, [if] one moment is now completely sacrificed for another one in the future, then the ethical obligation remains completely unfulfilled. How can we escape from this disharmony?

This becomes even more difficult and important if we consider not only one moment, but a great sequence of moments—the whole period of education. Among a great number of those to be educated, the intended moments [for the fulfillment of the education] are never realized. This is because the time of education is characterized by the highest level of mortality, making the sacrifice of an early moment for a later one lose any relevance for those who die early.[16] One might think it helpful to suggest: Even though children may express opposition—to whatever degree—against a pedagogical influence aimed at the future, the time would certainly come when they would consent to it. The assumption is that this later time is privileged and complete, and the positions taken in the incomplete state of childhood are to be ignored. And if one were to suspend the pedagogical influence because of [the child's] opposition, then the subject [i.e. the child or person themselves] would disapprove in the future, and the educator would be held responsible. This reasoning that is used to justify the sacrifice of the moment would be correct only if the child were also satisfied with substance of the pedagogical influence. However, one can never know this. And for those who do not reach a time when their consent can be given, the whole justification of the practice [of education] disappears. We therefore must consider another way.

Proceeding from the justification attempted above, we assume that there will be a point and time in the future when the child will consent to pedagogical practice. However, does this time come only when one uses that which has been stimulated through pedagogical influence in one's job or profession? We must not limit ourselves to this. To live in the present moment is only the province of the tenderest childhood. Remembrance of the past and anticipation of the future develop gradually in the same way. The time for [the child's] endorsement [of the pedagogical influence] is therefore given to arrive. By the time the future reveals itself to the child in a particular way, and the child is able to realize what he or she has to achieve in the future and starts to aspire to it, the child will also desire that education will take the future into account. Presuming that education takes the right path, we would therefore have to say that it will struggle with this opposition primarily at the beginning. The closer it comes to its endpoint, the more education withdraws from any opposition, and at the end, there will be no opposition for it to overcome. If education follows the right path, opposition appears to dissolve and disappear.

But our earlier observation [about the ethical obligation of education] is not eliminated. Because even this initial opposition [of the child] is not a state that can be sanctioned from an ethical point of view. From what has already been said, we only must gather that the corrective which we require and search out will be something that itself also dissolves and disappears. However, we cannot state at this point that in education as such, the relation to the future can be neglected in any way, since it is truly the nature of the pedagogical influence to be oriented toward the future. Inasmuch as we may want to weaken this orientation, we would eliminate the pedagogical influence as such.

The only way we can eliminate the contradiction is to decide the matter from an ethical perspective: That life activity, which has its relation to the future, must at the same time find satisfaction in the present; in the same way, every pedagogical moment that, as such, is related to the future has to provide satisfaction for the individual as he or she *is* [in the moment]. The more these two interpenetrate, the more ethically perfect the pedagogical activity becomes. And the less one is sacrificed for the other, the more both moments are able to merge together. If we were to say that pedagogical activity has to be strictly enforced with the most recalcitrant child—so that the child would have to abandon his or her satisfaction in the present moment for the sake of the future—then education as an ethical activity would be imperfect and morally damaging. If on the other hand, we were to say that in order for the pedagogical influence to be exercised morally without being damaging, pedagogical activity would have to be diminished to the point where satisfaction is granted in the moment. But in this case, we just would have displaced the difficulty and contradiction elsewhere. Or in other words: we would have asserted that for pedagogical activity to be morally perfect, it must be technically imperfect [i.e. without influence].

It is therefore [our] task [to achieve] such a unification in which no sacrifice occurs. But this only seems possible when on the one hand, we establish a relation to the future in a way that the moment is utterly and completely satisfying for the child. And as long as the approval to take into account the future moment cannot yet be given because of the child's limited consciousness of the future, we would realize this [unification] by avoiding everything that—which because it does not intrude into the moment—could excite the opposition of the child. If on the other hand the child gives his or her agreement or consent, and no opposition to taking the future into account has to be taken into consideration, we recognize the satisfaction of the moment in this act of agreement itself. In this case, the life of the child, even when it is interrupted in a period of education, is one that is ethically treated as an end [in itself], and the pedagogical influence is the satisfaction of their very way of being [*Dasein*]. Either the satisfaction lies directly in the moment, or in the agreement. All of education is a series of such moments of satisfaction, with any one giving way to the next.

But we cannot be silent about the fact that the formula we have just presented appears to suffer from an internal contradiction that must be eliminated. If we think of the time in which the child is already aware of the future, though in a way that they cannot take on fully but that sets their trust in those who are providing guidance: in this way, an intimation of the goal arises in the child. Pedagogical practice would actually not require anything more of that which appears as the mere satisfaction of the moment; the pedagogical influence itself offers satisfaction through the way the future is found in the spirit [*Seele*] of the child. The most immediate satisfaction of the moment through the present itself occurs when the pedagogical influence is interrupted. For the life of the child does not consist [only] of numerous moments [of education, i.e. ones] in which the pedagogical influence dominates. Such [non-pedagogical] moments, however, are not part of our investigation.

If now in opposition to the moment in life we [just] consider[ed], we look at an earlier moment in which the future is not yet found in the child, then we cannot assume that the satisfaction is provided through the pedagogical content of the moment. The satisfaction of one's entire life activity, as it is directly related to the [present] instant [*Augenblick*] in time will be the main focus without taking the future into account. According to this, we do indeed have two different periods in this connection [in how the child views the future]. Moreover, we cannot overlook [the fact] that there isn't a clear and distinct moment in which the future also enters into consciousness. It seems therefore as if we would need two different formulae. The first would consist of two parts/aspects: This moment is realized in terms of what offers satisfaction as a preparation for the future and of what offers satisfaction in the present. The second [formula] would only have one part or aspect: The moment is realized [only] as the satisfaction of the present. Nevertheless, education should be whole and complete, and every moment, inasmuch as it can be isolated, should be accounted for by the same formula. Moreover, if we consider that these two periods in life [as described above] are not distinctly separated, then, in relation to the fulfillment of our task, one and only one formula with the same content is to be postulated. How can we now arrive at a solution?

The relationship between the first beginnings and the further development of education, where there is the assent of the child for the future, necessarily becomes one that, in the progression of education, is severed. [The moment that is separated] into a practice that is oriented to the future [on the one hand] and to the immediate satisfaction of the present [on the other], is *not* separate at the beginning of education, but inextricable. The separation of these two moments happens gradually. It is a continuous development and presents itself completely when the consent of the child to take the future into account is given. Whether a specific gradation has to be assumed here, or whether education, like life itself, represents a gradual transition, has yet to be addressed. Here, we first have to achieve some clarity about this in itself. We call "play" or a "game" in the broadest sense that which, in the life of the child, offers satisfaction in the very moment without regard to the future. On the other hand, [we call] "exercise" the activity directed toward the future. If therefore education were to be consistent with the moral goal, our theorem must be as follows: In the beginning, exercise [has to be present] exclusively in play. However, gradually both [play and exercise] become separate to the degree to which the child develops an appreciation for the exercise and rejoices in it for what it is. The latter we have referred to above as the consent of the child.

We also find this theorem implied in the language of the ancients. It is but one and the same word that refers either to exercises which indicate something playful or to those which hint at something more serious. Music and some physical activity [μουσική, γυμναστική] are both: playful and serious exercises, a light exercise of playing and a serious undertaking. In this way and from this perspective, we would have then liberated education from any contradiction and have made it consonant with the common moral obligation. Furthermore, the child would be treated as human in every single moment.

However, it remains to be asked whether our solution—that in the beginning, exercise has to be present exclusively in the play—is actually possible. This question can be answered as follows: First, everything that we would refer to with the expression "play" or "game," inasmuch it is an activity, can only be an activity consisting of one specific practice or of several related and therefore united practices. Because of that, play activities are already exercises in themselves as it is a law of all human activities that every activity becomes easier through repetition. From what has become easier, one proceeds to something difficult. Imagining play to be in this way progressive, it appears at the same time to always be an exercise. Second, every human capacity is something that develops over time. And the human consciousness is complete only if it is of the same character [i.e. developing over time] and also expresses this. If one is conscious of one's development, this is the simultaneous satisfaction of both the present and future. In fact, the human begins in a state of non-consciousness, and the first occurrences of consciousness are fleeting moments. However, as soon as this imperfect form disappears and moments begin to connect with each other, a certain form of comparison of these more or less connected moments will have to emerge as well. [Further] consciousness has to follow, too, and growing out of this will be a consciousness of human capacities as being under development. Inasmuch therefore as play in its design is exercise as well, it is nothing but the complete satisfaction of the consciousness of the child in the present, because while playing, children are conscious of their powers and of the development of their capacities.

Notes

1. Two female members of this Romantic circle seemed to be almost swooning over the young chaplain: Although "he was not the greatest man [*Mann*] of his time," one wrote, "he was the greatest human being [*Mensch*]." A second effused how Schleiermacher possessed "so much understanding, so much knowledge, [yet was] so full of love and yet so tender," Vial, 2013, p. 12.
2. In writing "What is Enlightenment?" (1784) Kant famously defined "Enlightenment" as a kind of "maturity" (*Mündigkeit*) that allowed one to think for oneself.
3. Vial, 2013, p. 23.
4. It is worth mentioning that it is difficult if not impossible to find a commonly accepted formal definition of "education" in English. The *Oxford English Dictionary* (OED 2003), for example, defines education as "systematic instruction… received by a child, typically at a *school*" (emphasis added). If we then look up "school" in the OED, it is defined as the "institution for the formal *education* of children or young people" (emphasis added). The definition is circular: Education is what happens at school and school is where education happens. Handbooks and encyclopedia in education themselves generally also fail to provide entries focusing specifically on this term. Based on this lack of definition, Schleiermacher's point about the challenge in defining education arguably still stands today.
5. Translated by Norm Friesen and Karsten Kenklies (Strathclyde University, Glasgow)
6. *Theory* is meant here in the sense of the Greek word θεωρία (*theoria*)—meaning "viewing, speculation, contemplation, *the* contemplative life," but simultaneously also as an activity understood in its relationship to action and praxis. (Peters, F. [1967]. *Greek philosophical terms: A historical lexicon*. New York University Press.)
7. *Erziehungslehre*. The term "Lehre" in this compound word could be translated as principles regarding education. As just one example, Fichte's *Wissenschaftslehre* (literally, teachings of science) from 1804 has recently been translated as his "Science of Knowing."
8. Here, Schleiermacher is using the term "Geist" (spirit) as an adjective (*geistig*), speaking of the entire "geist-ly" being or essence of the child in general. We have translated *Geist* and *geistig* variously, depending on its association with individual or with a collective human way of being. In referring to individual manifestations, we use the terms spirit(ual), intellect(ual), mind/mental, inner or inward. When speaking of its collective manifestation, we generally translate it as culture(al), society/social and/or intellect(ual).
9. The term being used here is *Erfahrungslehren* (literally the teachings of experience). See footnote 2.
10. *Wissenschaftlich*: *Wissenschaft* identifies a semantic field much broader than informal contemporary understandings of "science" or "scientific" suggest. It includes all scholarly study and work—such as reflection and philosophical speculation.
11. Here, Schleiermacher is using the word "art" to designate not a purely aesthetic pursuit, but τέχνη or *techne*, a practical knowing and doing that involves craft and technique and that is variable and context dependent.

12   Schleiermacher is using the term "*Kunstlehre*" for "theory of an art." He also uses this term in reference to his hermeneutics (where it is also translated as a "theory of an art;" see: Schleiermacher, F.D.E. (2008). *Hermeneutic criticism*. Cambridge University Press.). *Kunstlehre* suggests a practical type of knowledge or teaching, one that is realized in practice rather than something that can be articulated explicitly. It is also in this sense that Schleiermacher describes the practice of education as preceding its theory.

13   *Einwirkung* is often translated in English as "influence," but it has stronger connotations than the English term suggests. It could be also translated as "effect," "control" or "intervention," but the very decisive, even deterministic denotations of these terms would be unsatisfactory for Schleiermacher's text. Schleiermacher generally associates the term *Einwirkung* with the action of the older generation that is directed to the younger, and his text emphasizes that adult action in the life of a young person is ongoing, of many kinds, and does not reliably result in a predetermined outcome.

14   *Bildung* is used by Schleiermacher here for development. Among other things, *Bildung* refers both to collective and individual growth and development; in both senses, it gives special emphasis to active self-aware engagement in this development.

15   Schleiermacher is referring to the relations of church and state that reflect the European situation at his time, and that still apply to some degree to this day: Some countries (e.g. Italy, Norway) have traditionally had an official church and a "state religion" (whether Catholic or Protestant).

16   The child mortality rate in the part of Europe that is now Germany was 34% in the early 1800s. This means that in Schleiermacher's time, more than one in every three children born would die before they reached the age of five (see: https://ourworldindata.org/child-mortality).

DEFINITIONS

CHAPTER FOUR

H. Nohl: Thoughts on the Educational Practice of the Individual with Special Reference to the Findings of Freud and Adler

Editor's Introduction

Herman Nohl (1879–1960) was one of the most influential pedagogical theorists in Germany in the 20th century. Married to a cousin of philosopher Ludwig Wittgenstein, he lived his life in relative comfort in Germany's cultural centers and picturesque university towns. Despite this fact, Herman Nohl's contributions to pedagogy, as one scholar recently put it, "can only be understood in terms of educational engagement with underlying experiences of crisis …with massive changes in society."[1] For example, after experiencing the enormous social and cultural crisis represented by the First World War, Nohl switched his academic focus from the *philosophy* to *pedagogy*. He came to see pedagogy as nothing less than a path towards the potential renewal not only of the troubled individual (as he outlines in the first text included here), but also of culture, society and its spirit in general (as he emphasizes in the second text, Chapter Five). There is "no other solution for the misfortune of our people," Nohl once famously said, other "than a new education of its youth toward a happy, courageous, bold creative achievement."[2]

The focus of the two texts included here is of course the pedagogical relation, one of the most enduring topics of modern German pedagogical theory. Nohl was the first to explicitly name and define the "pedagogical relation" as such, namely, as an emotionally charged relationship between an adult and a young person for the sake of the younger. Nohl first broached the question of this pedagogical relation—without naming it as such—in 1914 in a text titled "The Relationship of the Generations in Pedagogy." Here, Nohl begins with the question posed by Schleiermacher as the basis for his own theory of education (Chapter Three): "What [does] the older generation actually want with the younger?" In the face of massive social change—which can sometimes tend to pose more of a challenge to adults than children—Nohl's answer to Schleiermacher is that what earlier generations had once "wanted with the younger" is no longer sufficient. Nohl rejected what he called the "'original' pedagogy of parents and teachers," which he said "began with the goals of the teachers, and used coercive means—above all rules and punishments—for their achievement."[3] Education, Nohl insisted, could no longer be simply what parents and teachers wanted for themselves—their goals and ideals, their customs, habits and expectations. In their place, Nohl proposes what he refers to (in Chapter Four) as a "new pedagogy," one which is based on the goals, ideals and expectations of the young person being educated:

> This basic stance of this new pedagogy is decisively characterized by the fact that its perspective is unconditionally that of the one being educated. Its task, then, is not to act in service of objective powers, to draw the child towards the state, the church, law, the economy, towards a political party or an ideology that the child may be subjected to... That this child here comes to his life's purpose, that is the autonomous and inalienable task of the new pedagogy. (p. 65)

Nohl's insistence on the independence or what has been called the "relative autonomy" of education in relation to outside powers like the state, economy or ideology, has been both an important and controversial aspect of his "new pedagogy."[4]

Although Nohl also emphasizes the novelty of his pedagogy, he simultaneously makes no secret about the debt he owes to J.H. Pestalozzi (Chapter One). "Pestalozzi identified something decisive when he asserted that the family, and the child's relation to the father, mother and siblings is the cradle of all later relations" (p. 67). And like Pestalozzi, Nohl is concerned with the emotional dimension of these relations, particularly as it is experienced by the child, saying that pedagogy requires a "deep awareness of the individual who is to be educated, of his outer as well as inner constitution, of his socio-cultural [*geistige*] milieu, and especially of his [own] personal and pedagogical situation" (p. 67). Significantly, Nohl goes further than Pestalozzi in recognizing the importance specifically of the child's or young person's socio-cultural context. What is frequently needed, Nohl implies, is more than just food and clean clothes, but also "a change of milieu:" "not only the removal of an individual from a precarious social environment, but also removing him from disadvantageous personal relationships which cause personal problems" (p. 68).

A second important theme common to the two texts from Nohl included here is that of the meaning of pedagogy itself—pedagogy both as a set of everyday concerns in being with children and young people, as well as pedagogy as a specific discipline and also a more general way of looking at the world. As explained in the introduction to this book (and referenced in the introduction to Chapter Three), "pedagogy" is used by Nohl and others in this volume in a way that is different from the way it is used in English. It is neither simply a set of instructional techniques (e.g., constructivist pedagogy) nor a political program for teaching (e.g., critical pedagogy). Instead, as Nohl has already made clear, pedagogy is something that it is to be free of ulterior motives, whether these be ones of efficiency ("the state, the economy") or of politics ("a political party or an ideology"). He further argues that when it is understood in this way, pedagogy must also be seen to define both a "specific" disciplinary "field"—one that includes all aspects of engagement with children, from inclusive education to work with at-risk youth. But Nohl simultaneously insists that pedagogy is also a practical "stance" or "perspective" shared by parents, teachers and any adult engaged with children and young people. It is also in this sense that he is able to speak (in Chapter Five) particularly of "the *pedagogical act* of being a father, a mother or a teacher[, which] fulfills a part of our lives… [and] has its own purpose, a passion with its own joys and pains" (p. 78; emphasis added). As a further result, Nohl is able to speak of how psychology and medicine offer their own "perspectives," but still also insists that pedagogy offers a "basic stance" all its own.

The text included in this particular chapter, "Thoughts on the educational Practice" is only one of a number of "passionately moving lectures" that Nohl is said to have given "from 1924 to 1928" to those working with prisoners and troubled youth.[5] Problems with crime had increased dramatically on the heels of the collapse of the German economy in the mid-1920s. As was the case with Pestalozzi, a social crisis—this time of big-city crime and delinquency—presented Nohl with "a very specific educational borderline situation," one "at the outermost limit of human responsiveness."[6] It is in this context that Nohl came to understand the pedagogical relation in a way that Pestalozzi appears to have done implicitly before him: Namely, as a fundamental form of human interrelationship, one in which basic human needs and wants may need to be addressed at the same time as other types of learning and growth are being supported.

It is Nohl's response to one final crisis in his life and culture—that of the Nazi's coming to power in 1933 and their reshaping of nearly all of German science and culture—that negatively affects Nohl's reputation to this day. This is his decision to affirm National Socialism as a thinker and an educator. As a recent introduction to Nohl's life and work puts it, "his role in National Socialism [still] remains controversial."[7] On the one hand, "the key points of Nohl's pedagogy [like the autonomy of pedagogy] contradicted National Socialist propaganda on education, and he himself was forced into retirement" [during the Nazi era]. On the other hand, in the postscript to his pedagogical magnum opus (*The Pedagogical Movement in Germany;* see Chapter Five), Nohl says he sees the "creed of [his] pedagogical movement" as being "secured by the state." In the Winter semester of 1933–34, Nohl also gave a series of lectures titled "The Fundamentals of National Education"[8]

It is likely as a result of this controversial legacy that the "pedagogical relation" as Nohl both named and conceived of it, was almost entirely absent from the German-language vocabulary of education by the final decades of the 20th century. In the texts collected in this volume, explicit reference to the term disappears after Muth's 1967 text on "pedagogical tact" (Chapter Six). Despite this fact, however, questions of interpersonal relationships, specifically with children and the young, remain at the core of all of the subsequent texts included here.

Sources/Recommended Reading

Bollnow, O. F. (1980). Herman Nohl and pedagogy. *Western European Education, 12*(1), 89–106. doi: 10.2753/EUE1056-4934120189

Dollinger, B. (2008). Herman Nohl (1879–1960). Die Suche nach kultureller Einheit und ästhetischer Form. In B. Dollinger (Ed.), *Klassiker der Pädagogik: Die Bildung der modernen Gesellschaft*. Springer.

Friesen, N. (2017). The pedagogical relation past and present: Experience, subjectivity and failure. *Journal of Curriculum Studies, 49*(6), 743–756. doi.org/10.1080/00220272.2017.1320427

Friesen, N. (2020). "Education as a *Geisteswissenschaft*:" An introduction to human science pedagogy. *Journal of Curriculum Studies. 52*(3), 307–322. doi.org/10.1080/00220272.2019.1705917

Van Manen, M. (2015). *Pedagogical tact: Knowing what to do when you don't know what to do* (pp. 119–122). Routledge.

Thoughts on the Educational Practice of the Individual with Special Reference to the Findings of Freud and Adler[9] (Herman Nohl, 1926)

In a much-cited claim, Wilhelm Dilthey once wrote that true pedagogical reforms can only be achieved by consistent, laborious pedagogical work in the classroom, rather than simply by legal measures or theoretical reflections.[10] In view of the broadening of pedagogy today, classrooms are being replaced by the entirety of living pedagogical practice—with its constantly renewed experiments, successes and failures. And little supports the truth of [Dilthey's] claim more than the consolidation of [all these efforts]. The more one is convinced of this [truth], the more courage is required of the theorist in the ivory tower to speak to those engaged in the daily struggles of such work. I thus urge you to believe me that I speak with the greatest modesty—which is to be expected in a context where one's only vivid experience of youth, outside of the those who [...] are at risk, is that of one's own youth. This is a very narrow, subjective experience but is nonetheless significant precisely because of its subjectivity. There is no understanding of others that is not derived from one's own personal experiences. As a famous juvenile court judge once explained, it is the crimes he committed when he was young that is the reason for his success in dealing with those of other young people. [...] This constitutes the basic philosophy of the new pedagogy of which I am speaking of today… as an introduction [...]

This basic stance of this new pedagogy is decisively characterized by the fact that its perspective is unconditionally that of the one being educated. Its task, then, is *not* to act in service of objective powers, to draw the child towards the state, the church, law, the economy, towards a political party or an ideology that the child may be subjected to. Instead, it sees its goal [*with*]*in* the subject [the child or young person] and their physical and personal realization or unfolding. That *this* child here comes to his life's purpose *(Lebensziel)*, that is the autonomous and inalienable task of the new pedagogy. This is what we call its autonomy, which equips it with a measure of independence from other cultural systems and [gives it] the ability to observe them critically.

The results of this curious inversion [of the relative importance of the adult and child] must appear strange to other professions—for example, to the judge who represents "objective" justice and who consequently brings pedagogy into conflict with it. Nonetheless, these results are immensely far-reaching, and shape every aspect or moment of education. It is from this perspective that the inherent value of each individual step in a child's development is to be recognized—recognized as individual moments in life that should not be sacrificed to the future but each independently fulfilled. It is from this perspective that an inversion of the pedagogy for delinquent youth must be regarded, one where the young person is no longer seen as an enemy to be forced into a place in the social order, but instead as a troubled human being in need of help. The person who thinks pedagogically [in this way] not only views justice in relation to the crime, but to the offender. The point is not [just] to assist justice, but the adolescent himself.

It is a significant contribution of the school of Freud and Adler to have recognized and facilitated this inversion with great diligence and clarity [in the realm of medicine]. [...] These groups favor a doctor's perspective, which has the subject [or patient] and his will and life in mind. This [prioritization] brings it into conflict with other perspectives, such as that of the judge. This medical perspective has undoubtedly helped pedagogy in recognizing its fundamental stance.

The relationship of trust that a patient has with his doctor is grounded in the doctor's [own] basic stance which affirms the patient's life and will. In the same way, the peculiar relation of the child to the educator is based on the basic *pedagogical* stance, on the child's unconditional trust towards a teacher who affirms the child in the depth of his or her personality. This marks the *second* understanding of the contemporary [or new] pedagogy—although it is actually very old in that it expresses a relationship that arises perpetually in life. But it is only now fully appreciated. [This is the understanding] that the last mystery of pedagogical work is the *right pedagogical relation,* in other words, the inherent creative relation that binds teacher with the one who is to be educated. I cannot analyze this relation in all of its details—with love and composure on the one side and trust, respect, and a sense of one's need for proximity and help, on the other. The result is *the attachment* of the child to the teacher.[11] This pedagogical relation and the attachment it implies vary greatly, being different with regard to a regular child, a mentally challenged one or one who is mentally disturbed. Finally, it is also different for every individual. Rousseau was the first to establish its emergence according to stages of childhood development, but in one way or the other it is the prerequisite of any fruitful pedagogical work.

The sphere to which this is particularly applicable is the pedagogy of neglected and delinquent youth. In a truly pedagogical text, Isemann stated that the personal attachment between child or youth and teacher is decisive for the education of those who are mentally disturbed. Curt Bondy and W. Herrmann[12] argue similarly in their pedagogy of the prison. It is the being of neglected individual in particular which is characterized by a loss of human attachment and is often consumed by defiance and hatred. And it is for this person that the pedagogical relation must replace everything. [Its] love and stability has to soften this individual in order to re-awaken and develop his higher life. Whoever speaks of pedagogy, be it in regular education or at the judge's bench, in protective custody or in jail, has to make himself fully aware that winning this relation is his first task. Without it, all other efforts are futile. He [the pedagogue] furthermore must not forget that the pedagogical relation cannot be forced. Within this relation, irrational moments such as sympathy and antipathy are at play, and these evade both parties' influences. The teacher may therefore not be offended or resort to punishment if he is not able to establish the relation successfully, if "the lad simply doesn't want to." One would then need to strive to have him become attached to someone else, if such attachment can be established at all.

It is another significant achievement of psychoanalysis that it has recognized this relation as the precondition for rehabilitating a life that has gone wrong, for healing defiance and hatred by establishing a social bond which the Freudian school has called "transference." [...] Aichhorn dedicated a whole chapter to transference in his inspiring book on neglected youth.[13] Transference is the emotional relation between the patient and the analyst—and further between educator and the one being educated. Following psychoanalysis, it relies on the initial love of a child of his or her father and mother, which is later replaced by objects in the family and transferred still later to unfamiliar persons. Just as it is true that the child's experience of human relations within the family is of the greatest importance for later relations to others (as Adler learned from Freud), it is false to try to see all independent relations (such as the pedagogical relation) as derivatives of primary libido. This is simply the residue of a false view from the perspective of the natural sciences. It takes the place of the recognition that in the first relations within the organism of the family, the manifoldness, the totality of various relations within these first familial relations, unfolds in the rich variety of relations formed later in life. In this instance, Johann Heinrich Pestalozzi identified something decisive when he asserted that the family, and the child's relation to the father, mother and siblings is the cradle of all later relations—both civil and religious.[14]

Acknowledging the child's experience marks the *third* moment of modern pedagogy, which distinguishes itself from outmoded forms, which in this case have come down only on the side of ethics [i.e. deciding cases based on rules]. [Modern pedagogy] instead realizes its essential precondition as deep awareness of the individual who is to be educated, of his outer as well as inner constitution, of [his] sociocultural [*geistige*] milieu, and especially with his personal and pedagogical situation. The older pedagogy obeyed ideals and ethical claims, addressing the subjective character of the child or young person, as Herbart called it—[which could now be called] the ideological superstructure of his factual character. [This] ends up being a cloud of good resolutions, role models and rules that hang over all of our heads;

this is what the old pedagogy attempted to encourage by cajoling, admonishing, didacticizing and the like. What is most important, and what constitutes the particularly *pedagogical* accomplishment in this, however, is as Herbart clearly saw, [the influence of the young person's situation on] their objective character, the structure of the personality and its respective milieu. Psychoanalytic schools have undoubtedly had an uncommonly strong influence here.

First, they recognized more clearly than any other pedagogical psychology before them that this objective constitution of the individual was independent of their patients' particular knowledge and desires, simply because there are mechanisms at work which the patient cannot understand. For the individual, this marks a dangerous tension between objective and subjective character, the constitution of the person and his ethical requirements, which can lead to fear and feelings of guilt. Psychoanalysis has furthermore asserted the primacy of the *personal situation* of the patient, of those vulnerable or neglected, over an incorrect naturalism. [This means recognizing] the child's experience of relationships of love or of violence as well as the relation of his capabilities to his particular circumstances, which shapes in its own way his character and relation to others. It is only from this perspective that it is possible to understand how gifted children from the best social circumstances can end up on the wrong path. Also from this perspective, the intensification of such personal experiences of people belonging to the working class becomes clearer as well as the relationship of class hatred and individual character.

The one-sidedness of such schools [of thought], which focus either on the absence of loving relationships or the oppression of the individual and his subsequent feelings of inferiority, his striving for acknowledgement or the imbalance between his personal abilities and objective demands, should be left behind. These phenomena are instead based very vivid experiences, which create particularity difficult problems for pedagogy because each has two sides: One can experience too little or too much love, too little or too much pressure, too few or too many demands, too much or too little guilt.

This context makes it clear that the most primitive but often decisive pedagogical act that leads to change is a *change of milieu*—not only the removal of an individual from a precarious social environment, but also removing him from disadvantageous personal relationships which cause personal problems. Every medical pedagogy works with this experience: an infant who does not drink his mother's milk at home might start drinking immediately when he is at the hospital. The same holds for pedagogical difficulties in general: the misbehaving child can suddenly act like an angel in an unknown environment. Even some psychopathic phenomena and maladjustments vanish with a change of one's personal situation. A significant number of the successes pedagogues and particularly psychoanalysts appear to me to depend on this, and it is irrelevant whether one follows Freud's methods: When a new personal relation is established, one's whole orientation is changed.

Often enough, such a change, or the integration of a patient into a new personal relation (e.g., in protective custody) can be enough. But frequently, it is only the starting point for positive pedagogical work that addresses the difficulties that underlie the immediate symptoms. These *difficulties* are the central approach for normal as well as delinquent youth: they determine what we call *the pedagogical situation* of the child. The inversion I spoke of in the beginning now again becomes significant. The old education began with the difficulties that the child *caused*, the new one begins with the *difficulties* that the child *has*. Every difficulty that is caused by the child or young person is actually a difficulty he *has*, something often overlooked in the disruption of the social order [caused by the difficulty]. Aichhorn says:

> ...in our first contacts with a child we make it a rule to side with him in any discussion of the difficulties. We do this because it is of utmost importance to learn the boy's story from him, to understand his attitude toward life and how it is reflected in his behavior. We therefore ask him questions and are not disturbed if he lies to us because that is only to be expected. What we learn from outside sources serves to confirm and expand our impression. We accept what the boy tells us of his actions as a natural response to a given situation.[15]

Adler agrees with this point entirely: all of the young person's difficulties, according this school of thought, are the result of a maladjusted way of life. The treatment of those mentally disturbed also suggests that these person's difficulties are mostly their own and that education always has to begin by addressing them, by helping to find their underlying causes and by helping to overcome them.

In this act of helping, the *fourth* moment of modern pedagogy becomes evident in its turn towards the activity *within* the person receiving education. This holds for regular school pedagogy, which focuses all of its attention on such activities from kindergarten to post-secondary education; it also holds for the education of those at risk, for which the term "active pedagogy" has been coined. It also results in a new understanding of the youth correction process, in which the person in custody is no longer an object, having to suffer his own fate, but a subject who sees his sentence as a function, as a task to be accomplished through personal strength, a fate, but one he can help to shape. It is everywhere a matter of self-activity[16] and winning over the child or young person, in those places where the old pedagogy believed it could make progress with those at risk or in custody through drill, enforcement and control.

Liepmann quotes Wines,[17] who says:

> No system can hope to succeed which does not secure this harmony of wills, so that the prisoner shall choose for himself what his officer chooses for him. But to this end the officer must really choose the good of the prisoner, and the prisoner must remain in his choice long enough for virtue to become a habit. This consent of wills is an essential condition of reformation, for a bad man can never be made good against his consent. (p. 50)

Eliminating defiance and hatred by establishing a pedagogical relation, therefore, is not enough. A higher, value-driven life has to be awakened, which invokes the young person's active will and his sense of responsibility. But this again can only be successful if one puts oneself in the place of the youth: the substance of what drives him as well as of his goals and plans, which have to be respected. In this way, the interests that bind him to something larger can be awakened, and he can be reintegrated into the productive order of society. Psychoanalysis calls this the sublimation, the social redirection of these drives. If this means that a primitive drive is simply transformed into a higher one, it would be, as Scheler has said, a kind of false wizardry.[18] However, it means that the crucial point is to show the young person more than simply ideals which ignore his natural impulses and drives, and instead, to develop tasks that emerge from his situation, and that affirm the substance of these impulses and desires. This would be absolutely true, and the same in regular as well as delinquent education, which would need to "analyze" the young person's impulses and desires in order to subject these to higher goals and social purposes, making them not merely something more than just talents or achievements, but turning them into the weight of his entire system of values and interests.

Finally, I ask: How is our pedagogy to position itself with respect to punishment? Psychoanalysis forbids punishment: It does this for some because of the possibility of its sadistic perversion, for others, because punishment leads to a vicious circle in which crime is the result of demoralization, with punishment being only the means of even further demoralization. But we must then ask: Is crime *always* a result of demoralization? In the latest issue of the journal of individual psychology, lawyer Eugen Schmidt's essay argues passionately against punishment, speaking of the "very many cases" in which psychological degradation is the reason for the crime. He closes by saying: "Crime must be regarded as social demoralization and can only be understood as such."[19] This type of emphasis is typical in all of this literature.[20] Similarly to Schmidt, Egon Weigl asks, perhaps rather naively, regarding his methods:[21] "Is punishment a means of education?" "This cannot be," Weigl continues, "because it violates the first principle of Adler's psychology, which states that the demoralization of a child is the source of all human maladjustment." It is the great discovery of such schools of thought that a very great deal of what was earlier regarded as obvious has now been recognized as avoidance, withdrawal, the result of repression, or again, of demoralization. But proposing that *everything* negative coming from the young person arises in this way represents an exaggeration that only serves to oppose common sense to what is established as true. [For example, a] boy constantly goes to the movies: This could mean that he is escaping from the demands of a difficult life, or simply that his hunger for pleasure is insatiable. Another is always playing soccer: This could be an attempt at validation, and the result of demoralization in another area of his life. But it could, on the other hand, be the absolute devotion of a young person towards his passion. It "could" be this way! One must always think of alternate possibilities in order not to do injustice to the child. A university student might first give into his desire to drink, and then later drink because of demoralizing exam results; this is also something that happens. I do in no way wish to undermine the position of psychoanalysis. It is very profitable to look at its truths. There is, however, a type of unmitigated crime, a "natural" maladjustment, as opposed to the complexity of the one mitigated by other factors, leading us to ask: What does it mean to punish *this* form of deviant behavior?

From society's perspective, it is done for the sake of security, from the perspective of law it is understood in terms of atonement. We ask, however, what it means from a pedagogical standpoint? What consequences does it have if we regard it from our initial position, from "the perspective of the person who is being educated"? People have said that one should not punish at all, but instead only educate. But then, punishment would simply again resurface within education. Punishment is in itself nothing more than an expression of power in moral life, proving that the idea of a moral life is not merely a pious wish, [part of the] flowery language of pastors and schoolmasters, but a reality of the exercise of power. Where lower impulses [Leben] exert their power, it is punished by the power of moral life, as Plato understood. Again, seen from the perspective of the young person, such an experience of the gravity of moral life can have a tremendously constructive effect. In fact, each one of us lives on the basis of established values. When these structures of power disintegrate, character disintegrates with them. The reality of this power of a higher, moral life curbs that which is lower within us through a kind of fear, yet moral fear does not only work to discourage—as shown by the simultaneous fear and love of God in many religions. This fear instead elevates us, rather, because it frees us and opens a space for moral life. It was the truth of F.W. Foerster's position... in 1912.[22] He appeared to be wrong, since the circumstances showing the truth of his insight were not yet in place. In his time, the focus was on eradicating any thought of retribution from the practice of the penal system. And as long as our system of corrections embodies uncultured practices, consigning a child [to it] remains questionable. However, if psychoanalysis dismisses punishment altogether, even pedagogical punishment as well, it seems to misjudge the true structure of human character. As a pedagogue I have no choice other than to continue to take Foerster's side. Punishment is not at all the first concern of education but always the last, the true *ultima ratio* [or last resort]. That which is positive always comes first. Undoubtedly, punishment is so many times over the undeniable embarrassment of the educator, a sign of *his* failure. But it ultimately remains indispensable, because through it and only through it, the power of that which is higher is able to prove itself over that of the ego. Its deeper meaning, also from the perspective of the aggrieved party, for whom punishment is finalized in reconciliation and atonement, will be the subject of my next paper.

Notes

1. Dollinger, B. (2008). *Klassiker der Pädagogik: Die Bildung der modernen Gesellschaft*. Springer, p. 247.
2. As quoted in: Bollnow, O. F. (1980). Herman Nohl and pedagogy, *Western European Education*, 12(1), 89–106. doi: 10.2753/EUE1056-4934120189
3. Nohl, H. (1914/1967). Das Verhältnis der Generationen in der Pädagogik. In H. Röhrs (Ed.), *Erziehungswissenschaft und Erziehungswirklichkeit*. Akademische Reihe, p. 27.
4. For example, one critic of Nohl argued in the late 1960s that any conception of pedagogy is necessarily at the same time a conception of a larger social ideal: "The realization of pedagogical propositions ...including those envisioned by Nohl in his conception of the 'pedagogical relation'...is at the same time the realization of an image of society. The criteria for pedagogical valuation are at the same time those that belong to a particular understanding of society." K. Mollenhauer, as quoted in Friesen, N. (2017). The pedagogical relation past and present: experience, subjectivity and failure. *Journal of Curriculum Studies* 49(6), 748.
5. Bollnow, O. F. (1981). Der Begriff des pädagogischen Bezugs bei Herman Nohl. *Zeitschrift für Pädagogik* 27(1), 32.
6. Bollnow, p. 32.
7. Dollinger, pp. 249–250.
8. Dollinger, pp. 249–250.
9. Translated by N. Friesen and Sophie Zedlitz (Institute for Educational Studies, Humboldt University, Berlin). Sigmund Freud is the founder of psychoanalysis and is regarded as an early, key figure in the development of psychology. Alfred Adler was a student of Freud's who moved away from Freud's emphasis on sex and the libido to focus on societal factors and their significance to the development of the individual considered as a whole. It is Adler, rather than Freud, who remains an important influence in counselling associated with social work and general psychology today.

10 Dilthey's exact words were: "Real reforms are only achieved through steady and difficult pedagogical work in schoolrooms." See: Dilthey, W. (1890/1978) *Gesammelte Schriften: Die geistige Welt: Einleitung in die Philosophie des Lebens. Abhandlungen zur Poetik, Ethik und Pädagogik*. Vandenhoeck & Ruprecht, p. 85. Wilhelm Dilthey was a friend and colleague of Nohl's, and Dilthey is important in his own right as the founder of education as a "humanities" subject (*Geisteswissenschaft*; see: Friesen, N. (2020). "Education as a *Geisteswissenschaft*:" An introduction to Human Science Pedagogy. *Journal of Curriculum Studies, 52*(3), 307–322. https://doi.org/10.1080/00220272.2019.1705917)
11 Note that "attachment theory" as such did not exist at the time Nohl wrote this text. His use of the term "attachment" *(Bindung)* thus does not carry this connotation.
12 Both Bondy and Herrmann had been students of Nohl's.
13 Nohl is here speaking of the following text, which until recently, was also widely used in social work in the English-speaking world: Aichhorn, A. (1925/1984). *Wayward youth*. Northwestern University Press. Aichhorn was one of the first to bring psychoanalysis to bear on the education of at-risk youth.
14 See Chapter One, especially pp. 12–13.
15 Aichhorn, A. (1955). *Wayward youth: A psychoanalytic study of delinquent children*. Northwestern University Press, p. 132.
16 For a discussion of self-activity, see p. 98, below.
17 Moritz Liepmann was a professor in criminology and jurisprudence. The quote is from: Wines, E. C. (1880). *The state of prisons and of child-saving institutions in the civilized world*. Cambridge University Press.
18 Philosopher Max Scheler was known for his critique of Sigmund Freud's conception of "sublimation." In opposition to Freud, Scheler did *not* see humans as acting largely on the basis of unconscious primitive impulses that had to be "transformed" by culture. Instead, he saw these drives and impulses as being guided and pacified through deliberate human engagement. See: Scheler, M. (2017). *The nature of sympathy*. Routledge.
19 Nohl is likely referring to: Schmidt, E. (1926). Verbrecher und Strafe. In: Wexberg, E, & Adler, A., et al. (Eds.), *Handbuch der Individualpsychologie 2nd Vol.* (pp. 150–179). Springer.
20 Nohl appears to be speaking about the literature of "individual psychology," an area of study established by Alfred Adler which emphasized the importance of the whole individual.
21 Egon Weigl was a psychologist and neurologist who was deeply influence by Adler.
22 Friedrich Wilhelm Foerster a German educationist, pacifist and philosopher; however, it is uncertain which position taken up by Forster in 1912 that Nohl is referring to.

CHAPTER FIVE

H. Nohl: The Pedagogical Relation and the Formative Community

Editor's Introduction

If the text from Nohl provided in Chapter Four is the expression of an uncompromising educational reformer, the excerpt provided here is more of a Weimar-era conservative. In distinction from Chapter Three, the text introduced here also focuses more on educators' relations to the young child rather than to the (troubled) young person. Although first published in 1933, this discussion of the pedagogical relation has appeared in multiple publications as well as in Nohl's magnum opus, *The Pedagogical Movement in Germany*—despite the fact that this discussion is dated by its traditionalism. Regardless, the text translated here effectively provides an account of its main characteristics of the pedagogical relation as well as its canonical definition: "the basis of education is the passionate relation between a mature person and one who is becoming," Nohl explains, "specifically for the sake of the latter, so that he comes to his life and form" (p. 78). Its principal characteristics are:

- Its *asymmetry*: The pedagogical relation is not for the mutual benefit of those involved, but "for the sake of [the] one who is becoming" rather than the sake of the one who is already mature (p. 79).

- Its foundation in *love*: The pedagogical relation is passionate primarily in the sense that it is a loving relation, involving, as Nohl emphasizes, "an educating, bearing and organizing kind of love… [a love that] aims not at prolonging [the child's] obedience, but shortening it" (p. 82).
- Its particular *temporality*: "The relation of the educator to the child always doubly determined: by the love for the child as he is and by the love for his educational goal, the child's ideal" (p. 80). This means that the teacher or parent must balance their engagement with the child between the wants of the present and the expectations of the future (see also Chapter Three).
- Its proximity to *tact*: Building on the previous point, and also anticipating Muth's description in Chapter Six, Nohl explains: "The peculiar opposition and entwinement of two directions of work [oriented the present and future] constitutes the pedagogical *stance* and gives the educator a singular distance to his subject as well as to his student. In its most refined expression this distance is called pedagogical tact" (pp. 80–81)
- Its *impermanence:* When the young person matures and becomes an adult, their relations with other adults become mutual ones, and are no longer "pedagogical" as characterized in the points just above: "the pedagogical relation strives to make itself redundant from both sides—…a characteristic… unique to this relation as opposed to all other human relations." (p. 81)

As these points make clear, to understand the pedagogical relation as "the basis of education" is to see education as a matter of personality and emotion (rather than of cognition, learning and outcomes): "The central task of education" as Nohl emphasizes, "is the creation of personal thought and feeling" (p. 82) in the young person or child so that he or she can become mature. Although these and other claims made in Nohl's 1933 text may sound rather idealistic, they point to an emotional and interpersonal dimension of pedagogy that inevitably underlies aspects that today receive far more attention: Pedagogy, Nohl is insisting here, is above all about *love*—love for who the child *is* and for what he or she will *become*.

The Pedagogical Relation and the Formative Community[1]

Our lives are infused with exchanges of minds and the leadership of the spirit. A formative or educative moment subsists in every life context, in every conversation. Education and instruction accordingly appear only as one specific means among many others to accomplish the development and formation of both a single individual and an entire people. When speaking of education and child guidance, these formative engagements are decisive only when they are undertaken *consciously*, with the will to such guidance, which then comes to constitute its own means and institutions for this purpose. However, this planned and deliberate formation and advancement pervades life, and is to be found in every trade, in every factory and in the military. But this threatens the sustainability of pedagogy as an independent cultural and social function, making it into something universal, with its effects felt everywhere—wherever there is a meeting of minds of various levels, both formed and unformed. This then leads radical pedagogues to the conclusion that the age of the school is over; life must take such a form that it educates on its own, making the special profession of the pedagogue an impossibility.[2]

But from the rather different perspective of the one to be educated—and *his* formative experiences—this dissolution of the pedagogical is not something to welcome, but to oppose. Accordingly, the most fundamental educational experience is one in which [adult] individuals find themselves internally divided: As actively conscious, goal-setting beings, they have before them an instinct-driven carnal creature who wants to be educated. This type of purposeful action applies as much outwardly as inwardly; and as a fundamental way of shaping life itself, it gives this life its own pedagogical value. Gandhi once spoke of his life as being fully pedagogical; he made himself a solemn vow, and then used this vow to elevate his own life.[3] This process, in which people develop themselves is called self-education. But from this point, education can be thought of so broadly that it means the same thing as human development in general. Ernst Krieck skillfully attempted to disconnect education from the relation of the generations—and from the opposition of educator and the one to be educated—in order to find its most basic form in the development of the mind with its two forms: Self-education and, secondarily, the education of another.[4]

This approach coincided with the ideals of the youth movement of the time,[5] which sought independence from the older generation and valued self-education highly. As a result, however, pedagogy would disappear as a specific field yet again and the formative experiences of a young person can by no means be fully disclosed without reference to pedagogy as one's education by another. The term self-education is an analogical transfer of that true pedagogical act and process in which one person has an effect on another. But a child's primary formative experience is not one of a division of the self into one part that leads and another part that guides—that which prevails and that which is guided. Instead it is an experience of oneself being *in relation to* a guide: "Does not education begin only in that moment when the self is superseded by a higher entity which pulls us away from our self and frees us from our self?"[6] The formative experiences of the young person involve an intrinsic commitment to the teacher as well as to growing and being shaped by such an "other." The mere experience of an "ought" itself—if it comes alive in me at all outside of the larger formative community—is an ethical experience which has a great significance for pedagogy, but it is not yet an educational experience as such.

Education ends when a person becomes mature, which, following Schleiermacher, means: when the younger generation is equal to the older generation in working on fulfilling [society's] common moral undertaking.[7] Pedagogy thus has the goal of making itself redundant and of becoming self-education, a process which extends up to our death. This marks pedagogy's upper limit, which is defined as the boundary between pedagogy and ethics. Our higher self is not something that is given to us without any form of education; it has to be awakened, refined and solidified until *it* can educate. However, there is a moment of commitment and receptivity remaining in a religious relation that has a pedagogical quality. Thus, from the perspective of the formative experience of the young person, the basis of education is the formative community of educator and child's, with latter's will-to-development. In the same way, the pedagogical act of being a father, a mother or a teacher fulfills a part of our lives which is not only a means, but has its own purpose, a passion with its own joys and pains. The pedagogical relation is a part of the child's or young person's life and not only a means of becoming an adult—for all that, it still takes too long, and there are too many who never reach the goal. Among all relations that shape our lives, friendship, love, workplace affiliations, the relation between educator and one to be educated may be the most fundamental, significantly shaping and fulfilling our existence. Only when one understands the pedagogical relation from the perspective of the student and the teacher can its full significance for life be appreciated—a significance that makes it into a poetic motif of the first order with an inherently tragic note.[8]

The pivotal weight of the pedagogical relation becomes evident from yet another point of view. If the goal of education is to awaken a unified inner life, it can only succeed through such an already unified life, one's person can only develop from the person of another. The pedagogical influence[9] does not descend from a set of prevailing values but from an original self, a real person with a firm will, directed at another real human being: Its goal is formation from a whole. This is the primacy of personality and of the personal community in education as opposed to the primacy of mere ideas, as opposed to a shaping through the objective spirit[10] and the power of the matter at hand. As we mature, we begin following more specialized interests and devote ourselves to worldly tasks, but in the educative process our lives take shape only when we give ourselves to someone in whom such tasks come alive for us. Even then, we do not refer to a person's ideas, but to the person himself, his individual and ideal form, his word having become flesh. We gather from this the personal representation of a subject [or topic] rather than the subject itself, we perceive the person's devotion and verve, diligence and work ethic, his rigor in relation to himself, in short: his personal strength. My natural ability [as someone being educated] leads me to the object, but the educative relation also forms this ability—not from the object at hand, but from my own powers, to which objectivity itself belongs. That is why a great teacher can retain his effect, even if the content of his teaching is long outdated. The more fragmented and underdeveloped the *Bildung* of a historical era is,[11] the more important the representation of elevated life to the child or young person in the unified humanity of his teacher becomes. For it is the form of the educator that the ideal *Bildung* can be preserved, even if it has otherwise disappeared or is not yet present.

In this way, heroism gains educational relevance among young people; the Saints in monasteries become educationally charged as well as the figure of the last Mohican in boys' stories.[12] More generally, people also find such representations of a unified life in the personalities of prominent educator-personalities. All books with titles such as *Rembrandt as Educator*,[13] Bismarck, Goethe etc. as educators,[14] are characteristic of our unfortunate times. Their unqualified but longing portrayals offer the living possibility of a unified humanity. Goethe influenced whole generations in this way, not by his achievements in a range of fields, but through the unity of his life as a whole. One does not seek to learn anything factual as much as one wants to be liberated, elevated and formed by experiencing [Goethe's] way of confronting and engaging with life. Reading his work is so formative because each individual expression comes from the unity of an elevated life. Carlyle wrote his book *On Heroes* from this educative perspective.[15] Wilhelm Dilthey wanted to write a history of heroism of the German spirit, viewing poets in terms of the "highest quasi-pedagogical categories," to communicate "the degree to which they are leaders without our willing or knowing."[16] The special task which has been given to poetry in schools since ancient times has its ultimate pedagogical basis not in aesthetics but in portraying great people who became teachers of life and who displayed the human capacity to bear and even overcome life.

Thus, the basis of education is the passionate relation between a mature person and one who is becoming, specifically for the sake of the latter, so that he comes to his life and form. This educational relation is based on human instinct and natural expressions of life and family, e.g. being a father, a mother, a sister, a brother, an aunt or an uncle, even in being a grandfather. [...]

The true love of the teacher is of an uplifting rather than a desiring kind and the pedagogical relation is a true communion where the feeling of one side is matched by that of the other.

The relation of the educator to the child is always doubly determined: by the love for the child as he is and by the love for his educational goal, the child's ideal. These are not separated but intertwined: To make of this child that which is to be made, to ignite a higher life in the child, to lead the child to coherent accomplishment, not for accomplishment's sake, but because in it human life is completed. The pedagogical goal is not to simply breed a "type of life." The gardener who breeds a blue rose sacrifices thousands of roses for this purpose, but the educational love for the child is the love for *his* ideal. Nothing else should be imagined for him other than the form of life which he wants to lead. This must be the key to *his* life. Thus, pedagogical love requires sympathy for the child and his traits, for the possibilities of his educatability, always with regards to the consummation of his life. The difference between the mother's purely natural love and the father's pride in the son's achievements is clear, seeing realistically and desiring idealistically are here profoundly interlinked.

This directly correlates with the child or young person's desire for growth and commitment, which demands help and protection, affection and recognition. Again, this desire for growth and devotion only takes on an educational character where the interaction with a mature person is sought in order to gain vitality and form from him.

The tension that is felt by both educator and child is what specifically characterizes the felt and known nature of this reciprocal relation. As Herbart[17] once brilliantly remarked of the pedagogical interest:

> Interest in education is only an expression of our whole interest in the world and in humanity. Instruction concentrates all the objects of this interest—where our timid hopes will finally be saved—in the bosom of the young, which is the bosom of the future. Without this, instruction is of a surety empty and meaningless. Let no one say that he educates with his whole soul—that is an empty phrase. Either he has nothing to perfect through education (in the boy) or the larger part of his reflection belongs to what he imparts to the boy, and make accessible to him, belongs to his expectation of what more carefully cultivated humanity will be able to accomplish, beyond all that our species has hitherto experienced.[18]

This will to change and organize, however, is at the same time always slowed and, in its core, refined by a conscious restraint honoring the young person's spontaneity and individuality. In the same way, a work of art does not arise from mere neutrality but from the passion of a belief, while at the same time resting in itself and reliant on the outside world. The educator is not simply a teacher of his own bias.

The peculiar opposition and entwinement of two directions of work [mentioned above[19]] constitutes *the pedagogical stance* and gives the educator a singular *distance* to his subject as well as to his student. In its most refined expression this distance is called *pedagogical tact*—which does not "offend" the young person where educator wants to advance or protect him, and which allows the educator to sense when a great matter is not to be pedagogically trivialized. The student himself, regardless of his devotion to his teacher, essentially wants to be himself and act for himself—as evident as early as the child at play. Thus, regarding the child or young person's perspective, there is always a distance and opposition within his commitment. And the pedagogical relation strives to make itself redundant from both sides—which is the fate and tragedy of being a teacher. This is a characteristic, moreover, which is unique to this relation as opposed to all other human relations.

Schleiermacher once tried to determine the particular difference between the nature of art versus artlessness. The artless state is characterized by the simultaneity of excitation and expression inherent to it, whereas this synchronicity is essentially annulled within all forms of artistry: "another higher power intervenes, a moment of reflection already stops and breaks the brute force of excitation while simultaneously authorizing itself as a regulatory principle." It is thus this moment that distinguishes art from the mere process of nature, "it is the moment of conception in which what subsequently emerges externally is formed internally."

> An inner excitement must be given in advance, which awakens some outgoing function from slumber, but artistic activity arises only in so far as there is a strong measure of that reflection which elevates the activity of nature above itself and ennobles it to a revelation of the spirit which is conscious of it and dominates it.[20]

The will to change in pedagogy, which, contrary to politics, does not wish to change relations but people, only becomes a *pedagogical* achievement through such an exemplary conception—namely one which precedes unrestrained effect and whose *creative mystery lies in the difficult equation of the missionary will to enculturate and the spontaneity and personal ideal of the child*. All difficulty in educating rests upon this tension and the specific pedagogical tone is again based on adhering to the distance which respects the vitality of the child or young person and which culminates in his freedom of moral choice, regardless of the teacher's conviction of his own personal beliefs.

By the way, the duality of the relationship is revealed in the fact that we have two words for it, *Bildung* [formation] and *Erziehung* [rearing, education]. Recent scholarship has rather arbitrarily tried to define the difference between these two words based on systems of thought. Historically, the term *Bildung* first emerged in the second half of the 18th century, initially referring to the formation of oneself through a kind of kind of natural drive (*Bildungstrieb*) signifying the spontaneous development to a unique form from within; whereas "educating" (rearing) rather meant leading the child towards a predefined form. If the term "educating" is again the preferred term, this is a telling sign of a change of the pedagogical stance.

The formative community is at the same time a community of life; its spirit is the strongest formative force; it is the precondition of all pedagogical influence and all [pedagogical] methodology is altogether secondary to it. In this community, however, because it is a pedagogical community, the duality that was already touched upon in referencing motherly love and fatherly guidance again appears. In accordance with this duality of the love for a child as he is and the love for the child's advance—supported as it is through his enhancement—the pedagogical community is borne by two forces: love and authority, or, from the perspective of the child, love and allegiance.[21] These two forces determine the specific pedagogical structure of the educational community. In the process of life, both of these forces are united. But pedagogues favor one or the other depending on their individual inclination. Accordingly, the central task of education is the creation of personal thought and feeling. This demands from the educator a community of love existing between himself and the child. This is one that opens all doors in the child, and that collects and binds his whole little life in the trust of such love. When I trust, I myself act better; when I am trusted, I feel bound and gain strength beyond my measure.

This love is furthermore the basis of the focus of allegiance and obedience towards authority, which is nothing other than the conscience of that higher life and the model of that higher form to which the soul is to be given. Obedience does not mean to do something out of fear or to follow blindly: It means free acceptance of the adult's will into one's own will and spontaneous subordination as an expression of an inner relationship of will which is founded in the convinced devotion to the demands of higher life represented by the educator. This relation has its own certainty and a number of the most beautiful feelings are founded in it: awe, respect, piety and gratitude. Subordination and community are the formative powers of every society. Within the pedagogical community, these receive unique significance from the general pedagogical undertaking: this community is an educating, bearing and organizing kind of love, which is [eventually] substituted by a collective configuration of purposes in society. Society—or where its dominating organization of purposes appears—works to subordinate, concentrate and organize the will. The child's will grows only when challenged by a foreign will, and young people are up to it, because this demanding will is not just fate, but is also carried by love. It is—or was until recently—still "modern" to deny obedience because it can be abused, but all great pedagogical thinkers, including those of liberalism, Kant, Herbart or Schleiermacher, not to mention Hegel, have long known and emphasized its importance for education. Kant said that obedience is nothing less than the disposition of the child, that is, it is the first stage of the form of the soul held together from within, which we call character, and which the child gains only by it being so called. Zelter wrote into August von Goethe's family register: "Learn to obey!" Goethe himself then said that was the only sensible word in the whole book, and praises Zelter's excellence, saying he hit the nail on the head.

The double-faced structure of the pedagogical community and its different emphases give rise to its different forms and to different types of educators—biographies and novels are full of examples. Pedagogical love aims not at prolonging obedience, but shortening it, whereas the loyalty of the child prolongs it even when it is but a formality and, in truth, only love remains. Where authority does not always represent the ideal of the child, but only the force of the objective powers, it is denied pedagogical detachment described above. In this case tragic conflicts arise, which have made this relationship one of the few basic motifs in drama.[22]

Notes

1. Translated by Norm Friesen and Sophie Zedlitz (Humboldt University, Berlin).
2. See the discussion of "pedagogy" provided in this book's introduction; see also footnote 4, below.
3. Nohl is likely referring to Gandhi's autobiography, *The Story of My Experiments with Truth*, which was published in installments during the 1920s. In it, Gandhi interprets his life as an ongoing educational experience, and also describes his struggles with a vow made before his mother to live a pure and upright life.
4. Nohl is referring to Krieck's *Philosophy of Education* (1922), which outlined a theory of "functional education." This approach regards education (understood in the broadest possible sense) as multi-layered: the first and most basic layer consists of unconscious influences, obligations and relations between people which form the basis for social life (e.g. unwritten rules of social interaction). The second is captured in the phrase "everyone educates everyone," and occurs through conscious social action, for example, in the family or place of work, in which people "form" one another, whether in cooperation or opposition (e.g. following explicit rules of social interaction). The third layer is what we generally understand by "education" in English: A rationally organized education, ordered according to concrete intentions, methods and goals. As Nohl makes clear, this construction stands in opposition to the influential conception of Friedrich Schleiermacher in which the domain of educational theory is seen as defined by the fundamental question: "What does the older generation *want* with the younger?" (above, p. 46).
5. Nohl is referring to a movement that began at the end of the 19th century and flourished in first two decades of the 20th. The young in general sought to leave industrialized cities and the impositions of the Prussian education system to experience the relative health, purity and freedom of the countryside. They saw themselves as being able to constitute their own society separate from that of the old, with its own forms of (self-) education. In this sense, this development is reminiscent of youth movements of the 1960s and '70s.
6. Foerster, F. W. (1909/2005). *Lebensführung*. Reichl Verlag, p. 71.

7. Schleiermacher writes: "Education—which ends when [a person's own purpose] becomes dominant over the influence of others—should deliver the individual, as a capable 'work' of education who is *knowledgeable* or *capable*, to the communal life of the state and the church, and to free, convivial social intercourse" (Schleiermacher, forthcoming; emphasis added).
8. Nohl is referring to the fact that, when it is understood in terms of the eventual maturity of the student, the pedagogical relation must inevitably come to an end. It has as its ultimate goal to change from a relation between a mature person and one who is *becoming mature* into a relation between *two* mature persons which is no longer "pedagogical" in the sense articulated above.
9. The notion of the "pedagogical influence" (*pädagogische Wirkung*) described here also likely has its origin in Schleiermacher's understanding of the *pädagogische Einwirkung* (influence, effect, intervention), which Schleiermacher sees as constitutive of education in a broad sense (see Chapter Three).
10. Here and elsewhere, Nohl refers to "objective spirit" and "objective powers" in a sense developed by his doctoral supervisor, Wilhelm Dilthey. Dilthey saw all artifacts of culture (from books through biological science to buildings) as "objectifications" of human willing, feeling and thinking—or of what Dilthey called the human spirit or *Geist*.
11. *Bildung* refers to individual and collective "formation" and "self-formation," processes seen as intrinsically social and also necessary for a healthy society. This means that societies, cultures and historical epochs themselves can be considered to be characterized by robust *Bildung*, or by *Bildung* that is, as Nohl is saying of his own time, fragmented and underdeveloped.
12. See: Cooper, James Fenimore. (1826/1984). *The last of the Mohicans: A narrative of 1757*. In: B. Nevins (Ed.), *James Fenimore Cooper: The Leatherstocking Tales I*. (pp. 476–877). Library of America.
13. Langbehn, J. (1890/2018). *Rembrandt as educator*. Wermod.
14. Nietzsche's early text *Schopenhauer as Educator* (1874/1997) inspired a wave of other books which took famous cultural figures and examined the educative power of their thought and their lives (e.g., Zilchert, R. [1921]. *Goethe als Erzieher*. August Peters).
15. Carlyle, T. (1840). *On Heroes, Hero Worship and the Heroic in History*. James Fraser.
16. Dilthey, W. (1923). *Briefwechsel zwischen Wilhelm Dilthey und dem Grafen Paul Yorck von Wartenburg 1877–1897*. Niemeyer, p. 186.
17. See Chapter Two.
18. Herbart, J. F. (1806/1908). *The science of education: Its general principles deduced from its aim*. Heath & Co. p. 141. Just as pedagogy involves its own disciplinary and practical stance, it also approaches elements of education itself and of the world with its own interest. See the "Editor's Introduction" in this volume.
19. i.e. love for the child in themselves and love for what they can become.
20. Schleiermacher, F.D.E. (1833/2018). *Ästhetik (1832/33): Über den Begriff der Kunst (1831–33)*. Meiner, p. 459.
21. The original for "allegiance" is *Gehorsam*, which also translates as "obedience." Note that it is translated as the latter in Nohl's subsequent references.
22. Prominent English-language examples of the conflict between "pedagogical" authority and a young person would include Shakespeare's *King Lear* or Arthur Miller's *Death of a Salesman*.

CHAPTER SIX

J. Muth: Pedagogical Tact: Study of a Contemporary Form of Educational and Instructional Engagement (Selections)

Editor's Introduction

Jakob Muth (1927–1993) was born into a working-class family and was only six when Hitler came to power. At the age of 13, he was sent to the "Adolf Hitler School" for gifted students; at 16, during the closing months of the war, Muth was forced to fight as one of Germany's infamous "child soldiers." Like many in his generation, these kinds of experiences turned Muth into a sworn enemy of all forms of illiberal rigidity and exclusion—both in education and in the world at large.[1] Given that West Germany did not shake off many of the habits and frames of mind from its facist past until the 1970s, Muth was, for much of his career, a leading educational reformer. His advocacy was international in scope and focused especially on the integration of differently-abled students into the general school population—something that has only recently become commonplace in Germany. Muth's approach to education in general is also said to have been deeply influenced by J.H. Pestalozzi's call to be attentive to the inner emotional life of children (Chapter One).[2] A number of schools in Germany now bear Muth's name, and since 2009, Germany has awarded the "Jakob Muth prize for Inclusive Schooling" on an annual basis.

Muth's resistance to rigidity and exclusion is evident in the opening paragraph of the text included here. At this point, Muth singles out Elisabeth Blochmann, both as a woman and as a German exile during the war, as someone who is well positioned to reintroduce the idea of tact in a society in which it had been effectively suppressed for at least a decade. He speaks of how, for Blochmann, "the heinous uniformity and conformity of the Nazi era" represents "the diametric opposite of tact" (p. 88); and remarks later on the value of other studies on pedagogical tact appearing in Germany already in the 1940s.

The main focus of Muth's his text, however, is on tact neither in the context of history or politics, but on what makes tact particularly educational or *pedagogical*. Unlike Herbart (Chapter Two), Muth does not see tact so much as arising in the gap that opens between theory and practice. Instead, Muth sees it as emerging in the context of what he refers to as "the unplannable"—in the figurative gap that appears between pedagogical plans and what actually happens in the classroom: "Tact is not subsumed to the planning intention of the teacher. Therefore tactful action cannot be realized in a pre-planned educational operation, but always only in the unforeseeable situation in which the educator is engaged" (p. 89; italicized in original). Muth still sees both structure and planning as essential to pedagogy; however, he also sees "irregularity"—the unpredictable, contingent and capricious—as interwoven in this "regularity."

Muth goes on to emphasize an important quality of pedagogical tact that had received relatively little attention before him: Namely, that as a kind of action that is sensitive to the other, tact is just as much about what an educator *does* as what they *do not do*—a characteristic that he refers to as "reserve:"

> This reserve is manifest in tact through its non-influence, its non-interference; it is an omission rather than an overt act, something that is not possible without sensitivity. In the final analysis, reserve allows the other to be and to become—to become that which they are called or given, without abandoning them. It knows itself to be bound to this other. It attends to the boundaries of the other in that it does not transgress its own boundaries. (p. 92)

Echoing Pestalozzi (Chapter One), what makes tact an indispensable aspect of teaching for Muth is *not* student achievement or success, but rather their inner life, the "special sensitivity" that he emphasizes in the quote above. Indeed, it is clear that Muth at many points sees an emphasis on achievement and outcomes as the enemy of tact: "The person who intends their action only to achieve a desired effect [e.g., improved student learning] acts only for their own sake, and not for the sake of another" (p. 101).

Early on in his examination, Muth notes the significance of phenomenology in the study of education for understanding pedagogical tact (p. 89). Phenomenology refers to the study of everyday lived experience, of what both the young person and the adult undergo, what they sense and feel, both in pedagogical situations and elsewhere. And this lived experience, of course, is not only about what *should* happen pedagogically, but also about what actually *does* happen—including what is unplanned, accidental and even pedagogically unproductive or harmful. In referencing phenomenology, Muth points out something common to nearly all of the chapters in the remainder of this book: An emphasis on everyday experience, and also on how it reveals not only moments of pedagogical accomplishment, but also pedagogical failure.

Muth's discussion of pedagogical tact, of reserve and of the special, selfless, sensitivity for the needs of others that it requires is structured in three main sections: It begins with (1) a discussion of that which is unplannable in education, and then moves to (2) a brief history of tact both in general use and in education. In the last section, (3) Muth describes four aspects of the "General Conception of Tact in Education," speaking of how tact "expresses itself in:"

1. Authenticity of speech;
2. Naturalness of teacher action;
3. Prevention of harm to the child;
4. Maintenance of the distance necessary for the pedagogical relation.

Muth, like Nohl before him, sees tact as constitutive of the pedagogical relation, as working to preserve "the correct middle point between the educative help of the teacher and the possible self-help of the child" (pp. 107–108).

Like Muth's own advocacy for inclusion in education, the influence of his words and ideas on tact is similarly international, reaching as far as Japan. They are also taken on, largely unacknowledged, but sometimes word-for-word, by Max van Manen in English (e.g., 1991). Finally, in Germany to this day, Muth is regarded as having "bridged" early conceptions of pedagogical tact from the 19th century to more critical and historical analyses of pedagogical tact in the present day.[3]

Sources/Recommended Reading

Friesen, N., & Osguthorpe, R. (2018). Tact and the pedagogical triangle: The authenticity of teachers in relation. *Teaching and Teacher Education, 70*, 255–264. https://doi.org/10.1016/j.tate.2017.11.023

J. Muth: Pedagogical Tact: Study of a Contemporary Form of Educational and Instructional Engagement (Selections)[4]

Pedagogical Tact and the Unplanability of Teaching and Education

Pedagogical tact is a concept that one encounters frequently in today's literature on pedagogy and instruction. It seems to have a particular self-evidence. Authors from very different backgrounds seem to agree on what it means generally. It might be precisely because of such self-evidence and unanimity that there is still no deeper determination or at least description of *pedagogical* tact. Recently, in the years following the Second World War, Elisabeth Blochmann examined tact in two essays.[5] It is certainly not by chance that it is a woman, returning to Germany [from exile] after the war, who has addressed this issue. To her, the heinous uniformity and conformity of the Nazi era—which extended well beyond orthodoxy of thought to include elements like clothing—was the diametric opposite of tact. And at the same time, she must have seen the importance of drawing the educator's attention to the profound significance of tactful action in interpersonal engagement in the confusion of the early post-war period. For those who abandon their individuality to uniformity to become an organizational "category" obstruct possibilities for tactful action just as much as those who, in the disintegration of human relations, abandon all responsibility for others.

Elisabeth Blochmann starts from the conviction that pedagogical tact "plays almost no role in German education, at least in its theory" both in the present and "the past."[6] She is speaking here only of theory for good reason—since educators may well act tactfully without reflecting explicitly on their action. An expression of Johannes Buno, a didactician[7] from the 17th century is illustrative in this regard: "a clever school master will know to be suitable in his person, timing and opportunity."[8] Buno thus designates *tact* rather precisely in its substance without necessarily recognizing it conceptually, since his characterization also expresses the crucially elusive nature of tact. The educators of earlier centuries acted in an "unreflected" pedagogically tactful way—just as the concept is used today as it were self-evident. One difference may indeed lie a kind of power of the word "tact" itself, which—despite its being taken for granted—is realized through its knowledge and use alone. This allows tact to be relevant today. We must break through the self-evidence of this phenomenon—one which has meaning in everyday adult life just as in the education of the younger—since its self-evidence corresponds with a certain inattentiveness. It is on this basis alone that a presentation of pedagogical tact is justified.

Besides its self-evidence, the neglect of tact in pedagogical theory can be explained by the fact that pedagogy has for centuries primarily concerned itself with education as a *conscious leading*, a *deliberate effecting* and an *intentional influencing*. In other words, up to now, education has been understood almost exclusively as something that can be rationally planned. This certainly applies to instruction, which in school is always "educational instruction"—educational in the sense that it develops and gives order to the circle of thought from whose center the mature human acts. According to one perceptive didactician from the early 17th century, education is a "planned performance: the planning of instruction is an ongoing task for teachers."[9] Every plan, also curricular plans, are always identical with the anticipation of a future event, all of whose details are somehow foreseen in advance. For this reason, the preparatory planning of teaching itself must leave open the possibilities which, in principle, are beyond anticipation. These possibilities or gaps can be filled by the teacher who is gifted with pedagogical tact.

Only recently has a conception become popular which has [emphasized]... the significance of the *reserve of the educator* towards the child. It points to the *unintentional nature of original educational action*, which sees *the involuntary as pedagogically meaningful*.[10] In other words: Only recently has that part of the educational field been informed phenomenologically,[11] and this includes instruction, that part of which cannot be ordered through educational planning...

Only with the opening of the dimension of unplanability does the phenomenon of pedagogical tact become clear. This is because pedagogically tactful action eludes the purposefulness of advanced planning, both in actual teaching and in the life of the school. The location of tact precisely in the domain of unplanability allows us to determine the first and essential aspect of this phenomenon: *Tact is not subsumed to the planning intention of the teacher. Therefore tactful action cannot be realized in a pre-planned educational operation, but always only in the unforeseeable situation in which the educator is engaged.* However, the unplanability of tact certainly does not preclude acquiring or being trained in pedagogically tactful action.

Of course, understanding the unplanability of education should not lead on the one hand to an abandonment of educational intentions. On the other, it should not lead one to understand learning only as an event[12] should not result in abandoning the necessity of methodical instruction. Perhaps this discussion of pedagogical tact will help us to understand that the opening of the domain of unplanability places the pedagogical intention of the educator in a new, broad horizon—and that it gives education enormous responsibility. And because it is manifest in unplannable instructional phenomena, a decisively more intensive planning of instruction is needed in comparison to the time that a teacher would commit herself to slavishly anticipating, in a strictly determined sense, all of the events possible in the classroom. The eminent significance of pedagogical tact is thus not to be confused with a newly propagated pedagogical naturalism.[13]

The most recent references to tact in pedagogy fall into two groups:

As both a concept and a form of educational action, pedagogical tact has been taken up in education just as it is used *in the sphere of general human relations*. In this case, modification is not necessarily required for tact to become pedagogically relevant. This is because, in their engagement with the young in the school, the educator is called, for the sake of these young people, to be tactful just as they would naturally be outside of school, in relation to other adults.

On the other hand, in everyday language, tact is accompanied by a more discrete meaning. One speaks in this case also of pedagogical tact, but of a kind that is *instructionally directed in its meaning*, a meaning that is oriented to the educator's teaching and the student's learning. The realization of this type of pedagogical tact accordingly means an incursion into the realm of plannability, as is generally the case with instruction.

[The famous educationist J.F. Herbart (Chapter Two) had] the second, instructionally-oriented version of tact in mind [when he originally coined the idea of pedagogical tact in 1802]. This notion of pedagogical tact dominated during the remainder of the 19th century—but without entirely eclipsing the first "version" of tact. Those following Herbart knew to differentiate a tact that is specifically "educational" from one that is more narrowly didactical or instructional. On the other hand, in our century, the first version has been widely adopted, without the second being neglected. Today, both versions are granted the same weight in educational literature. Therefore, a book-length representation of pedagogical tact must have both versions in view.[14]

Pedagogical Tact as a Form of Educational Action

Its General Use and its Adoption by Education

In general usage, tact refers to "sensitivity," to an "inner sensitivity for that which is right and appropriate, a fitting and fine judgement," understood and articulated as "correct judgment," and as "reserve."[15] Thus understood, the concept came from the French language in the 18th century, specifically from the refined social culture of the Rococo era. Voltaire is said to have been the first to apply the Latin *tactus* to the sphere of human engagement just after it had undergone an important shift in meaning in the area of music.[16] Since then, this use of tact has coincided with *reserve* and *sensitivity* as its two defining moments. These moments can be described individually, but tact resists any definitive description just as any particular form of human action would. These two defining moments, however, give the original Latin term (*tactus*, i.e. touch) an entirely new, even opposite meaning: Tact as sensitivity and especially as reserve means above all avoiding bodily contact with others, and it is obviously not the concrete contact or even knocking or tapping suggested by its Latin meaning…

Although the contemporary use of the word tact is not directly related to its Latin etymology, it is perhaps not surprising that its conceptual connections are informative. The concept of tact clearly entered into the sphere of general human interaction from music. Sensitivity and reserve were still important as its defining moments in this context, since for music tact was a principle of order. And as an ordering principle, it must have arisen with musical polyphony back in the 10th century. The multiplicity characteristic of harmony and polyvocality require "tact" as a regulating unit of measure. Adherence to this unit of measure was enabled though hand clapping, foot tapping or with the help of a large conductors' baton, through which they lead with one blow after another on the ground or in contact with another surface. Only in [terms of these connections] is it possible to meaningfully see the adaptation of the Latin *tactus* into music. […]

Subsequent centuries were primarily the prisoner of tempo as the absolute organizing principle, which became self-evident as a methodological principle more generally. But starting in the mid-18th century, orchestral arrangements allowed the musical tempo to be maintained soundlessly—[expressed through] the reserve of the conductor, the inconspicuousness of his timing, and finally also his sensitivity for the music—which was no longer a question of simple time measurement. It is only at this point that the reversal of the Latin meaning could become possible, and it is only here that the concept of tact enters the sphere of general human engagement as does sensitivity and reserve, from which it would again be soon transferred—in modified form—by J.F. Herbart into pedagogy.

That peculiar inner connection has been sustained to this day. The folk song of the 19th century with its almost boring symmetry has its counterpart in educational practice in the formal and static hourly structure of a habitual methodical way of thinking, which does not have any connection to the subject matter at hand. On the other hand, songs composed today break any absolute principle of order, conveying a particular weightlessness and originality of movement. One must have a feeling for tact as irregularity in that which is regular. This is also the central characteristic of our contemporary understanding of specifically pedagogical tact: *It is distinguished as dynamic irregularity in static regularity.*

But we return to the more general meaning of tact, especially to the concepts of *sensitivity* and *reserve* as its two essential defining moments—as highlighted by our exploration into its conceptual-historical connections, above. The sensitivity which characterizes that which is tactful is a feeling for the "you" (or thou[17]), for one's fellow human being, for the singularity and singular rights of the other; it is a respect for the ultimate inaccessibility of the other. Like every feeling, it cannot be calculated in advance; it cannot be intended in advance. It is always realized in the concrete, unforeseeable situation in which one finds oneself suddenly confronted, needing to protect others, to help others—insofar as another is in need of help—in that one responds to the other, in no way hurting or imposing oneself on the other. Such action is possible because it arises from a sense of "security that comes from within," as Elisabeth Blochmann has put it—from a purity and impartiality of someone who does not reflect on himself, but is always turned to the other, and therefore experiences the experience of the other in his own being.

And the *reserve* that the tactful person exercises in engagement with others—as paradoxical as it may sound—is encompassed by agreement, since the one who is tactful restrains themselves for the sake of the other. This reserve is manifest in tact through its non-influence, its non-interference; it is an omission rather than an overt act, something that is not possible without sensitivity. In the final analysis, reserve allows the other to be and to become—to become that which they are called or given, without abandoning them. It knows itself to be bound to this other. It attends to the boundaries of the other in that it does not transgress its own boundaries. It does not denude the other in their intimacy—all while still engaged by and for them. Just like sensitivity, reserve is ultimately only about others, not about one's own wishes and pursuits. And just like sensitivity, reserve can only be realized in concrete situations in which the individual immediately finds himself. The person that calculatingly restrains themselves in advance because they do not want to get involved actually does not act tactfully. That is because they come to reserve not for the sake of another person, but for their own sake.

As expressed in the term *con-tact*, tact is always a *social phenomenon*—whether it is manifest through sensitivity or through reserve. One is only in a position to act tactfully only when one is released from egocentric self-attachment and is available to others—a self-attachment proper to the child, but which ultimately threatens any [adult] individual's humanity. Consequently, as Hans M. Elzer has put it, neither "condescending civility" nor "routine politeness" can be seen as the same as tact.[18] Also conscious, willful exertion has fundamentally nothing to do with tactful action. Indeed, all three of these forms— "condescending civility," "routine politeness" and conscious, willful exertion—have little to do with naturalness of action. They also lack the selflessness of the tactful. And this is the only basis on which interpersonal relation is possible.

Now the question arises: *how is it possible to translate the concept of tact from the sphere of general interpersonal relations to the domain of educational practice?* What is the educational structure of tact, such that its translation into the domain of educational practice would be justified? The first objection to such a transfer should arise from the fact that while a particular sensitivity is certainly appropriate in educational engagement, the restraint that would represent the omission of intentional interventions [in education] appears much less appropriate. This is supposedly because education is generally seen as possible as a result of a specifically educational intrusiveness (*Aggressivität*), one that consciously seeks to effect change. The reserve that is a part of tact, however, does not proceed from the goal of changing others.

A second concern or reservation arises from the fact that reserved engagement, as it occurs in everyday life without any deliberate object, cannot on its own be directly taken up in school, because it simply is not the case that life and school are equally educational. The potential of everyday life to miseducate or de-form may well be decisively stronger and more intensive than its potential to positively form or educate. In opposition to this second concern, however, tact has the potential to also release us cathartically from life's miseducation and deformation.

Tact expresses itself in any case in relation between persons. To be tactless [or alternatively, tactful] to an animal, on the other hand, is of course absolutely impossible—just as one cannot be tactless [and also not tactful] in relation to God.[19] In the same way, tactful action in relation to things is not possible. If one is challenged by something in the world of physical and technical objects, for example as a watchmaker repairing a watch, what is required is impartial objectivity and intervention along the lines of mechanical necessity. Tact belongs exclusively to the realm of the interpersonal; it can only be realized in interpersonal engagement in that it has to do with the being of the other, the very essence of the interpersonal; in subtle empathetic action or in a reserved forbearance in the face of inappropriate action. This alone leads to the improvement of our life with others.

The fact that tact is clearly located in the interpersonal realm grants it its pedagogical status. This status is also visible in that all educational engagement takes place in interpersonal relationships. As the singular relationship of an educator to a child, the pedagogical relation is always an interpersonal one.[20] This is characterized on the side of the educator by dedication to the child and on the side of the child by trust in the educator. And therein lies the educational structure of tact: The educational engagement of the teacher does not simply arise on its own; it arises through the child, through one who is in need of education and upbringing. That leads us perforce back to first objection mentioned above. It was again Herbart who saw the "malleability" or "educatability" of the child as irreducible and as the fundamental category for education.[21] And since that time, urgency, intrusiveness and the will to change (the child) have been seen as determinative factors in educators' actions. But when the need of the young person for guidance and direction calls the educator into dialogue, help and reserve become the central pedagogical categories. This is because, within the horizon of educational need, education is all about leading the young person to that which he is and what he is able to be, to the possibilities that he has been granted as his own. Put another way: the tactful educator knows to address the need of the child in such a way that the child finds their own substance granted through the educator—all so that, as Elzer puts it, "that which is granted is directed to the child themselves."[22] *The task of all education is placed here within a new horizon or context through reserve*, and in this way, the relevance of tact to pedagogy as well as to the interpersonal in general becomes evident.[23]

In education, the "childhood" of the child must not be seen as a deficit. This would make tactful engagement impossible. Instead, this "childhood" should be seen as a kind of "being other" when compared to the grown up or adult, since this alone allows for the emergence of respect for individuality and individual integrity of the other. As a result, the relation of the educator to the child from the first day of school onwards should be carried by that sensitivity which grows outwards from the teacher's inner security, and from that reserve which does not force itself on the other, but instead, finds him in terms of the measure of that which is gifted to him. Indeed, it is in this that the undertaking of all education lies. This helps to explain the fact that it is said in the education of young offenders: "Not only the mature, but also the maturing person must be treated with tact."[24] This is as valid for the student in this particular educational context as it is for the child in the first grade or the sixth grade of school.

Of course, action that is tactful (and also tactless) on the part of the child toward the teacher, toward other adults, or toward other children is always entirely possible. This is especially true as the child frees himself from his egocentric disposition and thus enters into interpersonal engagement. For at this point, the child achieves something important in relation to attention—specifically in the sense of "attending to someone" even in a small way. It is then as a kind of prefiguration of tact that children, in the course of being educated, experience the experience of others—specifically in a way that calls one to tactful action, allowing such an act to become the purest expression of our collective existence. However, this has little to do with specifically pedagogical tact, and thus will not be discussed here.

Incidentally, the guidance of children in tactful action should be possible through the unintentional *example* given by the teacher, through their tactful action in engaging with children.

The General Conception of Tact in Education

Fundamentally, no distortion or revision is necessary to take the concept of tact from the sphere of general human interaction to the realm of pedagogical practice and engagement, and to preserve the role of sensitivity and reserve as the carriers of pedagogical action.

[…]

Four specific forms of the expression of tact can be identified as different aspects of a single phenomenon. Let us now turn our attention to these four aspects.[25]

Tact Expresses Itself Through Authenticity of Speech

The natural authenticity or the "binding power of language"[26] presents a power which one cannot force, since it involves *more* than seeing language as a medium of understanding. And it is only through this power that the respect of the educator for the child, and their recognition of the child in his or her being as a child, shows itself. *The binding power of language establishes a field of interrelationship that lies beyond the level of understanding and that extends well beyond mere communication: it is the basis for communication, consensus and understanding....* Thus it is not simply all the same if a teacher finishes reading a child's name, and for the sake of expediency, simply moves to the next name, calling "Johnson!" Nor is it the same if they add a binding "thank you," or a correction—and then ask the next child by saying: "Lucas, now you please." Are such nuances mere trivialities? Authenticity of speech is of course not trivial because it founds a common space between teacher and student. And this lies at the very beginning of the tactful attitude of the teacher to the child—as well as of the guidance of the child to their own tactfulness. […]

But knowing a student's name and linguistic interaction in the everyday life of the school is more important still. To know and to say a name out loud is to elevate the child from the anonymity of namelessness in which he or she can be submerged, unrestrained and undisciplined. Without this "naming," the child knows him or herself to be unaddressed, and thus also is not placed under an expectation. Instead, the child stands outside of a binding relationship which is realized with the use of the name. The fairy tale of Rumpelstiltskin is a good illustration of this ("The queen will never win the game, for Rumpelstiltskin is my name."[27]) New teachers, or those taking over a new class must therefore see learning the names of the students in the class as quickly as possible as their first task. But this is not done simply to capitalize on these names and the children in a superficial way, but only because the name has a communicative power which can neither be grasped nor objectified.

Even the Herbartians[28] saw in the binding power of speech an essential form of the expression of tact. Karl Volkmar Stoy gave masterful expression to this in his 1884 lecture opening the University of Jena for the summer semester:

> The tactful person is one who has the right word for every occasion, the right content for his speech, the right tone, the correct emphasis, the right sequence in speech and action. And the educator who handles individual's natures correctly, valuing the meek and humble, not pressuring the slow, never harsh to the sensitive, patiently supporting the laboriously hard-working, collecting, calming and redirecting the distracted; whoever holds together the majority through their tone, through the right choice of words and the right tonal emphasis—briefly, these are the ones who exercise what is advantageous to every pedagogical situation—they receive from every unbiased observer the recognition of tactfulness.[29]

In her recent book on classroom management… Elisabeth Plattner contrasts the non-binding language of one teacher with the binding language of another in the following revealing way:[30] "In a class of twelve to fourteen-year-olds, a teacher showed the boys the notebook of a girl and said: 'Let your notebooks look like this. See it as your example.'" Plattner then continues:

> If one tries to spur young people on with such words, one expects and wishes them to think: "What she can do, I think I can do." Unfortunately, however, such well-intentioned words often have a different effect. Some respond despondently or defiantly: "The other guy can do it, but I can't." Then they will feel even more discouraged and even less able to do their best.

The second teacher in another class showed the girls the notebook of a boy and said, "'Do you like that? … I think you can also write so beautifully.'"
Plattner continues:

> When read quickly, one might think that both teachers said approximately the same thing. However, there's a big difference. In the given context, the second teacher like the first strove for good writing, partly through recognition and encouragement, partly through rigor, and by having any sloppy work rewritten. And like the first, the second teacher one day [comes across] some particularly carefully written work; she also wanted to show it to his classmates as an example. But she did it tactfully, happily avoiding a number of possible dangers.

And what was tactful about what she said?

> She didn't say: "This is what your notebooks should or must look like" but chose her words in such a way that they could not act as a reproach to those more sensitive. She also did not arouse secret resistance by calling for imitation. Instead, the teacher expressed confidence: "You can write so beautifully!"

Through such a way of speaking every child was actually called to themselves, but not to imitate a role model.

Such binding speech is of course something that can be learned, which is particularly evident in the use of questions or interrogatives; and if it is in fact a characteristic of tact, we can then see that tactful action can indeed be learned. That tact can certainly be learned [means it] admittedly exists in some tension with its principally unplannable nature. This is shown simply by the fact that the learnable binding nature of what is said has little in common with the naturalness of speech—or with a positive verbal atmosphere—which can of course exist in the family as well as in the classroom, and which of course cannot simply be "intended." *There is simply no uniformity in the binding character of speech*. That which is to be said at a given moment changes with changing situations in which it is said, and it also changes with the person I am talking to. The possibility of learning the binding power of speech is only a precondition needed for the teacher, with all of the intangibility and indeterminacy that this implies. [...]

This authenticity or binding power of speech is therefore something that must always be won anew; it is not comparable to something one possesses; something which teachers have at their disposal. Both the tactful expression of the educator as well as the educative engagement of the child constitute the singularity of the situation that requires tactful action. Above all, one must see both sides in connection with the unplanability of pedagogical tact: not only the action of the child, but also the resulting reaction of the teacher—both are in principle beyond calculation.

It is certainly the case that tactful action that is grounded in the naturalness of what is spoken is manifest in many different ways in different classrooms. This is independent from the dialogical tension that invisibly comes into being between teacher and child, and that holds the teacher... and invigorates them, but which is independent from the general verbal atmosphere which may reign in the classroom as a whole. This is referenced frequently, and Johann Wittmann speaks to it in his summary of "holistic" arithmetic in the first grade. He emphasizes the importance of the linguistic penetration of elementary mathematical matters, which must be clear to the child for the opening of this [mathematical] world:

> A good verbal climate must reign in the classroom. It is currently the case that the student speaks too little and the teacher speaks too much. The teacher needs to learn to speak less, and to allow the child to speak and to act more independently. A particular tact must inform the teacher when it is appropriate to speak or to allow the child to speak more and to act autonomously...[31]

"A *particular* tact must inform the teacher when it is appropriate to allow the child to speak or to be silent," Wittmann adds. Already the attribute particular in this case places tact in the position of being closed off to strategy and manipulation.[32] It does not allow itself to be contained, planned or calculated in advance; it does not allow itself to be "mastered"…one cannot use it at will, but as a teacher, one yields to it. One can connect with it, entrust oneself to it. But this hardly means that the teacher is completely delivered over to uncertainty when they turn themselves over to tact. On the contrary, those who are in the fortunate position of being able to entrust themselves to pedagogical tact have, with all their ease, a peculiar inner security and coherence in their pedagogical activity, which touches again and again those who are with a good teacher. The tactful teacher knows when it is appropriate to let the child speak or to remain silent; but they also know when it is their turn to speak or remain silent themselves. Even in general human relations the tactful person knows or feels from the inside when it is up to him or the other person to speak or to be silent. It is in the same way that he feels what is appropriate to say in this unique situation and to this one person. For that reason, the person who is immersed in a given situation cannot be wrapped up in himself, isolated and coolly distant. The being of other people must have touched him; he must be touched by others.

Precisely that silence which Wittman highlights is significant for a positive verbal climate in a classroom. It is certain that silence as the absence of speech belongs to tact just as much as active speech does. The moment of reserve in tact is given expression in silence; and the teacher must find a path to this reserve for the sake of the children's education. He should, as Wittman says, speak less than is generally the case; he should step back, for once *not consciously attempt to be a teacher* in the sense of the intrusiveness often associated with it—all in order to allow children to speak and act to a great extent independently. In view of the realities of the classroom, these thoughts on the authentic and binding character of speech can be formulated more decisively: *Only on the basis of the reserve of the educator, for example in speech, in help, in supervision and monitoring, and also in teaching and instruction is the self-activity*[33] *of the child possible, and with that, also his or her guidance to self-activity.* The teacher who, through reading or telling aloud gives away the meaning of the text being read, as is recommended in the literature for reading instruction, whoever in arithmetic would attempt to prevent every conceivable error, or cannot accept that there is such a thing as a "pedagogy of failure," the science teacher who conducts every experiment herself and forces his young students to merely be receptive, whoever prevents participation on fieldtrips through over scrupulous concern about the possible costs for every child and thereby prevents the concrete emergency from being educational; whoever takes away the resistance of a text to the exercise of translation through various methodological tricks and thereby cheats the student of the experience of this resistance, such a teacher can be called pedagogically intrusive and does not exercise reserve. Indeed, such a teacher effectively impedes the self-activity of the young person. It is this sense that as Werner Loch says that "the reason for the reserve of the teacher is to make the self-activity of the student possible."[34]

It is in this way that the pedagogical significance of tact becomes clear... However, this self-activity of the child, which is rendered possible by the reserved tactful action of the educator …is defined by the insight that that tact, as a social phenomenon, is a kind of doing *for another* and not for one's own sake. Only in this conception is self-activity relevant pedagogically and thus for our own humanity.[35]

Tact Shows Itself in the Naturalness of Teacher Action

For further insight into the naturalness of teacher action as an expression of tact, we can continue along the lines outlined above. In connection with what was said above about silence and reserve, one is of course tempted to think of the [radically progressive] work-school movement,[36] and its cardinal principle of the self-active nature or being of the child. However, the self-activity of the child, which corresponds to the reserve of the teacher, should not be exaggerated. Not all activity in school can be based on self-activity. A child in their activity can be taxed by reserve, silence, listening and contemplation on the part of the adult. Wittman expressed this [above], and in this same connection, Theodor Schwerdt strongly critiqued Hugo Gaudig [an advocate of the work-school movement], saying:

> The principle of free, mental, personal activity supports the idea that every school assignment should be completed by the pupil in an active way. With this principle, Gaudig lays out a single path, characterized by the active attitude of the student. But this raises the question of whether this single path is to be promoted [and] if all schoolwork can be fully addressed in this way. Certainly, in the majority of work, the promotion of an active attitude among students is to be affirmed.[37]

But after asking this question regarding the power of self-activity, Schwerdt continues: "But there are at times situations in instruction, when dealing with some of the most valuable educational goals, when the tactful teacher feels that the fruitful moment would be negated if one were to grant students one's silence and stillness."

One must recognize precisely this side of the work-school movement, with its overemphasis on the self-activity of the child, if one wants to come to a correct approach to pedagogical tact. Just as on the one hand a teacher's constant forcing of herself on children frustrates their attempts to act independently and thus hinders their path to independence, the teacher's stepping back from such activity is a necessity when a thing or a situation calls for quiet, for listening. For that, one only needs to think of the hearing of the word in religious instruction, of the deep plunge into the stillness of the word that the poet demands, on listening to the voices of birds in a nature excursion. In a properly understood approach to the school, it would above all become clear that the young person would attend to manifold claims made of him, whether these are met actively or through receptivity. Above all, the teleology of the *non scholae sed vitae discimus* (learning comes from life, not school) must be broken down, because school is not there for the child, as is commonly assumed; it is not an institution that meets the needs of those in early life as other institutions meet those of people late in life; instead, the child is there for the school, since school in the Western world is a task which all young people must face up to.[38] There is no other way to understand its current historical position in the West and in the present condition of human kind. As a result, to be a student is not something a young person "has." Instead, the task of being a student must arise anew every new day in becoming aware of the demands in the school world and in their fulfillment.

But this raises the question: How can the teacher encourage the student to attend to the claims of the school placed upon him? In all tentativeness, it is possible to respond: *Through the naturalness of the teacher's action, which enables pedagogical tact in him, and which indeed is virtually identical with pedagogical tact itself.* However, we must now try to address the wide-ranging generality of this answer. The natural action of the teacher can be described in three ways; the teacher:

1. Needs to step back from the demand which he is working to help the students with.
2. May not consciously and deliberately begin and end with purely academic results and purposes.
3. May not try to achieve naturalness as an educator through the artificial cultivation of himself as educator.

The naturalness of the action of the teacher coincides with the fact that in school, it is assignments and expectations that come to the fore. In other words: It is not the child that sets the standards for what happens in the school; this would condemn the school to irresponsible non-commitment. The school stood in danger of this when, at its outset, our century was declared the "Century of the Child."[39] On the other hand, teaching methods take a secondary place; they cannot be used as an independent instrument that is imposed formally, from the outside on all situations, and to which all situations can be subsumed without differentiation. Instead, one's method must be determined from within the midst of any given situation that the method is to address. As a result, to proceed methodically in the school is different every time, in keeping with expectations and situations understandable to the students. In the final analysis, it is not really the teacher who "educates" (if you like); but it is the tasks and demands themselves to which he submits and as whose speaker he appears to the children. This is the real depth of the natural action to which the teacher is called in our time. The teacher does not need to artificially cultivate himself as an educator; doing so would (among other things) only show that he does not inhabit the originality of being an educator. He does not need to see himself as a universal methodologist, since it is not at all a matter of one or another ability being ascribed to *his* "arts;" *what is alone decisive is that the educator is able to appropriately "open up" those issues relevant to the class, and to not distort them or deprive them of their essence through himself or through artificial methodological refinement.*

If one wants to clarify this through the traditional model of the didactic triangle,[40] one must then allow the teacher and the child to move into the background, since assignments and expectations—which have otherwise been referred to inappropriately as curricular "objects" or "material"—are to be accentuated. At no time in the history of the school has there been a "balance of forces" in the didactic triangle. Since the beginning of the 20th century, those following Herbart placed the accent on the person of the teacher, who has a formal method "at hand;" and since the beginning of the century, the progressive educational movement *(Schulreformbewegung)* did something similar in emphasizing the student. Representing recent pedagogical developments, it is the being of the student and of the teacher that comes to the fore in the school.[41] In addition, the received version of the concept "self-activity" as a kind of doing for another's sake manifests the same emphasis.

From the moment the teacher withdraws from the expectations of the situation that must occur in the school he is given the possibility to pursue "effects" through all manner of artificial arrangements. The person who intends their action only to achieve a desired effect acts only for their own sake, and not for the sake of another. They lose their naturalness and plausibility in their action. Their actions solidify into sheer power. As Gabriel Marcel says: "From the moment that I become preoccupied about the effect I want to produce on the other person, my every act, word and attitude loses its authenticity."[42] Indeed, if there is something like an "effect" in such situations, it evades the given situation.

The educator who is completely absorbed in his actions[43] never needs to pursue "effects." He is virtually forbidden from consciously and deliberately cultivating his being as an educator, and working towards an "effect," as soon as it comes the question of leading young people in the classroom. Whoever relentlessly wants to be an educator is deprived of the naturalness of their being as a teacher. They have a theatrical effect and will achieve the opposite of what is possible. In this sense, speaking of the "born educator"—one for which there is "no rulebook"—is not the same as pedagogical naturalism because an educator always "happens upon the right thing based on a deep, inner instinct."[44] This is because what is most valid here is the demand for clear action, not instinctive blindness. The idea of an "unintentional" education in this sense has a different meaning than in pedagogical naturalism.

Such failed forms of educational action mentioned above are, in the final analysis, an expression of the educator's overreach, not of the reserved naturalness of teaching and learning. We must finally have the courage, both in education and its practice, to open up and keep open the realm of the natural, the unintentional and the involuntary. This is of special importance since this domain is obscured by the means-ends thinking of our time that stops at nothing—with neither the school nor educational theory standing in its way. "Education has lost the paradise of pure [spontaneity] and now consciously serves at the plough for the bread of life," as Martin Buber puts it (2002, p. 106). This paradise can be reclaimed, but not in the sense of a pedagogical naturalism—but instead by having the circumstances of the school appear as unforced, since it is only in this way that are they reconciled with educational efficiency, which in any case escapes humans' grasp. Only through such unforced circumstances is it possible for the teacher to work in a way that is itself unforced or natural. But this does not mean that the planned and intentional action of the teacher is negated. It is to be seen in that place which proceeds the release of the essence of the claims imposed by a given set of circumstances. That's why the unplanability that is being emphasized here cannot be a genuine alternative to a planned course of action in the school. It would mean delivering the school to an ad absurdum, to instructional chaos, if one were to locate the naturalness of the teacher and his capacity for pedagogically tactful action exclusively within the horizon of a pedagogical naturalism. But this is not to consent to the idea of a "naturalistic tact."[45] ...With "naturalistic tact" however, our concern with didactic decisiveness comes to an end.

Tact Expresses Itself in the Prevention of Harm to the Child

In general human contact, that which is tactful is marked by the fact that it does not harm others. This is made possible by one's ability to take the experiences of others to an extent as one's own, and in this way, to respect the otherness of other. It is also possible to live our lives together in a mutuality that exceeds explicit articulation, one that draws attention to the other's space and privacy. In this mutuality, one is "invisibly" embraced by the other, and an injury to the other is experienced as one's own. Sensitivity and reserve circumscribe this stance or disposition just as much as does *consideration* of the other (*respectus*[46]). The reality of interpersonal contact is determined in such a way that the person who lives in the naturalness of tactful action doesn't really have to work explicitly to avoid injury to others. This is simply because his action is so infused from and by others, that there is hardly a situation in with injury can arise. The same holds for the interpersonal engagement in the setting of the school.

Since Rousseau and Pestalozzi, pedagogy has understood this experience and experiencing of others (this mutuality, our being "embraced" by others) as also affecting interpersonal engagement in school—specifically in the context of the so-called "individuality principle."[47] It is *precisely the tactful teacher who works to embrace the individuality of the particular child, and his special, individual situation through a kind of individual* "care-taking"—in this way avoiding any injury to the child. It is precisely the teacher who possesses the capacity for such individual caretaking, because he experiences the experience of the child in his own being and allows it to become the basis for his action. In this way, tact "is essentially not conformity to the situation, but instead the criterion for the singular case."[48] Illustrative examples are manifold and new ones are constantly being taken up in the literature. In order not to be lost in generalities, we will confine ourselves to three aspects of the individuality principle, which appear particularly important for pedagogical tact. These are (1) school-life in general; (2) instruction or lessons in a narrow sense, and (3) the problem of method.

School Life in General

A teacher, for example, cannot greet all children who come to school late in the same way, perhaps with the same sternness. If a child's mother repeatedly gets the child up too late, there is no reason for the teacher to diminish him or her in front of the class or even one-on-one—and there is little difference in this case. He or she should not have to stay after school; it is instead the mother's neglect that should be addressed. One should not diminish a child on account of the lack of order at home—or a child who [for example], despite many reminders, has not brought money for a fieldtrip. He should not be called before the class, since it's possible that his parents will only have money at the end of the month. Any child who is conscious of material impoverishment of their own household is already injured if this has been pried from their private life. It is with such cases, which lie outside of actual "teaching," where individual "care-taking" of children begins, and this appears in terms of the ability of the teacher to take tactful action. He can of course realize this himself by becoming familiar with the home life of the children.

Instruction More Narrowly

This caretaking of the individual which results from the tactful action of the teacher is both necessary and possible in lessons and instruction in a narrower sense. In a class which is being directed by the teacher from the front of the room, it is frequently difficult to avoid injury to children. This is because such traditional instruction always equalizes; one cannot take the individuality of the child sufficiently into account. This is expressed, as Langeveld says, in that the assignments and challenges made of children must be expressed "with tact, with the accurate understanding of the world as perceived by the—or rather, this—child; but at the same time, also with a correct estimation of the child's ability to carry the work and lessons assigned."[49] For example, in the context of a class dictation exercise, a child's inability to spell might exposed because the teacher does not come to an individual arrangement that can no longer be planned down to the last detail (and which is therefore more difficult to carry out). In this case, it should then not be surprising that the child is soon injured and blocks himself against a deeper penetration into the rules and irregularities of spelling and also against the teacher. [...]

Likewise, the teacher turns a blind eye to the possibility of individualizing tactful action if he commits himself exclusively to a given method. In this way, one can end up shifting all responsibility for the child's learning, which the teacher should actually bear himself, over to the particular method. For example, how simple is it to use a lock-step method in introducing children to reading their first words? This provides the teacher with a methodical procedure in which he knows every step, and it keeps the children of the class all at the same level.

Moving beyond the individuality principle, we can return to our discussion of schoolwork above to further consider tact as the avoidance of injury to the child. In other words: *Pedagogical tact is especially important in school work, when the child has given himself fully to the demands of the task, when he has given something of himself,* and through this dedication to the task, lets himself be present in these demands, indeed, positively enables the existence of these demands [for himself] in the first place. Even the slightest expression by the teacher, [for example] the exertion of some pressure based on progressing through the lesson, can disturb this dedication, and injure the child—as Martin Buber has so nicely said—because he has "ventured [so] far out on the way to his achievement" (2002, p. 105). This venturing "far out on the way to achievement" might appear in reading lessons when the child experiences fears and hopes, rejoices or despairs with the protagonist, or when the child is so deeply engaged in a mathematics lesson that he lives fully in the present, forgets the time and everything else around him. It is in this abolition of time and expansion of space something unique appears, something which is grounded in a kind of "selflessness." This is the structure of this "giving over" of oneself. Or when the child, in creative activity, lives in the task, and is freed from it, returning to him or herself, very often psychically accompanied by a sigh of relief after the demands of the task have been withstood and fulfilled. In the original "giving" of oneself, the child is like any person "within" the task, and no longer with themselves as a self, ego or "I." The teacher must assist this originary "giving" rather than disturb it when it occurs in the school, since to interrupt it is to injure the child.

On the other hand, the questioning look of a child who is uncertain about something often demands—as a form of help—an expression of the teacher so that the child finds his way through his situation. This expression, however, does not necessarily have to be in the form of spoken words, but can consist of a nod, a wink, a gesture or the unmistakeable tone of something barely spoken.

The injury of a child who is caught up in a task can of course also be caused by other children in the class. In this case, the ability of the tactful teacher to respond appropriately, his or her sensibility for that which is appropriate in the singular situation makes the avoidance of injury possible. For example: In a first-grade class, during a discussion of Santa Claus, a child might proudly yell out: "He isn't real!" The teacher, who may sense the injury of the other children—because they still live in a world in which Santa Claus is real—steps directly to the child. Laying his hand on his shoulder, he might look the child in the eyes, and asks quickly: "Would you like it if there were no Santa Claus?" The child's surprised "No!" restores for the other children their childhood world and simultaneously allows the conversation to continue. No teacher can prepare for such an unforeseeable situation—but the teacher is nonetheless challenged by it. Finally, the good teacher is actually very well "prepared" for such unforeseeable circumstances, since he is "quick on the uptake"—on the basis of his studies, his experiences, and through his constant efforts. On the basis of earlier understanding, he can constantly realize his "being" as a teacher anew in the singularity and instantaneousness of such situations. One is not a teacher by the sanction of one's certification; one's being as a teacher is accomplished and realized anew every day in the reality of the classroom.

Tact Expresses Itself in the Maintenance of the Distance Necessary for the Pedagogical Relation

Injury to the child is avoided to the greatest degree possible through the reserve of the teacher; this is because in such reserve, the teacher preserves the integrity of the child, and does not injure his privacy. Above all, it is in each case necessary that the educator maintains himself as educator, [solely] for the purpose of the education of the child. This requires a particular distance, one that is in itself not identical with reserve. Distance, in its substance, indeed lies very close to reserve, but it means something more. *In distance, the person attempts to preserve himself; for the educator, this would be to maintain his being as educator. Reserve, on the other hand, is always exercised for the sake of another.* That is why a distancing reserve is expressed in everyday interpersonal interaction—one indifferent to the well-being of others and meant to prevent direct engagement—results very often in a false safeguarding of oneself.

Nonetheless, there is a distance, one proper to the pedagogical relation, that is to be regulated through the tact of the teacher. This is because teachers and students belong to different levels, and they exist in different realms of duty or responsibility. The teacher represents the older generation, which carries the duty to educate and bring up the younger. To exaggerate somewhat, he lives in knowledge, whereas the child lives in not-knowing. This makes for a natural distance between the teacher and the child, which enables the former to educate and instruct. [...] A loss of this particular kind of pedagogical distance leads to the dissolution of the pedagogical relation. But this does not stand in contradiction to the fact that we have identified the "giving over of oneself" (*Hingabe*) as an important pedagogical task. In selflessly giving oneself over to a demand, that distance is overcome, and in this original giving over, one becomes human. But this is only possible where the need of the other demands interpersonal action. In the pedagogical relation, however, distance is needed so that the educator can do justice to his task; indeed, an important part of this relation is a distance whose essence includes the eventual obsolescence of this relationship itself in the course of the process of education.[50] Paul Gabele discusses this in an essay that is most informative:

> The educator simply sits next to the child. He sits at the same height, face to face, eye to eye. He doesn't have to say anything. It is enough that he makes an acknowledging sound, a nod; and the child senses it: He is with me, with me alone. With the youngest pupils, it is not uncommon that they often try to wrap their arms around their educator, and do not want to let go. Of course, this is much better than freezing in front of the teacher, but regardless, a danger doubtlessly remains: As near as the child should be to the educator, however much they might find the same language, the same rhythm, they should never simply be completely the same. How far [these similarities] might reach is a matter of personal tact.[51]

Writing further, Gabele rather dramatically describes those occasions where the equality or sameness of the teacher and the young students appears through a failure of tact, when in other words, a loss of distance arises:

> The educator who roughhouses with the children on the floor or plays a game of tag with them, he must be taken aside, because he's treating the children casually like

comrades, happily slapping them on the shoulder and greeting them: "Yeah! I don't want to learn today either!"

Significantly, there appears in education (as in life itself) many cases in which a loss of distance occurs in the moment of physical contact. It is not by chance that Gabele mentions things like roughhousing or a game of tag as examples since both involve bodily contact in which the natural distance of teacher and child is shattered. It would [also] be broken if the children were to give *the teacher* a comradely slap on the shoulder or to use an expression that negates the distance between them. Physical contact that happens in school… often arises unconsciously, for example, when getting children into place in a choir [or] in helping a child [with an assignment]. However, insofar as the teacher sets himself in the place of the children, a loss of distance—and with it, a break in the pedagogical relation—can result.

Those teachers who allow themselves to violate the distance required in tactful action, are also among those whose physical contact [with students]—however well intentioned—leads them to fail as teachers. (At this point, it is clear that our adoption of the Latin *tactus* has given it a meaning opposed to the one it possessed in the general realm of interpersonal engagement [namely *touch*]) [...]

With young children in elementary grades, as Gabele also indicates, this problematic is configured differently than it is in the higher grades. [...] [In this context] touch comes already in the form of giving one's hand in a greeting. Here, distance is created precisely in the act of reaching out one's hand—in which one must see an archaic mode of distantiation.[52] Distance comes further to fore in verbal forms of greeting, which sometimes amount to an establishment of the status of those involved in the greeting. And on the other hand, in the everyday reality of the school, a suspension of distance is virtually necessary, for example whenever a third person [i.e. a second adult] is present, who positions both the teacher and student in the same way, and thus encompasses both. One might also consider singing together [i.e. between teacher and students]. Such a suspension of distance, however, is not the norm in school.

The distance appropriate to the pedagogical relation in the uniqueness of a given situation and in the particularity of a given child is the measure of pedagogical tact. Although this tact is always directed at others and inaugurates an action for another person's sake, the distance through which the educator maintains himself as educator belongs as much to tact as reserve. This is because he preserves his being as an educator through distance ultimately for the sake of the child—for the one who is in need of education. His distance can be understood as one established for the child, rather than the isolating difference that is often exercised in life [for one's own sake]. This distance preserves the correct middle point between the educative help of the teacher and the possible self-help of the child. This makes it clear, as Herman Nohl has said, that pedagogical tact is the "most refined expression" of distance of the educator to the child.[53] Pedagogical tact is simply the criterion according to which the correct pedagogical distance can be judged; in its elusive intangibility, it is appears as nothing less than an "inner voice," one that cannot be replaced, one that the teacher must allow to "flourish" because it enables him to respond to the calls which are unpredictably addressed to him in the reality of education.

[...]

Tact allows one to find the right way in education, it allows justice to be done to the individuality of the unique child without going against set rules and established beliefs. It is precisely those set rules and established beliefs which sometimes prevent one from finding the correct path in education. However, it is simultaneously for this reason that these rules and beliefs are not at all superfluous. *Tact is indeed free from all rules but (given the predictability of education) is also effective as an exception to the rule, so to speak, as the irregularity in the regular. And as irregularity within the regular, tact at the same time creates an exaggeration of the regular.* This makes visible both its strength as well as its limits.

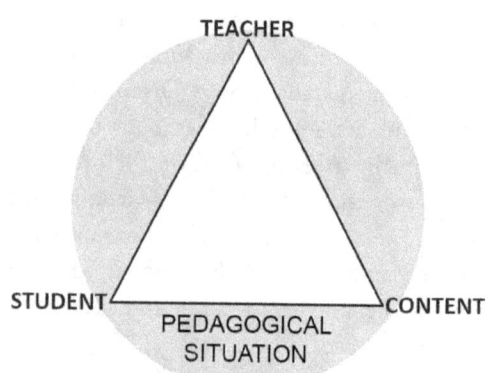

Figure 6.1 The Didactic Triangle, a prevalent heuristic for pedagogical thought.
(See: p. 101 above and p. 111, footnote 40, below)

Notes

1. Another example is Klaus Mollenhauer, who was born one year later than Muth and was also enlisted as a child soldier. Mollenhauer emerged as *the* representative of "critical pedagogy" in Germany in the post-war era. See: Mollenhauer, K. (2014). *Forgotten connections: On culture and upbringing.* Routledge. [Trans.]
2. See: Möckel, A. (1997). "Muth, Jakob." *Neue Deutsche Biographie 18*, pp. 642–644. https://www.deutsche-biographie.de/pnd129037435.html#ndbcontent [Trans.]
3. See: Burghardt, D., & Zirfas, J. (2018). *Der pädagogische Takt: Ein erziehungswissenschaftliche Problemformel.* Beltz/Juventa. [Trans.]
4. Translated by N. Friesen.
5. Blochmann, E. (1950). Der pädagogische Takt. *Die Sammlung 5*, 772–720; and: Blochmann, E. (1951). Die Sitte und der pädagogische Takt. *Die Sammlung 6*, 589–593. Blochmann was a colleague of Herman Nohl and Professor of Social and Theoretical Pedagogy at the Academy of Education at Halle. Because of her Jewish heritage, she fled Germany for England in the 1930s where she taught at Oxford. She returned to University of Marburg in Germany in 1952. [Trans.]
6. Blochmann, 1951, p. 589. Blochmann seems to be referencing the fact that, between Herbart's 1802 lecture and the postwar era, there were few if any studies devoted exclusively to the subject of pedagogical tact. [Trans.]
7. Didactics is a discipline concerning itself with modes and techniques of teaching and instruction. At the same time, it is also a rich European tradition of educational thought inaugurated by the Czech Jan Amos Komenský (Comenius) in the 17th century. See: Comenius, J. A. (1896). *The great didactic of John Amon Comenius.* A. and C. Black. [Trans.]
8. Buno, J. (1650). *Neues und also eingerimtetes ABC- und Lesebüchlein.* Dantzig: Hünefeld, (more recently republished as J. Muth. [1962]. *Fünf Fibeln aus fünf Jahrhunderten. Faksimiledrucke zum Studium des Erstleseunterrichts.* Dürr.)
9. This is the first sentence of a text from Artur Dumke (1959). *Grundzüge der Unterrichtsplanung.* Ehlermann, p. 9. Dumke is however completely open to the fact that there is much more going on in class than can be planned. He sees in that which is unplannable a type of "didactic artistry"—one that "makes every teaching situation always differently influenced and shaped" (p. 109). Precisely this identifies the didactic component of tact, something we have yet to explore here in detail.
10. See: Langeveld, M. J. (1954). Das Absichtliche und Unwillkürliche in der Erziehung und Erziehungskunde. *Die Sammlung, 9*, 29–37.
11. Phenomenology refers to the study of lived and embodied experience in everyday life. Since the early 20th century, it has been understood in Germany as a way or method for studying pedagogical practice. See: Brinkman, M., & Friesen, N. (2018). Phenomenology in education. In: Smeyers, P. (Ed.), *International handbook of philosophy of Education* (pp. 591–608). Springer. [Trans.]
12. Seeing learning as a sometimes unplannable *event* (rather than as an effect or *process*) means that it is not ultimately tied to methodical instruction. [Trans.]
13. See below for Muth's discussion of pedagogical naturalism. [Trans.]
14. Muth is describing two forms of tact that he outlines in his book: tact as it applies to the art of instruction and as it appears in the more general unplannability in education broadly speaking.

Muth discusses four specifically instructional elements of tact that are not included in the excerpt translated here: (1) "Tact expresses itself as certainty in a given situation;" (2) "Tact expresses itself as dramaturgical ability;" (3) "Tact expresses itself as a gift for improvisation;" (4) "Tact expresses itself in risking free forms of action in the school." [Trans.]

15 The first and the last two definitions come (respectively) from E. Wasserzieher (1950). *Woher? – Ableitendes Wörterbuch der deutschen Sprache*. Dümmler; and: Perkin, R. (1955). *Das deutsche Wort* 3*rd* Ed. Keyser. The longer definition of tact as an "inner sensitivity..." comes from the German Grimm Dictionary, see: http://woerterbuchnetz.de/cgi-bin/WBNetz/wbgui_py?sigle=DWB [Trans.]

16 In speaking of music, Muth is referencing the primary meaning of "Takt" in German. In this language, tact first of all refers to tempo, and only secondarily to the meaning it holds in English. Naturally, Muth is concerned with the second. [Trans.]

17 "Thou" represents an antiquated form of informal address in English and is used here in parallel with the German informal "you" to emphasize this immediacy and intimacy. [Trans.]

18 Elzer, H.M. (1949). Der soziale Takt. *Bildung und Erziehung, 2*, 81–92. It is noteworthy that this important essay appeared immediately after the Second World War.

19 Lennert, R. (1946). Versuch über den Begriff der Taktlosigkeit. *Die Sammlung 1*, 659. This essay, too, appeared right after the end of the war.

20 The pedagogical relation is interpersonal in that it is not defined by formal social roles, like those of "teacher" or "student." It instead involves mutual concern for the whole person (see: Chapters Four and Five). [Trans.]

21 "As defined generally, educatability or *Bildsamkeit* refers to a person's malleability, to a certain plasticity, to a person being adaptable, flexible towards new situations. [...] The perpetual unfinishedness of a person's growth and development process must be assumed to be the starting point for all educational and pedagogical action. In this respect, educatability is for Herbart a type of meta-assumption required as the unwritten point of departure for pedagogical action and education" Siljander, P. (2012). Educatability and *Bildung* in Herbart's theory of education. In: P. Siljander, A. Kivelä, & A. Sutinen, (Eds.), *Theories of Bildung and growth: Connections and controversies between continental educational thinking and American pragmatism*. Sense. p. 91. [Trans.]

22 Elzer (1949), p. 87.

23 Muth adds parenthetically: "The emphasis on the need for educational guidance and direction as opposed to Herbart's notion of *Bildsamkeit* now becomes more than a mere terminological distinction."

24 Patzschke, W. (1946). Der pädagogische Bezug unter besonderer Berücksichtigung der Fürsorgeerziehung. *Die Sammlung 1*, 665.

25 These are (1) The authenticity of speech, (2) Naturalness of teacher action, (3) Prevention of harm to the child, and (4) Maintaining distance as necessary in the pedagogical relation. [Trans.]

26 "The Binding Power of Speech" is the title of an essay in a book of the same name by Hans Lipps. Here is an example of what Lipps says: "The word 'sounds' as you feel it... And this means: that the word is not simply 'heard' here like the material structure of things may become audible. In contrast to the fleeting perception of what the ear 'carries to one,' hearing means recording, a letting [of something] sound again within oneself, so that one can, in turn, come back to it. One hears the word 'with the intention of its significance.'" Lipps, H. (1958). *Die Verbindlichkeit der Sprache. Arbeiten zur Sprachphilosophie und Logik*. Klostermann, p. 120. [Trans.]

27 Rumpelstiltskin is a fairy-tale recorded by the Brothers Grimm. At one point in the story, the Queen is threatened with the loss of her child. Her only recourse is to guess the name of an old forest imp. The Queen wanders into the forest before her last guess is to take place and sees the imp dancing around a fire and singing the line quoted above. [Trans.]

28 J.F. Herbart (Chapter Two) had many well-known followers, who produced versions of what were known as "Herbartianism." These followers often focused on lesson planning at the expense of Herbart's concern with tact or the development of student-teachers' feeling and disposition. [Trans.]

29 Soldt, J. (1935). *Karl Volkmar Stoy und die Johann-Friedrichs-Schule zu Jena*. Böhlaus, p. 35.

30 Plattner, E. (1960). *Gehorsam. Eine Hilfe für Eltern, Lehrer und wem sonst Gehorsam gebührt*. Klett. Muth does not provide the page numbers for the quotes that follow. [Trans.]

31 Wittmann, J. (1959) *Ganzheitliches Rechnen. 1. Teil. 5. Aufl.* Crüwell, p. 44.—When Wittmann speaks of a "certain tact," he is clearly not associating tact with a pedagogical naturalism. This is already clear in the first edition of his 1929 book: *Theorie und Praxis eines analytischen Unterrichts in Grundschule und Hilfsschule*. University of Kiel. There, he writes: "If the teacher has made himself fully familiar with the spirit of a particular method, and is secure in its practice, then his pedagogical engagement will gradually take on a form that one can best refer to as 'pedagogical tact'" (p. 64.).

32 Because it cannot be based on generalized principles and simply repeated. [Trans.]

33 Self-activity refers to "activity arising from one's [the child's] own initiative, according to the child's own goals. It can arise spontaneously or can be prompted." See: Böhme & Seichter (2017). *Wörterbuch der Pädagogik*. Schönigh, p. 430. [Trans.]

34 Loch, W. (1959). Die Aufgaben des Lehrers im Gruppenunterricht. *Pädagogische Arbeitsblätter, 11*, 49–59.

35 See: Muth, J. (1961). Die Aufgabe der Volksschule in der modernen Arbeitswelt. *Neue Deutsche Schule*, p. 26.

36 A movement that allowed children to follow their interests and inclinations in preparing them directly for the trades and the workplace. [Trans.]

37 Both this and the quote immediately below come from Schwerdt, T. (1955). *Kritische Didaktik in Unterrichtsbeispielen. 11. Aufl.* Schönigh, p. 127.

38 Here, Muth is challenging the progressive truism school should accommodate itself as much as possible to the wants and inclinations of the child. Such challenges are common in German language discussions of education and schooling, and are illustrated, for example, in Hannah Arendt's 1954 The Crisis in Education (https://thi.ucsc.edu/wp-content/uploads/2016/09/Arendt-Crisis_In_Education-1954.pdf). [Trans.]

39 This occurred in the work of Ellen Key (1849–1926) an early and radical proponent of child-centered education, who wrote a 1909 book titled *The century of the child*. http://www.gutenberg.org/ebooks/57283 [Trans.]

40 The didactic triangle is an elementary heuristic structure common in German educational theory and teacher education. It can be used to highlight and analyze the specific interrelationships and interactions between *teacher*, *student* and *content* (e.g., student lessons, exercises and projects). It sees these three key elements as being located in (and/or as constituting) a *pedagogical situation*. Generally, this structure highlights the tensions, mediations and types of equilibria that are possible between any two of the three components it interconnects. [Trans.]

41 Muth here appears to be talking about a new existential emphasis in education and its theory which saw as most important the authenticity of the student and teacher (as well as their interrelationship). A primary example of this is presented by the work of O.F. Bollnow (see: Koerrenz, R. [2017]). *Existentialism and education: An introduction to Otto Friedrich Bollnow*. Palgrave; see also Chapter Eight [Trans.]

42 Marcel continues: "From the very fact that I treat the other person merely as a means of resonance or an amplifier, I tend to consider him as a sort of apparatus which I can, or think I can, manipulate, or of which I can dispose at will. I form my own idea of him and, strangely enough, this idea can become a substitute for the real person, a shadow to which I shall come to refer my acts and words." Marcel, G. (1962). *Homo Viator*. Harper. pp. 17–18 [Trans.]

43 This is what Muth would call "naturalness" of teacher action—"the educator who is completely absorbed in his actions." [Trans]

44 Eduard Spranger also correctly characterized love as a pedagogical phenomenon in this way—but without having to negate rules and general beliefs about public education. See: *Der geborene Erzieher* 2nd ed. Quelle & Meyer, 1959, p. 23. Although Spranger in various ways describes the content of tact as a concept, he does not mention the term at any point in this text. Regardless, Spranger brought deep insight into the unplannable nature of education and of teaching. In a 1928 essay entitled "The Schooling of Germany," he had already written: "The school cannot accomplish that which is most refined and decisive in education, including in this the kind of 'moral tact that strengthens the soul.'" Incidentally, it is in this essay that the term fruitful or "pregnant moment" occurs, which Copei shortly thereafter explicated in his dissertation (which was supervised by Spranger). The fruitful moment also belongs in the same sphere as the unplannable. More recently, Spranger has cast one side of "unplanability" virtually as a law. See: *Das Gesetz der ungewollten Nebenwirkungen in der Erziehung*. Quelle und Meyer, 1962. But in this text too, Spranger does not use the term tact.

45 Referencing the Herbartian Tuiskon Ziller, Muth continues: "Ziller has already pointed this out." Muth here is contrasting the idea of a return to some naïve pedagogical naturalism (e.g. the lost paradise of pure spontaneity) to what he has been describing as the unforced and genuine "naturalness of teacher action" in which the teacher's personality and their being is expressed. [Trans.]

46 As the Latin root for the word "respect," *respectus* refers to "regard, a looking at," the "act of looking back (or often) at one." https://www.etymonline.com/search?q=respect [Trans.]

47 The term "individuality principle" appears prominently in a 1926 text by Georg Kerschensteiner, *Theorie der Bildung* (Springer), in which it is defined as "the idiosyncracy of the young person being educated, in all of his individual functions and acts, and at every stage of development" (p. 466). This principle is of concern to Kerschensteiner especially in terms of the young person's sensory engagement with the world, and how this engagement becomes part of this person's inner being. [Trans.]

48 Elzer, H. M. (1949). Der soziale Takt. *Bildung und Erziehung, 2*, 95

49 Langeveld, J. M. (1960). *Die Schule als Weg des Kindes*. Westermann, p. 63.

50 Insofar as pedagogical relation—and pedagogy as a whole—works towards a point where it will no longer be needed: "The pedagogical relation strives to make itself redundant from both sides," as Nohl says, Chapter Four, p. 81.

51 Muth does not give a source for this quotation and for the one that follows; none can be found.

52 E.g., see: Gasset, J. O. (1956). Reflections on the salutation. In: J. O. y Gasset. *Man and people* (pp. 176–191). W.W. Norton & Co. [Trans.]
53 Nohl, H. (1957). *Die pädagogische Bewegung in Deutschland und ihre Theorie. 4. Aufl.* Schulte-Bulmke, p. 137 (See Chapter Five, p. 81). On the question of distance, see: Spranger, E. (1952). Über die Höflichkeit. Broadcast by Hessischen Rundfunk on March 11, 1962.

RECONFIGURATIONS

CHAPTER SEVEN

E. Fink: The Questionableness of the Modern Educator

Editor's Introduction

Eugen Fink (1905–1975) earned his doctorate under the supervision of philosophers Edmund Husserl and Martin Heidegger. Fink remained Husserl's loyal understudy, even when the Jewish Husserl was abandoned by Heidegger and persecuted by the Nazis. The essay translated here is rife with the influence of both of these famous teachers, especially the later Heidegger. Like both Husserl and Heidegger, Fink held a chair at the University of Freiburg—although Fink's was in philosophy and *education,* disciplines which he saw as inseparably intertwined.

Education and philosophy are inseparable according to Fink because education is always based on "particular ideas about humanity or anthropological conceptions" (p. 128)—conceptions about who we are as humans. "The way in which human beings are seen predetermines the nature of education" (p. 128), Fink explains. For example, if we see ourselves as *homo economicus*—as acquisitive, competitive, economic beings—then we correspondingly see education as a technical or instrumental matter: How to get ahead as efficiently as possible and be "college and career ready." For Fink, this would represent "a technical-instrumental misinterpretation of education… in full force"—one that "is surely responsible for making the educator's understanding of himself harder" (p. 124). To avoid such distortions, Fink instead works to keep "the questionability of humanity… open," allowing him to consider "the basic event of education…in a more elemental way" (p. 129). Through this questioning, Fink comes to see that the human is a being characterized by things like striving, communal meaning and belonging and—perhaps counter-intuitively—games and play.[1]

Fink's questioning of education as a human phenomenon is not just an echo of the radical nature of Husserl's and Heidegger's influence; it reflects concerns that were both urgent and concrete in Germany after the Second World War. After the horrors of the war and the Nazi era revealed to Germans the monstrous cruelty of their countrymen (and of their society and themselves), the pedagogical worldview that has been articulated thus far in this volume became much more difficult to sustain. Fink's essay and the chapters that follow it reflect a break or rupture in pedagogical thought and reflection. Instead of looking to tact and the pedagogical relation as ways of enhancing education where roles and responsibilities are stable and self-evident, educational thinkers like Fink (and later, Bollnow, Lippitz and others) return to more basic questions.

Fink begins by recognizing that whatever we human beings may be, the "realization of our being is constantly troubled by the resonating question concerning ourselves"—the question of who we are and might become (p. 119). "The human being is 'his own task,'" Fink explains, "he must become what he is." This undertaking, however, "is not a mechanical necessity, but an *existential* one" (p. 132). In this life-defining task of discovering and becoming who we are, we of course help each other out and provide counsel for others who are struggling with *their* questions. Everyone, as Fink observes, "is a teacher of life to another" (p. 121). The ultimate result, Fink continues, is that "the educator" him or herself becomes "an anthropological key-figure of great importance:"

> One is not an educator like one is a weaver, streetcar conductor or bank director—but in the manner of being a worker, lover and fighter. "Educating" belongs to the central phenomena fundamental to human existence. This simple truth however is generally forgotten, obscured or distorted, because in the modern world, the 'educator' has increasingly taken the role of a specific functionary in the … process of social production. (p. 121)

The reason that the educator is so central to human existence is not only because we all need to work out our own "question[s] concerning our own selves" (p. 119); it is also because, in a basic sense, we all also strive to go *beyond* ourselves as individuals. Existentially, we reach beyond ourselves, our finite existence do this through what we leave behind when we die. We do so, as Fink explains, secure in the knowledge that "extinguishing an individual existence does not touch the basis of life" (p. 133). It is the fact that we can thus overcome our own mortal limits that forms the true basis of education: "The essential grounding of human education lies in the entanglement of [individual] mortality and supraindividual perpetuity" as Fink puts it (p. 133).

For Fink, this does indeed place the educator beyond other mortals. It means that they not only help others with their questioning and striving, but also that the ultimate effects of their work go well beyond just those who immediately surround them. Educators are thus nothing less than the keepers and perpetuators of our (still questionable) human essence; they both represent this essence and keep it open for the future: "The educator, the true educator, belongs to the circle of those rare human beings who exist in a representative way for fellow human beings, who keep the question of life's meaning alive" (p. 135).

Sources/Recommended Reading

Fink, E. (2016). *Play as symbol of the world: And other writings*. Indiana University Press.
Mickunas, A. (2008). Philosophical anthropology of E. Fink. *Problemos, 73*, 167–78. http://citeseerx.ist.psu.edu/viewdoc/download?doi=10.1.1.525.297&rep=rep1&type=pdf

E. Fink: The Questionableness of the Modern Educator[2]

The human being is that mysterious creature of nature that does not simply exist like a stone; this being does not grow to the light in the sky from the dark grounds of the earth like a silent plant; and this being is not led into safety by instinct like an animal. In everything it does and allows, the human being is for itself a constant "problem." The realization of our being is constantly troubled by the resonating question concerning our own selves. All human life bears the misleading character of an experiment or attempt. The authority of religious faith, the stability of traditional custom, the certainty of scientific knowledge all seem to contradict this. But religion, morality and science are all interpretations of Being that don't eliminate its problematic character but instead presuppose it. And prior to such "answers" to the question of the meaning of life, the human being is sustained by an incomprehensible, elementary trust in life that is opaque even to himself and makes him—aware of his own mortality as he is—think and care beyond himself: He founds cities and states, works and labors, he sows and reaps, and gathers harvests in the store. Provision and welfare that are based on trusting faith and science are founded in questioning. In human life, the seemingly contradictory fundamentals of the familiar and the strange, of the secure and the dubitable interpenetrate. The human being is the creature most alienated from nature, but nonetheless he has not escaped Mother Nature completely. He as well is carried by the ebb and flow of life forces, of the seasons, of sex, death and procreation. The human being is searching for his way precisely because he is human, he is wandering aimlessly like Ulysses.

The way of the human being is a lost way—all paths one takes in one's life history are overshadowed by the uncertainty of not being *the* right way. Especially since the human being is *not* like the lilies of the field and the birds in the sky, he has to care and work and eat his bread by the sweat of his brow, he is able and bound to pray and educate [*bilden*], to research and think. Who are we? What is the human being? This is not at all an abstruse academic question for philosophical speculation but is instead *the* inextinguishable burning question of every human existence. The old saying of Delphic wisdom, "Know Thyself" was not a demand for harmless psychological introspection and soul searching. It was the shibboleth of a passionate will-to-truth of those people who stood at the dawn of the Occident. Since that time, work towards human self-understanding and to the rational penetration of that which is human continues in the footsteps of the Ancients. [This is despite the fact that] the course of the Western history has led us far from its antique origins: Christianity and modern science have brought with them completely new themes for human life [*Lebensmotive*], different terms and definitions of technical human power and superhuman authority. [Despite this fact,] the desire for *insight*, as part of the heritage of the Greeks, has remained. Even when humankind has submitted to God's orders, it wanted to know why it thus submitted itself. And to the degree that humanity has stood on its own, it has wondered about its capacity to do so. The meaning of every [human] form of life [*Lebensgestalt*] is derived from an inquiring and discriminating awareness. This is true for everything humans do and allow, for all dispositions and involvements, for every social status and profession, but foremost for the profession of the educator.

The educator, from a general point of view, is a tragicomic figure: Someone who gives lessons to others, but who may not be able to follow them himself, who uses grand idealistic words and yet remains all-too-human, who pretends to have precise knowledge about life and its meanings, but who is himself tortured by qualms and doubts. [The teacher is someone] who cloaks himself in pathos at work but is revealed as banally middleclass in his spare time. This is the familiar caricature. It is based not only on lazy everyday habits of mind but has deeper roots in centuries-old misconceptions of what an educator is. Maybe it is not only the educator who is tragicomic, but *humanity as such*. This human is the only creature on earth and under the blue sky who is *free* but still can't completely free himself from the spell of nature that binds every living thing. This tragicomic characterization, when interpreted correctly, is not a *critique* of the true educator because it also gives witness to the paradoxical character of human nature. Reflection on the nature of the educator is always necessarily a reflection on human being itself. The educator is an anthropological key-figure of great importance because 'educating' is not simply one action among others, or something that human beings carry out just any which way.

Human existence always subsists in the element of teaching, everyone is a teacher of life to another, everyone can serve as a good or a bad example to another. And it is only the old and wise who educate those young and restless. Occasionally, a specially gifted child is capable of rising above the wisdom of age, like the 12-year-old [Christ child] with the scribes in the temple. That which is educational is part of the substance of being human, not simply a random side-effect. One is not an educator like one is a weaver, streetcar conductor or bank director—but in the manner of being a worker, lover and fighter. "Educating-belongs to the central phenomena that are fundamental to human existence. This simple truth however is generally forgotten, obscured or distorted, because in the modern world, the "educator has increasingly taken the role of a specific functionary in the divided labor of the social production process, one specialist among countless others.

Being a teacher is never just an isolated part in social roleplay, something that a person takes up from time to time. The human "substance" of the craftsman is not exhausted through occupation, no matter how much he might love it. The educator however not only acts as an educator during his "work hours." If the life of an educator is real, if he really is someone who has a calling, his existence has the character of a great passion. And it is a strange passion, one that comes from the depths of existence itself and that mostly remains mystifying and incomprehensible even to himself, because public opinion always already decided on the status and reputation of a given calling. In this public sphere, the office of the educator is already ranked. It has a certain use-value insofar as training of the younger generation in skills and abilities necessary for life falls on the educator. This office has moral value in context of the character-formation of the youth and cultural significance in the custodial transmission and imparting of so-called "canonical knowledge." But it is questionable whether this everyday social perspective allows even the slightest glimpse of the *essence* of the educator.

If some thoughtful points about this essence of the educator are to be attempted here, it is not with pre-existing presumptions about that essence or nature; nor is it done as if one were speaking from within it. On the contrary; our attitude to it is a searching and questioning one. Our thoughts proceed in three steps: we start with the current *social situation* of the educator, then try to determine the *nature* of the condition of the educator and finally draw some conclusions from these insights.

Part I

The present social situation of the educator seems quite contradictory at first glance: he is *courted* perhaps like never before, and he is at the same time undervalued and his very own dignity is misjudged. This mistake is blatantly but not exclusively expressed in the material undervaluation of his merit.

In the 20th century, human society took a course whose destination was unclear, not even clear to the prophetic critics of culture who were shooting up like mushrooms after the rain. They were bemoaning the "Decline of the West"[3] or arguing that the "old world" should be given a chance, seeing the direction of world history headed to one of many different continents. The meaning or purpose of this uneven movement is probably still in the dark, but we all feel the precariousness of our living conditions, a chaotically brewing will to change, the wrestling of many and countless opposing trends. A fight *of* the human being *for* the human being has broken out with intolerable intensity. Dignified traditions are being fiercely attacked and fiercely defended; the whole history of morals and customs with its traditional values is being put on the scale, the fabric of society trembles in a storm that is sweeping over the entire planet. Different cultural domains have lost their shielding from each other; they now compete against each other with varying conceptions of life. And even within our own culture, the unquestionable security of previous values is gone. Closely linked to this spiritual-moral crisis is the industrial revolution, the result of modern science, which now claims—against the mythic-religious interpretations of the world—to be the true and actual understanding of reality and thereby able to determine the true relationship of humans to the world. This industrial revolution changed the face of the world—and even more, it has changed the structure of society—the dwelling of human being in the midst of that which *is*, the social connections of humans to one another.

In the turbulence of this human crisis, the situation of the educator is, as said before, strangely ambiguous. All groups of power try to persuade and engage the educator for their own purposes. This is a result of the prevailing conception of education as the most effective instrument of leadership and governance. Education is said to be the most noble means of war in the battle for power—power over souls. With this instrumentalist view of education comes a corresponding instrumentalist conception and treatment of the educator. Whoever can educate has the ability to form the youth and whoever has the youth has the future: At least this is how it appears in the open or in the sometimes secret reasoning of rivals for power. The educator is approached as a valuable tool, a useful instrument, a lever of power. But such solicitation actually shows the greatest contempt possible for the educator; it shows the greatest disregard of his real social duties and his professional dignity. He gets reduced to being an instrument of a foreign will to form humans, to force the educator into an undeserving servitude. This is even more true when a certain group can temporarily use state power to coerce educators as servants of the state. With this we touch on a delicate issue. The business of education is a social service of the greatest importance. The professional educator is entrusted with the most valuable resource of the nation. He can only prove himself worthy of this trust through the most significant development of his skills and by tirelessly improving himself. It should be the right and duty of the state to ensure suitable training and continuing education for all teachers. In this regard, the state here acts as a trustee of the whole nation. The youth of a nation should certainly only be placed in the most capable hands. But this intention is not guaranteed by exam regulations and efforts in school administration. Instead, it depends on the state authority *not* acting as an external, foreign power against educators, but rather with a genuine understanding of the phenomenon of education. Even better would be for the state authority itself to be represented by outstanding educators in the field of educational administration. The professional educator may be an employee of the state; however, the educator is ultimately not the servant of the *state*, but the servant of the *people*. It is precisely because the educator in a significant sense *serves* or lives for others, that he should not sink to become the servant of a political party that might temporarily be in power. It is a contemporary myth that human beings are simply programmable, that any purpose is attainable through proper influence and propaganda—and that education just happens to be the right tool to achieve the desired formative effects in human beings. Such a misanthropic view is almost entirely ignorant of the secret of human freedom. But freedom is *the* genuine, vital element of true education—not the false freedom of incoherent irresponsibility that flees from the law, but a judicious, reasonable freedom that also accepts the eternal limits of human power. The educator has as little right to deform the youth in just any way as the state does in misusing the educator as a "means" to its ends.

It is not for the educator to sell himself to the highest bidder, but to fulfill his inner life-mission within the community. This internal mandate is the precondition for the educator's decision to enter the profession and to let himself be employed by the state as a representative of the people. The official nature [of the teacher's position and employment] is never the primary goal, but a secondary result. The calling or vocation follows the call. Here, the [German] saying that "to whom God gives an office he also gives a mind" is surely wrong. Here, intellect, interest and passion must come first. This means that the educator responding to an inner calling cannot be satisfied with passing down a traditional, pre-existing education. He cannot serve simply as a means of transport for the continuity of cultural context. Instead of his own accord and with his limited abilities—but also with the greatest intensity—the educator fights, in thoughtful contention, for a position on what it is he is teaching. Only then is he more than a used or misused vessel, more than a mere technician in the transfer of cultural power that dominates in a particular nation. He takes an active part in this power, takes part in shaping it, takes part as a subject—not as a subordinate, dependent functionary.

At the same time, this characterization of the state of affairs is too simple. The present situation of the educator is not only threatened by the powerful and dogmatic—who, while they happen to be in power, try to dictate fixed educational goals for educators employed by the state. More dangerous is the decline of our moral world, the anarchy of values and measures of value. It is no longer a given that every individual is included in the moral conventions of the state. The fissures reach to the depths of society.

The shadow of nihilism, today greater and darker than ever, darkens the task of education. Some might ask critically whether education is even still achievable. Can the individual, on his or her own, arrive at a conclusion here? Others, when the "guidelines" for education are outlined before them by someone else—thus relieving them of their doubts and deliberations—see it as [nothing less] than a salvation. In other words: Even educators are endangered by the temptations of resignation and escape, to follow the force of social "massification" which seeks to avoid all risks in life. The general state of the educator is determined today by a dilemma—namely that he can't rely on an intact moral world of the people when confronted by the encroachments of the state. When governmental forces demand that he become a tool of their ends, to become a technician for meeting their purposes, to become a mere functionary in the processing of the young, his refusal, his decision to say "here I stand, I cannot do otherwise" does not simply or already have its moral grounding. He has to create this moral ground himself, has to gain it through difficult decisions laden with responsibility. The technical-instrumental misinterpretation of education that is in full force is surely responsible for making the educator's understanding of himself harder in our times. But also the profound sociological change, the reconfiguration of social relations that we are in the midst of, has a limiting but also compounding effect.

We don't yet have a proper perspective on these new conditions. In the first instance, the radical changes described here mean a transformation of the human relation to nature. Over the course of thousands of years, nature has been experienced as that absolute and superior power which grants humans their circumscribed lives and provides them with food. It is also something that humans could "work away" at, but not exhaust—despite the most titanic efforts. The modern-scientific technical and industrial revolution gave new self-awareness to modern humans; nature has been disenchanted and lost its magical qualities of daemonic superiority; technology becomes the actual magic that testifies to the "power and glory" of the human. But it is the truism of our advanced millennium that our technical control over nature has not been matched by similar progress in human moral conscience. The inner balance of human spiritual energies is unsettled. And together with the displacement of humans' primary relation to reality toward the technical natural sciences, a reinterpretation of the common truths of religion and philosophy into so-called "worldviews" (*Weltanschauungen*) has also taken place. A worldview can be seen as a statement about the whole of being, but it also contains within it a moment of subjectivity. It is in each case our, my, and your worldview. One professes it and fights the opposing worldview. With the emergence of the notion of "worldview" in the modern world, the subjective principle got unleashed that leads to the dispute of each against all.

The permanent dispute of ideologies necessarily confuses the educator who is seeking out the final goal for pedagogical results. The large number of existing recipes for living betrays the drastic decline of the moral substance of a humanity that used to be manifest as separate, self-contained peoples. Party divisions now split the closest natural societies, families and communities, and reach beyond countries and cultural groups. At the same time, a massively overgrown apparatus accompanied by anonymity and bureaucracy overshadows human relationships to life and in many cases brings with it a manifold and hopeless coldness, indirection and abstractness. The modern human increasingly loses his naivete and the unproblematic healthiness of life; he is squeezed out of simple and clear circumstances and loses his home and proximity to the Earth. These are not processes that can be viewed and addressed as random aberrations. A destiny similar to the ponderous unfolding of the industrial revolution prevails here. One can assume that the usual and predictable characterizations of this frightening change fall short because—in the midst of this roaring current—we cannot foresee its end. Another aspect of the situation is the expansion of the school across the population. It is not just the result of philanthropy. The complex apparatus of contemporary life forces the distribution of knowledge and skills throughout the whole population. Even in the South Sea Islands one can no longer remain illiterate. While education and self-cultivation (*Bildung*) used to be reserved for a social minority, today a general vocational training (*Ausbildung*) for work life has almost universally taken its place; the function of knowledge in a social world that includes monks and knights is different than in a society constituted by machinists, airplane pilots, bank employees and shock troops.

School—in the broadest sense—is transformed at its core; increasingly, utilitarian traces appear in its image; increasingly, it is conceptualized in instrumental terms, configured as a means of gaining mastery over one's own life. Although the old school of culture and cultivation (*Bildungsschule*) still has its advocates, in many cases, this advocacy appears more as a preference for an antiquated world of *Bildung* no longer vivid in the present, but sunken in the past.[4] There is an intense ideological dispute about types of schools; educators are divided into many camps; a large and unified conception of school is missing. Different types of schools exist unconnected side by side and have no real inner coherence.

The educator receives his value based not on the type of school in which he teaches, but solely from the degree of the originality of his pedagogical passion and from the extent of his openness to the problem of human education. The less he is only an instrument of a foreign cultural will, or rather, the more he acts as a responsible subject to *help shape* the cultural will of his society, the higher his value—regardless of his position at an elementary school or a university. Value is decided by proximity to essence.

Part II

Up to this point, we may have filled in the current situation of the educator using rather dark tones. But we are not at all primarily interested in formulating a critique of our time, but rather in a reflection on that which is essential. What ultimately is education anyway? Based on the nature of education, we have to search for access to the essence of the educator.

In its countless forms, shapes and institutions, education, as mentioned above, is a well-known, common and familiar phenomenon. But something that is familiar [*Bekannt*] is not necessarily something that is recognized [*Erkannt*] for what it is or might be. In the final analysis, we are standing too close to this phenomenon to experience it at all in a way that it would appear strange or enigmatic. Everybody knows education and everybody has grown up experiencing it for himself. But still, when asked exactly what education *is*, one quickly ends up in confusion. We also don't have an adequate conceptual terminology to capture the phenomena of education; we operate with unsuitable categories taken from other areas of human life.

First of all, general opinion presents a series of familiar theses aimed at particular aspects of education but designate these with incommensurate concepts. The technical term labor [*Arbeit*] for example plays a fatal role in the pedagogical domain. The educational formation of humans comes to be understood as a form of production and fabrication, analogous to the transformation of a natural thing into a thing of art. The relationship of a human being to wood or stone from which one might make an axe or a club is—according to some—the same as the educational relationship to a child or student. The young person is seen in terms of uncontrolled growth, as something natural and wild that is to be re-created, to be worked over and refined. This means that education is understood as e-*rud*-ition [etymologically, to bring out of the rough or the "rude"], as rarefaction, as a guided and methodical abandonment of an original raw and wild state, from a barbaric natural condition to one that is sophisticated, cultivated, civilized and "humane." Education in this sense is understood as a methodical intrusion into human nature, as a "modification" that requires a kind of tempered and rational force or violence to break a defiant and primitive barbarism.

This conception of er-rud-ition plays a countless variety of roles in pedagogical theorems. For example, [it is important] in the opposition of the rustic and urban, of the common and distinguished, the primitive and the cultivated. Through the educational influence of the child, it is said, the historical development of humankind repeats itself—as a path of "progress" that gradually leads upward. The education of the child proceeds in the same way as our collective progress from a wild and primeval state to one more advanced, purified and improved. The child moves from a dull being driven by instincts through manifold steps to become a man of reason, from a small selfish creature to become a valued member of human society, practiced in virtue and consideration, tolerance and public spirit. This paradigm of progress belongs to the conception of education as er-rud-ition as much as the notion of the teacher as an instrumental craftsperson working upon the student. This conception is related to the notion of domestication. Just as early humans captured and tamed wild horses and cattle through habituation and training, it is the educator's task to subdue the wild, untamed nature of the child. It is said that this is not about destroying the child's vital energy but about refining and sublimating it. There is an incredible naivete that underlies any interpretation that would reduce the relationship of parent and child, teacher and student, master and apprentice, to the terms of domestication, to the relationship of humans to animals. But for the most part, this naivete goes unnoticed.

A radically opposed position is presented for example by Rousseau; he attacks the ideology of progress, domestication and amelioration. It is civilization and its deviation from the natural that for him is the original sin of humankind. Human beings should not be led out of a state of nature into a culture of refinement, but from the corruption of culture back into the purity of a natural existence. Culture, which for Rousseau is the feudalistic culture of the *ancien régime*,[5] is a perversion, a deformation of the natural order, a collective lie with false idols and backward values. True education for him is not one that leads to the life of a particular estate in a feudally ordered society, but to natural humanity *per se*. Education is in this sense the perversion of what is already perverted, the reversal of an already reversed societal order, the restoration of a free state of nature in which all humans are equal. It is necessary to let humans grow according to their own law and to help them carefully realize their talents and skills through unrestrained natural growth, to allow their natural gifts to unfold. Rousseau operates here with a concept of development that is to be seen as part of every living thing. However, he is not a biologist in any simple sense, his understanding of nature is influenced more by the Stoics than by the biological sciences.

Another common model for understanding education is the correlation of "immaturity" [*Unmündigkeit*] and "maturity" [*Mündigkeit*].[6] The task of the educator is viewed here as a way of gradually leading the immature student—who does not yet have power over himself—to gain control over his own life. The child cannot reasonably decide on his or her own yet, and the educator is consequently the advocate of the child's future. He has to work to make himself effectively redundant in the realization of the child's education by strengthening and encouraging everything that would lead to the child's eventual autonomy.

What, then, is education? The refinement of the primitive barbarian, the domestication of a wild creature—or the sublimation of a being driven only by instinct—or the return to a state of nature, through the reversal of the perversion that is civilization? Or is it the effort of making an egoist into a fellow citizen, a social person—or the conversion of a magical-mythical human into an enlightened being of pure reason? Or is it yet another possibility: A conversion of the irreligiously indifferent to true Christians or to true heathens? All these are common educational programs. But can we learn from them what education really is?

After some thought, it becomes clear that underlying all of these conceptions of education are particular ideas about humanity or anthropological conceptions. The way in which human beings are seen predetermines the nature of education. Maybe the right definition of education simply depends on right understanding of human "being" [*Dasein*]. Anthropology knows plenty of interpretations. As a member of the animal kingdom, humans represent a kind of mammal, differing from the anthropoids by their intelligence—as "homo sapiens." As *homo faber*, the manufacturer of tools and machines, the human being stands out from the animals. He has the capabilities of *technē*; a single path leads from the primitive beginnings of Stone Age weapons to modern technology. There is another perspective: only the human being knows law and jurisprudence, he alone among living beings has personal property and marriage, knows of both peace and war. He alone among the mortal creatures of nature knows of his own mortality, knows of death. Because of this awareness of death, aspiring but fearful hearts demanded "immortality" long ago, and wise men and seers have preached the celestial life of the soul. Only the human being is conscious of freedom and is what he makes of himself. Only he can laugh or play in a real sense. What then is this human being who offers so many possibilities? What is this "unknown" or "indeterminate" creature as he has been called? Which anthropology takes precedence over the others? Is it the human being as a creator of cultures, a user of tools, the "animal rationale," [the incarnation of] freedom, or an immortal soul—or something else altogether?

Of everything that breathes on this Earth, human beings are the biggest riddle, the strangest of all creatures—especially as they appear to themselves. It is *not* the Sphinx that is the strange beast that threatens the city, throwing itself into the abyss after Oedipus solves the riddle of its identity, the creature who walks on four legs in the morning, on two at noon and three in the evening—only to give the answer: the human being! The tragedy of Oedipus is that the riddle of the "human being" was solved all too easily and that the mystery of the departed Sphinx came back with menacing vengeance in Oedipus' own life: Oedipus had to guess again—responding to the oracle and revealing himself to be the murderer of his father and the violator of his own mother. This was the [riddle's] horrifying solution. The cheerful, clever Oedipus who outwitted the Sphinx and who was the proud king, shaken by horror, transformed himself. He became a thoroughly cursed suffering human who renounced his ruling powers and who cut out the eyes—his own eyes—that had looked into the human abyss. While we, as relative latecomers, might be far from the depth of this ancient understanding of life, the human being remains a dark mysterious Sphinx to us. This is despite our many positive sciences like psychology, ethnology, cultural morphology, the social sciences, etc. If a definite and reliable definition of the human being is no longer possible, does that mean that any prospect of understanding the phenomenon of education also disappears? Not at all. Because when the questionability of humanity is kept open, the basic event of education can be considered in a more elemental way. This requires further elaboration.

More powerful than any of the anthropological approaches mentioned above is the concept of the human being received from Western metaphysics. It forms the basis for a whole set of interpretations diametrically opposed to those listed earlier. This metaphysics characterizes the human being as the *zoon logon echon*, the "rational animal," the creature that is able to reason. As long as *logos* or reason were considered absolutely divine to the Greeks, the human being could be situated between animal and god. But the human being not only exists in a hierarchy of beings [*Seiendes*] between animal and god, he is open to himself in this in-between position. The human being is seen as that animal which, touched by a ray of divine light, strives to rise above his animality and tries to come closer to God. He is seen as a confused animal, one startled from its peaceful natural condition, within whom a divine spark is burning. The longing to get closer to God, the *homoiosis theo* according to Plato, the patriarch of metaphysics, is the prime motivator for human existence. The metaphysical tradition that has shaped our history tried to comprehend the human being based on the animal on the one hand and on God on the other. This tradition thus positions education as the means by which humans are able to transcend their animality and move towards God. In this tradition, the starting point for all education is the animal, and its goal, the "divine." It is said that the educational dynamic of the human being—whether as self-development or as the practical assistance for those growing up—oscillates between "animal" and "god."

Whether one regards this Western [metaphysical] tradition as right [or wrong], it is likely to be surprising to situate "education" as a lived phenomenon between the polar opposites of "animal," and "God." Is education indeed a means of mediation between these poles? Do human beings in education actually take part in the being of the animal and that of God?

It is the human being that alone educates.[7] Animals cannot and God need not be educated. Animals and God are each in their own sense "perfect"—only the human as the imperfect being is able to educate and also always needs education. For the zoologist, there may be many traits of animal behavior known to show an astonishing similarity to the behavior of human parents to their children; you can find a "nesting instinct," a touching attentiveness to offspring, a care of the young of surprisingly direct practicality. But animals do not "educate" their young, they act instinctively, following innate patterns of behavior; within the category of its species, an animal is complete and perfect, its development is a biological unfolding of dispositions and capacities—it does not happen through the image of an inner "ideal" based on a self-awareness of life in and of itself. Just as wrong as the interpretation of forms of animal behavior as "primitive forms" of raising of human offspring is the opposite tendency to look for animalistic traits in human behaviour towards their offspring, for example to interpret the love of the mother as a muted "animalistic drive." The mother nurses the child not like the cow nurses its calf but standing in an infinite inner experience of her motherhood; the notoriously "animalistic" conditions of the human being are not dull and animal-like, they are characterized by a peculiar form of "naturally-oriented understanding". There is no *existential* [*seinsmäßig*] relationship between the human being and the animal in the way that they relate to their respective offspring, even though there we undoubtedly see external behavioural similarities. The animal "arrives" according to its kind, it is not "on its way," it stands firm within its nature; it *is* formed and shaped; unlike the human being, it does not have to first move towards its form and shape. Therefore, the animal can never educate and can never be educated. Animal training is an entirely different matter.

God is also "perfect" in a rather different way than the animal; generally speaking, we think of "God" as complete and perfect, the *summum ens* [highest being], with nothing wrong, missing, or unachieved, whose being is not scattered in time, who is always gathered in the totality of his nature. God is not on his way to becoming himself, he is not in need of having to fulfill his being; he does not stand imminently before himself as a task, he cannot become anything else because he is always already the highest form of all beings. He is who he is. He does not need to form himself because he has no amorphous materiality that lacks shape; he is immutable in his eternal being or essence. Plato already thought of God in this way, but he argued against this myth, because there [in Classical Greece] the gods appeared as changeable beings. For Plato, the divine is instead the unchangeable constancy of the idea. The Christian concept of God interprets Him as infinite perfection, as the eternal maker of time and of the "world" within time. In both the ancient-Platonic and Christian senses, God does not "educate" himself, he does not first bring himself into a way of life. Where the Christian faith speaks of the secret of the Trinity, it does not think of the "son" of God as a "student," as someone who is to be brought up, for whom the father undertakes the work of education. The son is said to be eternal like the father, eternally different from the father but still one with him. It is also said that God "educated" humans through his son made flesh, providing them with the revelation of new and meaningful life. But the thought of the "divine instruction" of humankind is not a need on the part of God; he has no obligation to educate humanity.

But the human being simply must educate; he forms himself when he shapes his offspring; the human being is not fixed by the imprint of an established species as is the animal. Unlike God, he does not rest in his complete and perfect being. The human being does not hold his being or essence as a kind of possession within himself, he has to first realize it [for] himself and he is for himself a project or task. The imperfection of human existence is neither a blessing nor a curse but the condition of the possibility for our experience of the highs and lows of fortune and accomplishment. Because we simply do not lead our lives like the animal, because we move within an open range of possibilities of our choosing, the blessing and the curse of the freedom to choose falls upon us. As a result, we are forced to seek *counsel*. Since we are without fixed shape, we need form; because we are in danger of suffering the fortuitous rush of things [around us], we need constitution and support. Human existence gains counsel and support, form and constitution, in the fundamental event known as "education." *We are* a priori *without orientation and strength, formless and undefined.* Only the imperfect living being can and must form and constitute itself. *We need education to overcome our existential plight.* Only a creature in need can educate and be educated. [...] Certainly the animal also finds itself in need, but it does not relate to its needs with understanding. [Such understanding] is the mark of the human being. He lives in relation to himself through understanding [*Er lebt im verstehenden Selbstumgang*]: He places himself into practical relation to his own existence [*Dasein*] and to the Being of all beings. However, such self-relation is not a consequence of "consciousness," it is not a conscious reflexivity, but rather a much more primordial and tension-laden existential structure. The human being is "his own task" [*ist sich "aufgegeben"*], he must become what he is, must look for and fulfill his essence or being. This is not a mechanical necessity, but an *existential* one. Our life is not only objectively imperfect, it is above all an incompletion that we feel, experience and suffer. It is not only in the eyes of the Greek god that the human being appear as a torso, neither complete nor inexistent in its being, but a kind of inexistent existence [*nichtiges Sein*] or an existing inexistence [*seiende Nichtigkeit*]. The finite nature of their being lies open before human beings themselves, they become even more acutely aware of it when they sense the completeness and self-sufficiency of beast and flower—or the perfect and eternal divinity above the clouds and the stars. Because both animal and God are perfect [in their own terms], no amalgamation of the two could render the imperfection that is the human being.

This calls into question at its base the anthropology defined by Western metaphysics that would see the human as being between animal and God. We are the imperfect beings in a universe that is otherwise filled with perfect things and creatures; we are a cosmic exception and an ontological paradox. The concern of the human being with and for himself does not mean, as one might assume, the relation of the single individual only to himself. The distinction between "I" and "You" presupposes on its own the relation of existence [*Dasein*] to itself. It is a fault of common pedagogical theories to start naively from the relation between educator and student. But where does this relation come from? From where does the interest of the educator in his pupil arise? Am I and you, we and others simply given facts of the social world? Is it enough to point out these facts, or do [we] first need a fundamental awareness, to experience and express the pedagogical meaning of such social references in the first place?

Education can only be found where a difference between the generations exists, where those who are older feel responsible for the younger. This apparently does not exist in spheres of the divine. But animals, like humans, live through constant generational change. They exist in herds, packs and flocks containing clearly differentiated age groups arising from natural processes of origin, procreation and birth. Isn't it exactly the same for human beings? Certainly, human beings also have family lines, mates and offspring who themselves go on to have their own young. But the basic difference is that human beings do not solely live in a sexual way, that they live in relationship to their sexuality, with one example of this being identifiable as shame. One does not only live in groups, one puts oneself into a relation to these groups—such as family and kin—in piety and veneration; he does not only have offspring but children for whom he feels responsible. The human being is not temporally limited to his own life span like the animal, he puts himself into a relation to this limitation, he is walking toward his own death wherever he goes. The animal does not anticipate its own death, it has no relation to time *as* time, it cannot take precautions for the future, cannot be concerned about how its offspring will fare after it dies. Human knowledge of death is always at the same time knowledge of the possibility of the renewal of our own life in our children, in a tribe, in a people. Knowledge of individual mortality is also knowledge of earthly, collective *im*mortality in the progress of generations. The deep interest that adults take in their children, their endless care for them, is not some mute, internal natural instinct but comes from the intuition that extinguishing an individual existence does not touch the basis of life, that what is now present in ourselves is passed on even as all else passes away. Sociality sees in children its own "immortality." God is not able to educate in a human sense because he does not die. His eternity is not something repeated in time. *Our strange interest in earthly immortality in the form of living on through one's children and through their children is the innermost deepest root of educational love.* The human being alone educates, education is the business of mortals. In the end, our relation to death is the basis for all relations within our human existence [*Dasein*]. And it is on this basis that any form of self-formation and self-conception, which means any form of education, finds its ground. The essential grounding [*Wesensgrund*] of human education lies in the entanglement of [individual] mortality and supraindividual perpetuity. The will to immortality resonates in the passion of the educator in the same way it does in the statesman.

The educator is the servant of the people—but this now has a different resonance: He is accountable to immortal life, not just to those who happen to be present. In this way, those who educate are wrested from that belittlement which idolizes the child *per se*. The educator serves his people if he contributes to and helps to shape the historic formation and living perpetuation of the moral substance that is nothing else than a comprehensive relation to world of a certain humanity. The legitimate [*rechte*] educator is one who lives in the manner of his community, but not through blind and unreflected routine. Instead he puts himself in a questioning and scrutinizing relation to what prevails, and he himself exemplifies a point of awareness and is involved in envisioning the guiding ideal.

[...]

Part III

Let me summarize. I wanted to direct attention to the often forgotten problem of the mode of being and belonging to education *per se*—and thereby also to the basic question of the nature and the value of the educator. We have a great many excellent methods and proposals for reform. Hardly any epoch has thought so much about the process of education, about psychology, sociology, etc. in the service of pedagogy, and has risked so many experiments. But all of this has not led to a sufficient determination of the nature of being—the ontological structure—of the phenomenon of education. What is missing is the phenomenological notion[8] of education. This highlights more than just what one might think of as a gap or lack in "theoretical" educational studies.

This lack or absence inhibits the self-understanding of the educator and forces him into traditional forms when he attempts to give account. For some, established and generally accepted moral standards serve as the self-evident condition of education. The educator recognizes himself as someone who "applies" moral principles in practical life situations for his students and who judges situations on the basis of rules. We find a different approach in the so called [conservative] "liberal education": it makes the person who can form human beings into a mediator and messenger of cultural values, to a courier with the torch of the "holy fire." Still different is the perspective which views social partnership, collective responsibility, as the desired end for educational influence.

Morals, culture and state are certainly significant reference points for education, but there is never a store of absolutely predetermined meanings that stand before a given pedagogy. Education does not act retroactively, *a posteriori*, on these meanings; it does not confront them in complete dependence on them. Education is instead a way of working productively—in practical situations but always also with broader relevance—on the lived development and continued shaping of humans' normative relation to the world; and it is a productive "working" not just only on the student but just as much on the person who is educating.

It seemed [at the outset of this text,] that a renewed question after the mode of existence [*Seinsart*] of education was in doubt; that a deep suspicion hung over earlier definitions of education derived from the situation of the human "in-between" animal and God. It could be that the traditional proximity of the human being to those differently perfect beings of animal and God impeded the recognition of the strange incompleteness, the existential imperfection of human being [*Dasein*] as the condition and precondition for the educational imprimatur.

Education is the means towards human self-relation that is most necessary to life. The educator occupies the most essential function in humanity and is from the very start politically or communally formative. Strictly speaking, there is no separate and isolated educational "trade." Educators only *appear* to form a guild, a profession; they are instead a class of beings in which not self-interest but the general will, the interest of the Polis, is glowing. The significance, value and rank of the educator can therefore never truly be understood and grasped from the secondary perspective of social division of labor.

From this perspective, the following essential demands follow: the professional educator always has to take himself out of the character roles that society would push him into—he has to live from the awareness of his inner assignment, not of the outer contract of employment. Only then is he protected from demeaning servitude. With his great respect for given customs he has to combine the courage to always question traditions—particularly insofar as he derives his dignity from being a co-creator of the moral world, not simply its intermediary. The educator, the true educator, belongs to the circle of those rare human beings who exist in a representative way for fellow human beings, who keep the question of life's meaning alive.

But what society for its part can and must demand of the educator is the purity of his ethos—one that is to prove itself as incorruptible will-to-truth and as sacrifice in aid of life. Society is never allowed to degrade the educator to the status of a mere tool, to a dependent and submissive instrument.

A basic demand on behalf of the state and society on those who educate is the entitlement to an optimal [teacher] training—meaning higher education for all teachers regardless of where they will teach.

The educational path of the child to maturity and free self-determination in sufficient knowledge of the world follows a single course—in the same way the nature of the educator is unified and should not get lost in the fragmented educational organisation of various rivalling groups. The internal rivalry among the educators can only end with the realization that they all do the same thing—and that they are all endangered by the outer powers. *Arche* and *Paideia*, power and education are from time immemorial divided and as Plato has said, there is no end to misery among peoples until education becomes the center of being of the Polis—until the free, thinking relation of everyone to themselves is recognized as the basic life-shaping human-forming power.

But this is in no way a declaration of the absolute sovereignty of the human. Freedom is a great reward but also an enormous risk. We don't gain it by our own strength. Freedom is apportioned to us: we can and must educate because we are forced out into freedom—by a superhuman power. From the expulsion of the human being into the dangers of freedom, the poet says:

"And like the eagle father throws his young out of the nest, so that they hunt their prey in the field, the gods smilingly drive us out."[9]

Notes

1. See: Fink, 2016.
2. Translated by N. Friesen and J. Türstig. From: Fink, E. Die Fragwürdigkeit des modernen Erziehers. *Die deutsche Schule* 51, 149–162.
3. The Decline of the West (1918, 1922) is the title of a two-volume work by Oswald Spengler, a critic of modern culture and civilization.
4. *Bildung* in the sense being invoked here would refer to things like a knowledge of Latin and Greek and of prescribed cannons in art and literature.
5. This refers to pre-revolutionary and pre-democratic France (i.e. before 1789), ruled by royalty and aristocracy, and bound to quasi-medieval structures and customs.
6. In "What is Enlightenment" (1784) Immanuel Kant famously defined enlightenment as "man's emergence from his self-incurred immaturity (*Unmündigkeit*)."
7. This is adapted from Kant's Lectures on Pedagogy. In: Zöller, G., & Louden, R. B. (Eds.), *Anthropology, history and education*. Cambridge University Press. [Trans.]
8. Fink appears to be appealing to Heidegger's understanding of "phenomenology," specifically as the study of *being* or *Dasein,* an anti-subjectivist analysis of what it is to be—or the ontological structure of being—in the world. See: Schacht, R. (1972). Husserlian and Heideggerian phenomenology. *Philosophical Studies: An International Journal for Philosophy in the Analytic Tradition, 23*(5), 293–314.
9. Hölderlin, F. (ca 1799/2007) Voice of The People (*Stimme des Volks*). In: *Selected Poems and Fragments.* (pp. 83–96). Penguin.

CHAPTER EIGHT

O.F. Bollnow: Risk and Failure in Education

Editor's Introduction

Otto Friedrich Bollnow (1903–1991) initially earned his PhD in physics; but while working on this degree, he came to know Herman Nohl (Chapters Four and Five) and subsequently decided to devote his energies to philosophy and education. Still later, he undertook advanced study under philosopher Martin Heidegger. As a result, he developed a pedagogical orientation that incorporates the existentialist emphases of Heidegger's early philosophy while still embracing many of Nohl's pedagogical insights. Both influences are evident in the text on risk and failure translated here, an excerpt from one of Bollnow's most popular books, *Existentialism and Pedagogy* (1959). On the one hand, without explicitly mentioning tact or the pedagogical relation by name, this piece effectively focuses on the risks and challenges associated with a pedagogical relation that is marked by trust, authority and allegiance. It also considers the implications of moments marked by an *absence* of tact. On the other hand, though, Bollnow's many references to "borderline" experiences and the individual's "innermost core" reveal the influence of existentialism—which also emphasized the individual's authenticity, freedom and responsibility.

Such attention to questions of teacher–student interrelationships and individual authenticity were particularly important in postwar Germany, after 12 years of Nazi rule (as Muth's opening comments [Chapter Six p. 88] also suggest). For during these 12 years, adults revealed themselves to be deeply fallible and flawed as well as utterly tactless. To define the pedagogical relation as "passionate relation between a mature person and one who is becoming, specifically for the sake of the latter" (as Nohl had; Chapter Four) appeared much more problematic after the darkness of the adult psyche that had been exposed during this time. In addition, teachers could no longer claim to simply be "a wise guide from afar [speaking] well-timed, penetrating words and powerful actions" (as Herbart put it, Chapter Two). Instead, adults had *failed*—indeed in ways much more serious and far-reaching than those portrayed in Bollnow's discussion of "risk and failure" below.

Despite the particular historical context in which it arose, Bollnow's writing remains eminently relevant to education today, for example, to issues of "promoting," "facilitating" and "enhancing" student *learning*. Bollnow reminds us that in all these tasks, there is always a personal dimension at stake that involves risk and trust. We are not simply confronting either learning "brains" or even "learners" themselves—entities whose purpose it is to process information or to construct knowledge—when we educate others. Instead, as Bollnow makes clear, we are "dealing with those who are free and also fundamentally unpredictable in their freedom" (p. 140). Even the best promoters and facilitators of learning do not reach their achievements "through cause and effect," as Bollnow correctly asserts. Instead, they rely on a "voluntary moment" from the child or young person—one that "can only arise through the process of education" itself (p. 146). This makes us educators liable to a wide range of types of failures with students, and also more vulnerable to failings on our own part:

> That something goes wrong in education, that the educator does not achieve a desired goal, that their relationship with the child [or young person] becomes a struggle in which they are ultimately defeated—or even that they finally fail with the entire enterprise: these are all things which are all too familiar from experience. It's the painful dark side of the teaching profession… (p. 139)

Bollnow brings what could be called a "phenomenological" sensibility to his examination of the educator's experience of failure. Following phenomenology as the study of felt and lived experience, Bollnow can also be seen to frame questions of the pedagogical relation and engagement as ones between the self of the teacher and the "otherness" of the student (or the one being educated). This question of the "otherness" of the child or young person is something taken up in all the remaining texts collected in this volume: Lippitz (Chapter Nine) takes questions of the "otherness," "foreignness," "alienness" and "alterity" of children and young people as their central concern—and also sees adult risk and failure as being ever-present realities in this context. In Chapter Eleven, Zirfas, as mentioned above, defines pedagogical tact itself precisely as "resonance with the openness, dynamics, variability and unfathomability of the other" (p. 192).

In short: Following Bollnow, it is not so much the themes of tact and the pedagogical relation themselves that are of explicit concern to scholars of pedagogy in the late 20th and early 21st centuries; instead, it is the question of how and what we can and *cannot* know about the experience of the child or young person in our care that is paramount.

Sources/Recommended Reading

Bollnow, O. F. (1959). *Existenzphilosophie und Pädagogik* [Existentialism and Pedagogy]. Kohlhammer.

Bollnow, O. F. (1972). Encounter and education. *The Educational Forum, 36*(3), 303–312. 10.1080/00131727209338979

Bollnow, O. F. (1974). Practice as the human way. *Education 10*, 61–75. https://normfriesen.info/files/Bollnow_(1974)_Practice.pdf

Bollnow, O. F. (1989). The pedagogical atmosphere. *Phenomenology + Pedagogy, 7*, 5–11. https://doi.org/10.29173/pandp15109

Bollnow, O. F. (1989) Theory and practice in education. https://www.researchgate.net/publication/333295910_Bollnow_1988_Theory_and_Practice_in_Education

Koerrenz, R. (2017). *Existentialism and education: An introduction to Otto Friedrich Bollnow*. Palgrave.

O.F. Bollnow: Risk and Failure in Education[1]

Risk as the Essential Moment of Education

That something goes wrong in education, that the educator does not achieve a desired goal, that their relationship with the child becomes a struggle in which they are ultimately defeated—or even that they finally fail with the entire enterprise: these are all things which are all too familiar from experience. It's the painful dark side of the teaching profession, one that teachers don't like to dwell on. So it's not surprising that these things are rarely dealt with in pedagogical theory. Failures are generally regarded as accidents, as events which happen to humans as imperfect beings, and as incidents that could have been avoided with a better and more efficient educational programs. No one has yet considered the possibility that failure has a far deeper meaning, one that it is actually founded in the essence, in the dignity of education. In reality, risk belongs to the innermost essence of education as long as it is a way of dealing with those who are free and also fundamentally unpredictable in their freedom. The child or young person can always evade the intention of the teacher or even turn against and thwart him for inscrutable reasons. That is why the possibility of failure is inherent to acts of education from the start. One must accept it consciously if one wants to take on education in the full sense.

The connection between education and failure was hidden as long as education was understood as a kind of "craftsmanship." Even today, education is still viewed this way, even if few own up to it. Just as the craftsman or the sculptor produces what has been commissioned from his material, so too does the educator wish to shape the "material" represented by the student—in this case, according to the rules of psychological knowledge and the given educational goal.[2] If this shaping does not succeed, it is either due to an error in the educator's craftsmanship or to a defect in the material itself. In principle, the failure need not have happened at all. The success of educational activity in this case depends solely on the efficiency and care with which it is carried out.

The same also applies, by the way, if one starts from an understanding of education as a kind of organic development. In this case, educational activity is limited to avoiding disruptions while the [child's or young person's] development takes place according to its own laws, which are seen as infallible.[3] Regardless, if the educator's expectations are not met, this means that the educator has either misjudged the potential available in the young person or has not sufficiently guarded against external disturbances. In both cases, failure could have been avoided, with success again being a matter of careful human planning. An illness or a substantial misfortune might violently destroy promising initial development. But in this case, it is an external circumstance that could not have been anticipated at the outset. So the educator need not blame himself. It is a mishap, but not an actual failure, because it has affected the educator only from the outside, but not penetrated his inner core.

Both views of education (as craftsmanship or as facilitating growth) are clearly relevant within their limits; both can meaningfully illuminate certain aspects of the educational process. But from the start, both miss the actual core of education: Namely, that one free being confronts another with certain expectations and that the educator must take into account the freedom of the *other*—a freedom which is fundamentally beyond all pre-calculation. To recognize the freedom of the other means also to affirm the fundamental uncertainty, risk and audacity of education. For education contains the possibility that from this freedom there arises action which rejects my attempt at education and destroys it. This is something quite different from a lack of plasticity or the unsuitability of the material to be formed and reshaped.[4] This is also something different from fate intervening from outside. It is instead the active rebellion of the other's will against that of the educator. And I must include this possibility if I want to acknowledge the other person in his freedom at all, a freedom to move toward what appears to me to be the very opposite of my educational goal. The person being educated has the possibility of thwarting a well-intentioned attempt at education. And this is no longer a mere failure of the educator in an isolated task; it is a failure in his innermost self. To eliminate this audacity [in educating] and thus avoid the danger of failure necessarily reduces the other person to a mere object of manipulation, violating both *their dignity* and at the same time the dignity of *education* itself.

The possibility of failure constitutes the difficulty and sometimes also the tragedy of educating as a vocation; for this failure in education is different from failure in any other profession. In other contexts, failure is generally something occurring in certain practical tasks which the person can address by simply turning to other tasks and without being inwardly affected. The educator, however, fails in his innermost core because he breaks down in a situation with which he has identified himself existentially with all his strength. Every day, the educator must overcome not only the passive resistance of his teaching materials but also the possibly of the active resistance on the part of his reluctant students. This is the basis of the draining and demoralizing nature of the profession—one that leads so many educators to appear old beyond their years. To fail in this way is the tragedy of the profession of education. It weighs all the more heavily in that it is not glorified with a heroic aura but is only eroded through the curse of ridicule. The real tragedy of the educator has not yet found its poetic form, and thus also seldom the understanding of fellow human beings.

Attempting, Gambling and Risking

To clarify the essence of the genuine educational venture, we must first attempt a conceptual clarification. We need to distinguish it from two phenomena which similarly can involve failure, but without being "risks" in the proper sense: The "attempt" and the "gamble." Both are undeniably part of the experience of the educator and are similar in some ways to risk. We will first try to highlight the essence of these terms in a general sense and then inquire into their specifically educational meaning.

A person can *try* something; more precisely, he can venture, attempt or undertake an *experiment*. This happens with any purposeful physical action. One tries something new to improve an old process that seems inadequate: Can a common material be replaced by one that is better or cheaper? Or one tries a new technique or manufacturing process, etc. You just give it a try. "The proof of the pudding is in the eating" is a common saying, and it can be taken to mean that preliminary calculation only goes so far, and that the new experience of an actual attempt is decisive. The results decide whether the attempt "worked." But an such an attempt or experiment can also fail—although "fail" might be too harsh a term here. That an attempt does not work out is the most common thing in the world; and it does not need to affect the being of the person involved. Of course, there may be an unfortunate loss of time and energy, but an unsuccessful attempt also means that you have to find another way. By constantly trying new things, one learns.

Attempts of this kind are part of being human. However, modern natural science has since developed "the experiment" to establish rigorous findings of cause and effect. Such findings can be reproduced by others, and specific factors can be carefully varied. Such an experiment is not simply a random attempt but is a carefully planned procedure in service of knowledge that is being constantly and systematically expanded. However experiments of this kind are not our concern here.

One can attempt something by taking a chance, by gambling. This takes us in a different direction, one which cannot be readily compared with the experiment. For example, you can test the strength of a rope by pulling it with your weight; or you can take a chance and simply put it to use to see if it works out. In an attempt of this kind one simply wants to learn, to discover the general principles behind it. In gambling, however, one exposes oneself unpredictably to chance. One is in a sense passive with no influence on the outcome of the event; one just lets it play out.

Such a gamble is sometimes unavoidable. For example, the business person necessarily takes a gamble because their business depends on markets and other unforeseeable factors in the future—even if today's insurance attempts to reduce these risks. Nothing ventured, nothing gained, as the saying goes; and that is exactly what is meant with the term "gamble." At the beginning of a vacation, one takes a gamble with the weather; indeed, all of life is in this sense gambling—sometimes less, sometimes more—and with every plan, one attempts to assess the degree to which it *is* a gamble.

But taking chances that are entirely avoidable is called negligence or carelessness, and when it is not simply about entertainment, but about more serious concerns, this negligence can become criminal. Whoever gambles with their own life, for example is irresponsible. For one's life should not be a question of good luck. Something that is gambled is something that can be lost, and to gamble one's life would be to lower it to this level, to treat it as a matter of relative indifference. One might end up risking one's life for something, consciously facing grave danger for the sake of a deeper responsibility, but this is quite different than simply gambling with it. In this case, you would not be gambling, but taking on a real risk.

To accept risk in a venture of some kind takes us to a still different domain. The difference is determined by saying: There is always something at stake, but in the end I risk myself. When I truly risk and venture something, my whole person is on the line. From an ethical point of view, a gamble may appear indifferent and even hazardous, but taking a real risk is always a matter of genuine ethical responsibility. That is why failure in the case of risk has so much more weight. If one loses in a gamble or a matter of chance, it remains a factual matter, and does not affect who one is. When something "goes wrong" in a gamble, it can be painful, but it only touches the person from outside.[5] But if in taking a risk, one fails, then the person who ventures it is deeply affected. That's why every real risk in this sense holds the possibility of real failure.

Translating into Educational Terms

All three forms—attempting, gambling and risking—reappear in forms of engagement that are particular to education. The teacher who wants to meet the changing demands of his profession has to attempt and experiment with many things. He may try a new teaching method, watch the students respond to this or that type of material, and also try to accommodate their interests. The teacher remains alive only if he is constantly trying something new. Such attempts can be carried out more systematically as a partially scientific experiment. But with this we are already in the field of educational research and no longer discussing educating itself.

An attempt in education, or rather, in instruction, can fail. For the educator this means nothing other than the general failure of an experiment in teaching. One might regret it, but one would also learn from it and be encouraged to try new attempts. Such trials (and errors) are part of the craft of education and help significantly in improving its methods. That is why even a failed try, attempt or experiment is far from a genuine failure.

[...]

In education towards freedom and ethical independence, there is simply no way to avoid risk. Exaggerated protective caution and anxiety prevent the adolescent from maturing. The mother duck, helplessly squawking as her ducklings eagerly take to water, is an apt image for the protective urges of equally helpless educators.

Also, real risk is clearly different from mere adventure. The adventurer seeks danger and actually enjoys it for its own sake. He dares everything, but not for the sake of the goal, but for the thrill of the dare itself. There are also adventurous educators… They are the ones who are intoxicated by their influence on youth and who drive the young entrusted to them into dangers likely beyond their coping abilities. But the true educational *venture* differs from mere *ad*-venture in that it is necessary and carried by a high moral of responsibility.

This risk comes in different forms. I can only tentatively attempt to explore some typical possibilities to illuminate the common factor of risk that underlies them. This exploration is difficult because we are approaching something very close to the limits of what can be said, and we must be satisfied if a few characteristics can be derived from it, with these then becoming the basis for still further attempts at clarification.

A Simple Example as a Starting Point

It may perhaps be best if I illustrate the risky commitment of the educator with an example that is closest to my own educational experience—even though it is atypical for most educators: the relationship of the professor to his doctoral student. If this student starts their work under the professor's guidance, it is then a joint enterprise, one in which not only the student, but also the teacher, can fail. Simply to suggest that a student look at a particular topic is already a risk, since every student needs to have their "own" topic, and one cannot know in advance how a particular person will come to grips with a given subject. Fewer students today have an understanding of the fact that one must first find a topic, that one must try and also give up on certain possibilities, until one's ultimate question crystallizes out of multiple opportunities and possibilities.

But what is important is not this process per se, but the tensions that arise from the distance one takes as it unfolds. For example, a teacher may see that the student is on the wrong track, and even though it is important for everyone to have their own experiences, the teacher may try to shorten the detour involved. Or this teacher may see the student struggling with tasks that apparently exceed their strength and would then advise them simply to let go. This, too, is difficult because the person concerned usually hangs on to these difficult and uncertain questions with special tenacity. And it is even more difficult when the student has proceeded down a false path for some time and has adopted wrong ways of thinking. In these cases, a real intervention may be required. And examples of such intervention immediately make the sensitivity of such educational ventures clear.

Everyone is fond of their own thoughts—or is at least very close to them. That is why quiet encouragement may be insufficient. One sometimes has to be blunt and even sometimes harsh in one's criticism in order to get the other person to listen. One must occasionally even bring about a crisis through direct censure. Then the work can be redirected and liberated so that it can truly progress. But it can also happen that the person will be taken aback by harsh critique and incited to contradiction. Then the success of the work as a whole becomes questionable, and it is not only the student that fails, but the teacher as well.

There is, so to speak, a soft and a hard way to supervise work. The soft way is to persuade the student, to support them on their own path, to hold back one's own reservations, and to hope that everything will be sorted out in the end. But often everything is not sorted, and then you have to try the hard way. This entails more direct critique, identifying weaknesses openly, and attempting to give the work new direction. Just how far one can and must go is precisely the question of risk: One can achieve a breakthrough with critique that is fruitful, but one can also bring the whole work to an end by discouraging the student or making him suspicious. One cannot foresee which possibility will be realized, yet one must risk the intervention. Moreover, the teacher is often unexpectedly placed in a situation in which the momentum of a conversation drives things quickly forward, meaning that one must act in the moment without being able to weigh the consequences. And it often happens that honest help can result in irrecoverable disaster. In this case, it is not only the student but also the teacher who has failed. And even though this does not receive widespread attention, it is manifest in the isolated consciousness of one's own pedagogical responsibility.

This is both visible and painfully felt from my own perspective. There are corresponding difficulties in every form of education. One must make decisions and assessments at a moment's notice without being able to see the consequences in advance. These are not experiments made for the benefit of experience or in order to produce results for disinterested observation. Sometimes it can almost seem to be a gamble because one hopes that one's decisions are correct. But it is a real risk, because I am completely committed to it myself and consciously take responsibility for the outcome. That is why failure is not an unfortunate mishap, but a real one which affects the person concerned down to his innermost core.

Risk in the Use of Authority

We now analyze some more typical examples of risk and failure in education. One illustration of unavoidable risk is evident in everyday challenges with discipline, which are for some a greater, and others a lesser, part of the nature of education. When I simply force the child to obey me, whether through physical superiority or enforcement of the school rules (which are in turn are part of the general social order), I am not in the realm of education. Instead, education begins only where I can knowingly ask for something whose fulfillment cannot be forced. I frequently find myself in a situation where I must tell students what to do if I want to achieve the goal I have in mind. On the one hand, I can give such instructions because

I trust that the child will follow them on their own initiative, based on their own practical or ethical understanding. But a moment of unavoidable risk and uncertainty is always involved. This is because whether this understanding in the child exists and whether it will become effective at this moment is simply unknown. Here, I am not just considering cases where I believe I know I will be obeyed—because then my instructions are only a kind of a purely technical directive and do not actually have an educational character. Of course, I must also give instructions in cases where I cannot be sure that they will be carried out. From this the real risk of making authoritative requests arises, one that educational responsibility requires me to accept.

With this we come to the problem of the use of authority in general. For making requests and giving instructions means I must always put my authority on the line. But it is part of the nature of authority that it does not force another through cause and effect, but rather that it turns to a free being who is ultimately to submit voluntarily to it. This voluntary moment, however, can only arise through the process of education. In this way the educator repeatedly enters that border zone where he must face misconduct, disorder or rebellion with nothing to back him up other than the power of his moral sincerity. Knowing that he is outwardly powerless, if he nevertheless confronts the reluctant child or young person in this border zone, there is always a risk. This is a risk which the educator must consciously decide to take on and which he must then enter with the full force of his humanity: It is only through this risk that educational success is achieved. And the more convincing the educator is in his whole person, the more certain this success becomes. But the educator can never be completely sure. The venture can always fail, and then not only does his risk-taking fail, but he has failed in his practice. In everyday life, the power of a given authority is tested when the authority itself has already come into question. If the educator, in the rare case, turns to external powers to restore his authority, this means he is truly destroyed in the eyes of those he is educating. After such a defeat, he cannot hope to ever become an authority for them again. His failure in this sense is permanent.

The Risk of Trust

Another possible illustration of unavoidable risk is to be found in the trust that the educator must place in the child. I have explained in more detail elsewhere how healthy human development can only occur in an atmosphere of trust.[6] The mistrust that I might have of another changes them. It may make them just as lazy, stupid and treacherous as they are in my own mistrustful mind. And vice versa; every moment of trust transforms the other in a positive sense into the better person that I have already envisioned in my trust. You can make other people better simply by thinking they're better. "The moral energy issuing from one who believes is in a high degree an educative force," Nicolai Hartmann once said. Belief "can transform a man, towards good or evil, according to what he believes."[7]

It is especially important to bring such trust to the young person in critical situations where an educational intervention (for example, a punishment or reprimand) has abruptly taken them from the wrong path to where the vulnerable beginnings of new life are timidly emerging. Perseverance in this new purpose really depends not only on them alone, but also on the trust placed by the educator both in them and in this new purpose. If, for example, a person honestly promises an improvement after a series of errors, their strength for this new turn depends on the fact that the educator to whom they promise it also believes they will keep their promise. Without the help of this trust, even the firmest of intentions have no reliable foundation. In fact there is nothing colder and more discouraging than when an educator bluntly declares that after so many disappointments, he cannot believe the promise that the young person makes. Although such skepticism may be based on a great deal of experience, it still has a destructive effect because it deprives the youth, with all his honest will, of the strength to realize it. This will always depend on the faith of the one to whom a promise is made. That is why the educator, in spite of so many disappointments, has to constantly reawaken this power of trust within himself.

But such a reawakening is not simply a routine mechanical process; it does not produce its result automatically. Instead, it is also based on a risk which the educator must venture time and again. Hartmann continues the passage quoted above by emphasizing: "All trust, all faith, is an adventure. It always requires something of moral courage and spiritual strength. It is always accompanied by a certain commitment of the person." He continues: "The trustful person… puts himself into the hands of him whom he trusts; he stakes himself… he who trusts exposes himself to danger. If his gift is trampled underfoot, he himself is trodden upon."[8] That is why the risk of trusting the child can succeed—and then the educational effort is proven to have been worthwhile. But this venture can also fail, and then the educator is the one who appears to lack the necessary caution, and who seems to have acted irresponsibly in naïve good faith. He must bear students' mockery in addition to the failure of his own efforts.

A similar situation existed, for example, in a radical early 20th century experiment in reformatories where locked doors and other barriers were removed. Trust was extended so that the young people kept there would not simply run away. The great successes that came from this experiment are well known. But such trust always remains a risk where, like any other risk, the possibility of failure is always present. Such a risk can therefore only succeed when the effort is backed by all the internal strength available to the teacher, and it will fail immediately as soon as this strength recedes and trusting becomes a matter of routine.

Trust always means to deliver oneself over to something unprovable and unenforceable because trust depends on the unpredictable free will of another human being. For this reason, the one trusting always exposes himself, commits himself with all his human strength and thus also opens himself to possible failure. And because he may unreservedly put his whole person on the line, failure would correspondingly also affect him in his whole being. Not only is the reputation of the educator damaged through failure in such a commitment—meaning that he has in this sense failed with the other students as well—but he has also decreased his chances of succeeding again with the one who has let him down.

This is important: The educator does not fail because he has made a mistake that could have been avoided through better insight. We are talking about failure in a rather different way. For the educator can also fail even when he has done everything perfectly correctly. That one's trust in another can be suddenly and fully disappointed is part of the nature of risk, because risk is not about predictable causal relations. It is instead a thunderbolt of destiny that intervenes in education and that negates everything accomplished through human planning and care.

One could try to minimize the risk necessitated in trust simply by telling the child (or anyone for that matter) that "I trust you," since we already know that the child needs this trust in support of their development. But the educator would then not identify himself fully with this trust, would restrict and reserve himself through his "realistic" knowledge of human weakness, and would thus accept disappointment to already likely be the case. Such an approach may be very realistic and could offer the educator some security, but in educational terms it would be worthless. It is not enough for the educator, for pedagogical reasons, to act *as if* he trusts; he must himself instead be fully convinced of this trust, he must commit himself completely to this trust—otherwise he would not appear trustworthy to the child or anyone else for that matter. That does not mean, however, that he would carelessly or credulously buy into cheap illusions. He needs all his clear-eyed skepticism. In his own soul, however, he confronts this knowledge, and hazards to trust in spite of it. Despite all his knowledge of the dangers of disappointment, he must honestly trust himself if his trust is also to bear fruit for others.

The need to extend one's trust in these ways is something particular to educators. It is also necessarily their fate to be deceived and to fail in their trust. The danger of resignation or embitterment is obvious. And it is unavoidable that many educators fall victim to this bitterness and practice their profession just by going through the motions. But it is the task of the educator to constantly break free of this resignation and, in spite of the disappointments involved, to repeatedly summon up the power of trust. This can go almost beyond human strength, and it can be said that educators are constantly overtaxed by the demands made on their trust. This excessive demand is probably ultimate reason that so many educators are exhausted before their time. On the other hand, it is also true that the vitality of this trust may grant the educator a kind of inward youth.

The Risk of Unreserved Openness

Another type of educational risk arises from the fact that the teacher must not only expect what a child is developmentally capable of accomplishing, but that the educator must also go beyond it. For example, the educator speaks to the small child not at the child's own linguistic level, but at the one just above it, to incentivize further development, to create a kind of developmental impulse which moves the child forward. But this is also a risk because the challenge can easily become too great. The child may then deny it and become discouraged. At least temporarily, the teacher must in this sense ask something of the child which approaches the limits of the child's own strength, not only intellectually, but also morally—in the sense of the child's self-sacrifice and self-overcoming.

This means that risk is extended still further, given that the developmental impulse coming from the teacher does not just apply to measurable skills and knowledge, but to the realm of students' emotions—even touching on what is deepest within them. This is the case, for example, in encounters with a great literary work or in questions of human morality in general. Children must be presented with possibilities that go slightly beyond what they are willing or able to accept. There is always the danger that these opportunities will be met with reflexive resistance, or that they will result in an entrenched negative attitude. In taking these anticipatory risks, teachers expose something that is innermost to them, for there is always the danger that they will become suspicious or even ridiculous to the children in what concerns them most deeply.

That leads to a decisive point: Teachers always must invest themselves in the values that they seek to impart; consequently, they cannot exclude their students from the feelings and convictions that a person usually conceals in their vulnerable innermost core. Consequently, they must open this innermost sphere to the still immature other, because this is the only way to lead them into this realm themselves. Every other person has the right to protect from others those things that touch them most deeply. They have the right to a mask behind which one hides one's deepest feelings, only rarely revealing these to someone they really trust. Only the teacher is repeatedly required to stand and speak of these kinds of things without knowing how they will be received. The poet is here in a much better position, because he can write down his innermost feelings in solitude and does not have to present these directly to listeners. Only teachers—and in a similar way ministers—as placed in a situation where they must speak of things which touch them most intimately. Don't misunderstand me: This does not mean that teachers are speaking to the class about themselves and their own emotional lives. That would be shameless and would violate the distance that should remain between teacher and student.[9] But in speaking about things with sincerity and without irony, the educator reveals his own feelings. This is not to be avoided, but rather, reflects a commitment the educator has to make many times over: to hazard the risk of this openness each time anew.

At the same time there is the danger that these innermost things will become mere teaching "material" presented to others without inhibition—if not also with a sense of satisfaction. The result would be a sentimental or maudlin tone embarrassing to listeners; for genuine listeners experience the same wary reticence as a good speaker. They are moved only when the speaker's reticence is noticed—one that is necessary in order to speak of sensitive matters in public.

The inner life of the teacher always struggles with the natural need for protection—a need which must be overcome in order to speak of things that are decisive. Only then will the teacher succeed in conveying what is most important. And like Orpheus, who forced the wild beasts to be quiet through the strength of his singing, so too the teacher, through his unrestrained openness, brings things within reach of his students that they never would have gained by themselves. He may succeed, but risk always remains—together with the danger that the teacher will appear strange and may even gain nothing but ridicule from the students regarding a point which affects him most deeply. The teacher, we can say, must wear his soul on his sleeve, whereas everyone else is free to protect and hide their own. Through the constantly renewed risk of openness, the teacher is endangered, and in a special sense is placed in the hands of his students.

Failure

Consider a genuine apology on the part of a teacher to his students—for example, for unfounded suspicion or an undeserved reprimand. Although this type of apology is related to failure, it is by no means a failure on its own; and such an apology can remain in students' memories for decades. What is striking, however, is that the error that the teacher apologizes for has a much greater effect than anything that an error-free education could have achieved. But what is the basis for this profoundly disproportionate but unexpectedly positive effect? The reason might be that the teacher here has descended from his blamelessness and has realized a kind of equality with the student, one which abolishes the usual relationship between teacher and student. The student is elevated through this recognition, while the teacher does not necessarily sink in the student's eyes but may actually rise. The strength demonstrated through the teacher's voluntary apology may earn him still greater respect.

But one can go further and point out cases where educators have failed in a very real sense because student resistance broke them down in human despair: this can happen that the failure or desperate breakdown of the teacher (something which is not at all "pedagogical") has an extraordinary effect on young people. Their unexpected success turns out to be something that affects them to their core. That they succeed in their reckless venture may be accidental; but it not only demonstrates the senselessness of their endeavor but also the superiority of the teacher as someone who does not defend themselves against such ruthlessness. Such is the crushing experience of a regretful conscience: "I didn't want to take the joke *that* far." Put more bluntly, the one who arouses respect manifests a certain purity precisely because he is vulnerable and unable to protect himself against treachery. It seems to be the case that one cannot achieve such an experience of respect by merely observing others, but only through the shameful experience of having damaged it oneself.[10]

Although this kind of destruction of respect need not always happen, it becomes shockingly apparent in the defenseless failure of an educator. It will occur, however, mostly to those whose susceptibility already has become obvious in another context. And that is why success as a teacher is ultimately not something to be realized through conscious planning—just as little as a teacher would carefully plan in apologizing for a mistake. Anyone who would try to bring about such events deliberately would degrade their seriousness, turning it into mere spectacle—something which students would recognize as utterly inauthentic. Rather: It is only at the limit of conscious planning, only at the limit of education as an intentional enterprise, that a genuine crisis arises that shakes the individual to their core and allows for a clean break. This is a real borderline experience in education in which something absolute fatefully breaks into everyday life.

This borderline character means that we should be clear that such events do not belong to the everyday life of education. Despite the fact that the dangers of failure always threaten it, one must not exaggerate this side of education. Certainly such a failure is terrible for an educator, but fortunately, such an event is rare, and certainly not part of the educator's normal everyday life. It is not failure *itself*, but only the *possibility* of failure that is involved in everyday risk and trust in education. Failure fortunately remains the exception, but it is an exception that does not simply enter into education by accident; it is instead inherent to the nature of education from the start. But above this undercurrent of dark possibilities, the life of planned education continues its normal course. Needless to say, the importance of careful planning and of guarding against unnecessary disturbances, of course, remains uncontested.

Notes

1. Translated by N. Friesen. This is the final chapter from the book: Bollnow, O. F. (1959). *Existenzphilosophie und Pädagogik: Versuch über unstetige Formen der Erziehung*. Kohlhammer. See also: Bollnow, O. F. (1959). Wagnis und Scheitern in der Erziehung. *Pädagogische Arbeitsblätter zur Fortbildung für Lehre und Erzieher, 10*(8), 337–349. [Trans.]
2. With this analogy, Bollnow can be seen to be referring to methods like those of *direct instruction* which overtly directed students to produce changes in their knowledge, behavior and disposition. [Trans.]
3. This analogy sees the natural development and curiosity of the child as the basis for education. It corresponds to *indirect* or *student centered* approaches to teaching such as exploratory, inquiry-based and constructivist methods. Together with the more directive techniques implied in Bollnow's earlier analogy, these two approaches can be seen to mark opposite extremes in a continuum of ways of engaging in education. [Trans.]
4. The German world for plasticity here is *Bildsamkeit*, which refers, in part, to a child's or young person's "form-ability." See Chapter Two, p. 36, note 15. [Trans.]
5. Gambling in this way takes on some characteristics of risk when it becomes pathological, for example one gambles all of one's savings.
6. Bollnow later developed the theme of trust in the context of the "pedagogical atmosphere:" O.F. Bollnow. (1964/1989). The pedagogical atmosphere: The perspective of the educator. *Phenomenology + Pedagogy 7*, 37–63. [Trans.]; A. Nitschke. (1952). Angst und Vertrauen. *Die Sammlung, 7*, 175–80.
7. N. Hartmann. (1932). *Ethics, volume II: Moral values*. Allan & Unwin, p. 295.
8. Hartmann, 1932, p. 292.
9. Readers can refer to Chapter Six, where Muth describes how pedagogical tact maintains "the distance necessary for the pedagogical relation" (pp. 105–108). [Trans.]
10. On the connection between reverence and shame in general, see O. F. Bollnow. (1958). *Der Ehrfurcht* (2nd ed.) Frankfurt.

CHAPTER NINE

W. Lippitz: Otherness and "Alienness" in Pedagogical Contexts

Editor's Introduction

Wilfried Lippitz (1945–) is the first author in this volume whose formative years were spent entirely *after* the Second World War. His membership in this postwar generation effectively means that his text, like all of those in the remaining chapters in this book, is marked by a critical take on scholars who were active during (but only in some cases complicit with) the Nazi regime (Herman Nohl, Jakob Muth and O.F. Bollnow; see Chapters Four, Five, Six and Eight). It also means that Lippitz's work reflects the ubiquitous post-war influence of the critical theory of the Frankfurt School of Social Research—theory which also laid the foundations for critical pedagogy and critical race theory. This means that this chapter, as well as the ones that follow it, are characterized by a critical, historical and theoretical *self*-awareness and sophistication that is not present in some of the earlier chapters of this volume.

What Lippitz undertakes in this chapter can be seen as a kind of deconstruction of well-known moments in the history and theory of education. However, instead of covering the likes of John Locke, John Dewey, or Noah Webster's books and reforms, Lippitz takes as his examples texts and individuals familiar to a German or continental audience: A famous picture book by the Czech-Moravian reformer John Amos Comenius and figures like G.W.F. Hegel, Theodor Litt and

Martinus J. Langeveld. In developing his critical interpretation of these and other sources, Lippitz also references—directly or indirectly—a number of scholars covered earlier in this volume. For example, in the section titled "The problem of pedagogical understanding of the other and the foreign," Lippitz invokes Schleiermacher (Chapter Three) in pointing out that difference, otherness and "alienness" need to be clearly recognized in the relationships between the older and younger generations. In this same section, Lippitz also critiques what he refers to as the "human science pedagogy" of which Nohl, Muth, and Bollnow are important representatives.

On the other hand, Lippitz *follows* Bollnow in embracing a broadly phenomenological view on questions of pedagogy, teaching and learning; and he appears to approvingly reference Bollnow's account of education as necessarily being a matter of risk and failure (see Chapter Eight; see Lippitz, p. pp. 168–169). But even more important for Lippitz is the question of the significance of the terms "other" and especially, "alien" in the title of his paper—terms derived from the phenomenologies of Edmund Husserl, Emmanuel Levinas and Bernhard Waldenfels. Lippitz begins his paper by admitting that the "word 'alien' is not easy to define either positively or decisively." One cannot say directly what the alien is. Rather, the alien, Lippitz emphasizes, can only be described "in relationship to something that is *not* seen as alien" (p. 156).

What is least strange and alien to us is, of course, that which is familiar, those things corresponding to "me" or "mine"—things are part of us or belong to us. In the phenomenological tradition, this is referred to as "ownness," with Edmund Husserl, the founder of phenomenology, describing each of us as having a "sphere" of our own "ownness."[1] This sphere is characterized by affiliation, familiarity, availability, be it of one's own lived body, one's clothes, bed, apartment, friends, children, one's generation, home country or profession. From within this sphere, within this sense of being "at home," then, the alien is not encountered directly as we might encounter another person the other. Instead, it is experienced as something coming from the outside, as an interruption, a shock, even a violation. It is experienced not as knowledge, but in terms of an immediate emotional response, for example, to an utterly unexpected action or behavior on the part of a child. The child is in this case the other, but what they might say or do is alien.

While the other may thus bring with her elements of the foreign and utterly unfamiliar, this other is in a more general sense symmetrical with us: We can meet this other face-to-face, eye-to-eye, and likely also share the same language and culture. The other is to the self like apples are to pears, or day is to night. The alien is (more) different. This difference in the case of the alien is not complementary (like day and night); as discussed, it is an uncontrollable event that occurs from the perspective of the first person. To clarify the distinction between own and alien is to highlight the kinds of limits that, in recent German scholarship, have been seen to be relevant to questions of pedagogical tact and especially to the relations that are characteristic of pedagogy—without these being termed "pedagogical relations" as such. After all, despite its complexity, the alien, as Lippitz puts it, is a "relational concept," one that can be understood only in relation to another, to that which it is *not*. But this is conceived by Lippitz not only as marked by particular types of risk and failure, but as part of a much deeper dynamic between adults and children. This deeper dynamic is revealed—in part—in adults, parents and teachers being "rendered alien to themselves through their children" and children being "rendered alien in the eyes" of those caring for them (p. 172).

Sources/Recommended Reading

Lippitz, W. (1983). The child's understanding of time. *Phenomenology + Pedagogy, 1*(2), 172–180. https://doi.org/10.29173/pandp14873

Lippitz, W. (1986). Understanding children, communicating with children: Approaches to the child within us. *Phenomenology + Pedagogy, 4*(3), 56–65. https://doi.org/10.29173/pandp15023

Waldenfels, B. (2011). *The phenomenology of the alien.* Northwestern University Press.

W. Lippitz: Otherness and "Alienness" in Pedagogical Contexts[2]

> The encounter with the other always means the encounter with the unknown. The unknown can be easily misperceived. As a result, the child can be systematically misunderstood, assimilated to the model of that which is known or familiar, and the unknown will consequently be reduced in terms of the grown-up or the cliché.
> Martinus J. Langeveld, 1966[3]

Introduction

The word "alien" is not easy to define either positively or decisively. That which is alien does not belong to any set of binary oppositions, such as friend or enemy, self or other, in or out, subject or object, me or you, bad or good. If one uses a phenomenology of the lifeworld[4] to ask not what the alien *is*, but rather, how it *appears* and *reveals itself*, then an initial definition emerges: "Alien" is a relational concept, referring to phenomena that always appear and achieve articulation in relationship to something that is *not* seen as alien. That which is alien is thematized through our systematization and ordering of the world, in all of its dimensions:[5]

1. In the axiological, concerning values: between good and evil, same and different, familiar and unfamiliar, beautiful and ugly, etc.;
2. In the praxeological, concerning practice: between convergence and divergence, integration and differentiation, super- and sub-ordination, acceptance and rejection, etc.;
3. In the epistemological, concerning knowledge and perception; between knowledge and ignorance, familiar and unfamiliar.

Described in relational terms, it is clear that "alienness" is something that, to various degrees, doesn't fit into available structures, and that even tears through the warp and woof of the textures of the everyday. In so doing, it leaves behind fibers, fragments or traces of the contingent and arbitrary. Every human order is built on continuity, regularity and dependability.[6] These orders constitute themselves—insofar as they are able to secure and maintain their own identity—in processes of the inclusion of that which belongs to it, and of the exclusion of that which is other, that which is abnormal or alien. In the radical sense of an anarchic element or event, the alien cannot be integrated into such an order. For it is part of the realm of the unordered, of the unrestrained and unbridled. It eludes every effort and exertion of force that order might bring against it. Instead, the alien remains something which continues to irritate, which disrupts or interrupts, and destabilizes the given order. It is evident from such disruptions that any achievement of order remains precarious. Order has its origin in the pre-predicated and pre-reflexive[7]—an origin which cannot be comprehended in terms of order's own norms and rules. That which underlies order, in other words, is also largely invisible and unstable, and ensures that the order itself does not become ossified. In this way, orders remain dynamic and unconfinable systems. They can be compared to languages. They are not preserved in fixed vocabularies and grammars but remain alive and develop further in creative processes of concrete speech and in contexts of symbolic and pre-symbolic activity that cannot be planned in advance.

If we understand the study of education and our own pedagogical reality as an active and reflective practice which arises and is changed and maintained in systems of order, then education—like other social fields—is thoroughly interpenetrated by alienness. As an example, schools have continuously been given the task, as organizations, of dealing with the problem posed in every society, that of its social reproduction. This consists of the integration of new generations into the existing society through exclusionary and homogenizing practices and processes. For the social system of the school, its entering students, its newly arrived clients, are in a certain sense alien. A flood of literature—scholarly and popular, practice-oriented and autobiographical—deals with the first day of school, with the transition to school, and with the performance of rituals to deal with the newness and otherness that these phenomena present.[8] The attempt is to deploy specific aspects of practice and normalization to make students out of children who have thus far only known the family or the kindergarten, and to curb the "pathologies" or irregularities that readily accompany such assimilative processes.[9]

Of course, when they begin school, new experiences lead children to feel alienated and insecure. They enter into a new place, one that follows patterns different from those they are used to. Punctuality is required, and is almost physiognomically embodied in the austere face of the clock in the classroom, which inexorably and admonishingly indicates to latecomers their breach of academic order. One meets the functionality and the impersonality of the institution in the monotony of the architecture of the school and the classroom. Also, there are manifold duties and assignments—whether one likes them or not—that are all subject to official inspection and evaluation. Breaches of rules and irregularities are seen in such institutional orders as bringing with them clearly specified consequences. Finally, it is in the school that strange grown-ups appear in *loco parentis*: teachers, principals, counselors and others, each with their own claim upon the child.[10]

Out of this multiplicity of manifestations of the alien in its "normalcy" and "everydayness," I would like to select a few more or less dramatic aspects of alienness for further consideration. Although they may be novel and foreign to English readers, I believe these aspects to be interesting in their own right. Also, they show alienness as a central and timely problem for pedagogical thought and action. I will articulate the significance of foreignness with reference to the dimensions presented above:

1. Epistemologically and praxeologically in terms of the question of personal formation, socialization and development;
2. Epistemologically, axiologically, and praxeologically in terms of ongoing discussions about pedagogical understanding and about basic conceptions of pedagogical practice;
3. Intergenerationally, in terms of the formation of the interrelationships between age groups central to social reproduction.

Between Cosmological Education (Amos Comenius) and Neo-Humanistic *Bildung* (Wilhelm von Humboldt)

In the following, I will present two different, historically localizable aspects of the pedagogical encounter with alienness. Both are associated with periods that have important places in German cultural and intellectual history. One of these periods is from the transition between the Middle Ages and the early-modern period, and the second, from the 19th century. The first aspect of the pedagogical encounter with alienness to be considered here has to do with the material, epistemological and axiological side of formation and development. It finds its specific historical location in what is likely the greatest attempt by any scholar to establish a pedagogically significant order of the known world. This is undertaken by John Amos Comenius in his *Orbis Sensualium Pictus* (1658; *Die sichtbare Welt/ The Visible World*). The other aspect has to do with the rather theoretical side of the formation and growth as it is conceptualized in the neo-humanism of Wilhelm von Humboldt.[11] Specifically, this formation and growth is conceived of as a movement or dynamic, as a self-directed, enriching experience occurring as the self-encounters and assimilates the other and the alien as these are presented by other languages and cultures. Given their importance in German thought, both of these historical understandings—the medieval-humanistic and neo-humanistic—have important practical and cultural implications. For example, Comenius' cosmological view of the world can be said to lead to a canonization of the material form of education, which connects the social utility of skill and knowledge with the moral disposition that is bound up with it. The formal, neo-humanistic concept of education, of the dynamic development of the abilities of the individual, appropriates that which is other or alien from an idealized, past culture for the purposes of higher education. Education in this sense then becomes an end in itself, a general process of formation without the utility of an ultimate occupational justification. These differentiations are clarified in greater detail, below.

But what does Comenius' *Orbis Sensualium Pictus* have to do with alienness? It arose as an attempt, on the universal and cosmological scale, to create order out of the political and social chaos of the Thirty Years' War (1618–1648). The divine order, of whose existence Comenius is still convinced, is understood to be hidden by the confusion of war and religious strife. The world is no longer the familiar home it once was; it has become strange and foreign. God's order, on the other hand, is hidden, and it must be artfully re-created in trust and belief in the presence of the Holy Spirit. It must be imparted to all people through an ambitious and systematic effort of education. The invisible order of the world is made visible and accessible through reading and learning, through the careful and methodological arrangement of word and picture—and the juxtaposition of the common German with the elevated Latin language. All of these linguistic and imagistic forms and contents are combined to achieve a Christian legitimation of the world in its totality. Through the careful combination of text and image, alienness is made accessible for learning in the broadest possible manner. This includes the literalization of forms and contents in word and picture; it also includes separate or even isolated places of learning and systematic instruction. Such an intensely mediated didactic presentation of the world attains the status of a true and divinely sanctioned "reality," ontologically primary to chaotic, everyday realities, and elevated above the merely factual and empirical world of the senses and of action.

To exaggerate slightly from our (post-)modern standpoint: The simulacrum is more real than the real itself, and presents a didactically artful, cosmologically scaled artificial world to the student, who inhabits a world rife with the familiar and unordered. And this artificial world is oriented around nothing less than the learning of its human inhabitants. What pedagogue would not be inspired by such an education-centric cosmology? The metaphysical principle of a progressive order or hierarchy leading from physical and visible up to the invisible heavenly realm of ideas is typically Christian, Medieval and even Greek in origin. The invisible, intangible and divine is the exclusive purview of the soul, of that which is eternal in human beings. It alone exemplifies the rational order of the whole, and the more disorderly, earthly world of the human must be brought in line with it. According to this way of conceptualizing order, alienness is only transitional, a type of "sickness" or "sinfulness" that can always be healed in the great beyond. Alienness has no value in and of itself in the sense of the contemporary understanding described earlier (in which it serves as the basis for order itself).

Earlier, I indicated that orders are created through the selective processes of inclusion and exclusion. These "orders" suppress disorder in specific ways: they privilege some things in particular, and at the same time, through processes of exclusion, segregate that which is considered different, alien, of less value or simply as incapable of integration.

I would like to comment on one specific example of an attempt to create order that is evident in Comenius' work. It concerns a central site of the civilizing process of the modern individual. This civilizing process is, and remains today, one of the tasks of the education, a central part of raising a child. This is the cultivation of an individual's table manners, a type of cultivation, education or discipline which places significant emphasis on the body. As Norbert Elias has shown in his studies of the history of the civilizing processes of modernity, this process or program involves the cultivation of those less civilized—or even those seen as "barbaric"—takes place by adjusting the threshold of embarrassment and shame.[12] Certain bodily functions and associated organs are made alien and strange. They are expunged, rendered taboo both in speech and action. They are silenced, often withdrawn from that which is part of the desired, moral and cultural order, and from that which is seen to constitute the "humanity" of human beings. This is also the case for the way that food is handled at mealtime. A treatment of this particular subject is provided in Comenius' *Orbis Sensualium Pictus* (1658). A facsimile of the image and text used by Comenius is provided here (Figure 9.1) and is illustrative of his treatment of dozens of other subjects—from water to warfare—undertaken in this landmark work.

Cleanliness and order are maintained through a range of instruments and arrangements, from processes of handwashing, through the pouring of beverages from pitcher to glass, to the roles of guests and host. But to return to Elias, it is above all cutlery, listed near the top of Comenius' vocabulary ("Spoons," "Knives," "Forks"), that keeps a distance between food and the body. At the same time, these instruments—indispensable to civilized culinary conviviality—touch one of the most intimate parts of our body, namely the mouth. Other intimate places and organs, specifically, those for elimination and reproduction, are correspondingly rendered foreign and taboo. These taboos are rearticulated in the pathologies and neuroses of later generations of Puritanical or Victorian bourgeoisie.

But that is another topic that cannot be considered further here. What is important at this point, however, is that in the *Orbis Pictus*, in which Comenius generalizes the manners and customs of the higher Medieval classes to a universal benchmark for education. These manners and customs are to reach the lower classes and social groups in the course of modern processes of civilizing and social discipline. In Comenius' richly illustrated text, the everyday lives of those *not* part of the privileged classes is effectively rendered invisible. According to Comenius, education is something that applies to everyone, including those less privileged.

When a *Feast*	Cum *Convivium*
is made ready,	apparatur,
the table is covered	Mensa sternitur
with a *Carpet*, 1.	*Tapetibus*, 1.
and a *Table-cloth*, 2.	& *Mappa*, 2.
by the *Waiters*,	à *Tricliniariis*,
who besides lay	qui præterea opponunt
the *Trenchers*, 3.	*Discos* (Orbes), 3.
Spoons, 4.	*Cochlearia*, 4.
Knives, 5.	*Cultros*, 5.
with little *Forks*, 6.	cum *Fuscinulis*, 6.
Table-napkins, 7.	*Mappulas*, 7.
Bread, 8.	*Panem*, 8.
with a *Salt-seller*, 9.	cum *Salino*, 9.
Messes are brought	*Fercula* inferuntur
in *Platters*, 10.	in *Patinis*, 10.
a *Pie*, 19. on a *Plate*.	*Artocrea*, 19. in *Lance*.
The Guests being	Convivæ introducti
brought in by the *Host*, 11.	ab *Hospite*, 11.
wash their Hands	abluunt manus

Figure 9.1: A Feast (Convivium) from Comenius' 1658 *Orbis Sensualium Pictus*.

As a result, the issue of alienness is tacitly raised and at the same time, also expunged in Comenius' conception of education. And this selective inclusion of order and exclusion of alienness occurs along lines of social *class*. Less privileged elements have no place in the order of the whole as it is presented and integrated into a divine and all-encompassing cosmology.

Creating order out of chaos is an unavoidably imperial gesture. In making one thing privileged and familiar, order unavoidably makes another alien. This is basic to everyday experiences of education as it occurs in the supposedly central or paradigmatic order of the school—something which Comenius anticipates in its basic structures and implications. Comenius' optimism regarding education, how-ever, does not hold in our present age. The order which he elevates and universalizes is now generally denigrated as particular and exclusive. Since the school has become one of the central authorities for socialization and teaching, it must deal systematically with problems of the selection and justification of appropriate content for learning. Like Comenius, the school must attempt to present the world in literalized form in its textbooks, and to give it canonical order in its curricula. In this way, it accordingly excludes from its institutional logic and its inherently middle-class orientation other social and individual characteristics. These become, in effect, alien objects in the school, since they apply to the role neither of student nor teacher. It is precisely this that has resulted in the alien nature of learning in school, in the many negative experiences to which generations of students have given expression. The order of the school and classroom is experienced as senseless filler and alienated learning.

As a student in school, the child, in his or her person, is split: On the one hand, there is the individual in the plenitude of the child's own biographical experiences and adventures—which remain alien to the teacher. On the other, there is the child in their role as a student, a role which is an alien imposition, ultimately remaining external to the child. However, it goes without saying that the creation and maintenance of this order—and of the alienness and alienation associated with it—is undertaken in the school with ever less success and conviction. And the remedial impulse in reform movements makes this its explicit program: To bring into the school the extra-scholastic reality, the biographical and experiential dimensions of learning, the transparency and even the bodily and sensual proximity of learning contents so that education may be more relevant to life's meaning.[13]

Let us now turn to the neo-humanistic discussions that use a different term to refer to education and human development: *Bildung*. *Bildung* is a term which has no direct equivalent in English, and was given broad but canonical definition by Wilhelm von Humboldt as "the linking of the self to the world to achieve the most general, most animated, and most unrestrained interplay."[14] In its breadth, *Bildung* is viewed as an emphatically autobiographical process through which this interplay defines who one becomes—as one simultaneously gives definition to the world around one. However, in his famous discussion of *Bildung*, von Humboldt also makes reference to alienness and alienation. Alienness appears, however, only as something preliminary and temporary. In its ideal form, *Bildung* is understood in this context as self-*Bildung*, as an experiential process that arises through negative events and alienation. The subject of *Bildung* in this context is understood in terms of a theory of dialectical identity. Starting with the individual subject, *Bildung* in the broadest sense is the reconciliation of the individual and the particular with the general and the universal. Experience is dialectical in nature and is ultimately consummated only through a long and arduous confrontation with and assimilation of the other. *Bildung* happens through learning, unlearning and relearning; it is occasioned through formative experiences that are negative in a dialectical sense. Through such experiences, I alienate myself, in that I deal with things unfamiliar and unknown—for example, a foreign culture or language—which demands significant effort and assimilative labor.

This general process is perhaps presented most dramatically in the Hegelian dialectic or struggle between master and servant. They are both engaged in a fight for recognition, one in which self and other are pitted in a contest, literally to the death, to become autonomous. In the end, this struggle results in the appropriation of that which is other and alien by the victorious self. If it succeeds in its self-assertion, the self then subjugates the other and thus renders it familiar—eliminating its alienness. Of course, in this struggle of the self against the other for autonomy and recognition, the self is itself changed and becomes something different.[15] It is strengthened and enriched, and it is able to enjoy new experiences at a higher level of consciousness. In other words, the self integrates the alien and other, and in doing so, comes to know itself better, becoming in a sense transparent to itself. The path of *Bildung* starts in imperfection and in a dearth of self-consciousness. But it ultimately leads to consummate self-knowledge and self-awareness in the form of what Hegel has called "objective spirit."[16]

In keeping with the traditional modern metaphysics of the subject, the self in this scenario establishes its own identity through the reflexive encounter with and adaptation of the other. This dialectical experience enriches the self by providing it with the distance necessary for it to come to know itself better, and to be better taught about itself. That which is other and alien becomes simply a means of *Bildung* and carries no other purpose in itself. When the other or alien becomes knowledge, it is always presupposed that this otherness or alienness is not fundamentally different in comparison to the consciousness which experiences and reflexively appropriates it. It ceases to be something that is known even its alienness and becomes a part of reflexive consciousness. The initial difference between the self and other, the starting point of the self and the knowledge of the other, is effectively erased. It disappears in the sameness of reflection. The other and the alien are figures of passage, not insuperable barriers to thought and understanding.

Theodor Litt, a philosopher of education well known in Germany, provides an example of how this abstract model of *Bildung* is concretized.[17] Explicitly situating his thinking in the type of philosophy of dialectical identity described above, Litt makes the following argument: The general *Bildung* of adolescents should include a foreign language. In this way, Litt explains, the adolescent will be removed from the familiar and unreflective speech of his mother tongue and will gain distance from it. Only in that way, can the adolescent achieve two new experiences that are closely interrelated: First, he or she will learn a new language, and with it, a new culture and way of life; second, this learning process will provide a mirror in which the old, familiar, and trusted, appears changed. The first language or mother tongue is made reflexive; it is made to appear as something special, with its own grammatical, semantic and syntactical idiosyncrasies. Accordingly, learning a foreign or "alien" language means simultaneously to learn something about that language and also to learn much about one's own language. However, Litt goes even further, and in doing so, follows the integrative, totalizing dynamic of the Hegelian dialectic of mentioned above: Learning a second language, Litt argues, can be tantamount to overcoming its foreignness. Through learning and reflection, as Litt would have it, one can come to "know" a second language with the intimacy and familiarity with which one knows one's mother tongue. Learning a second language, Litt continues, not only illuminates both languages, but can also shed light on the "objective spirit" of language "in itself"—as a manifestation of that objective spirit which is transcendent of both the individual and their time: The "objective spirit" of language becomes "wed" to the individual undergoing *Bildung* and to his mother tongue in such a way that that "the general" is truly manifest in the particular and the individual. This bold construction of the philosophy of identity guarantees that in the final end, the self, as well as the other and alien, are made structurally identical.

In these neo-humanistic accounts, alienness thus appears only as a transitional, temporary phenomenon. Universality and generality has logical precedence over individuality and particularity. If one translates this model of language learning as a whole to the process of *Bildung*, then one can say the following: *Bildung* in its essence succeeds when one's own goal and that which is alien are conjoined to a common purpose. And this purpose is itself the fundament of the subjective and the individual. With this guarantee of identity, *Bildung*, however, loses its individual and processual character. This character consists in the fact that new experiences of the alien do not complete themselves in some form of finalized, general knowledge. Whoever looks at intercultural learning and communications processes, for example in their historical manifestation in the European colonization of the alien or foreign world since the 15th and 16th centuries, will be shocked at their violence and destructive power. In the name of the so-called universalism of European cultural and religious understandings, that which is other and alien was violently "appropriated" and "understood," nearly to the point of obliteration. This occurred with the help of ever more refined methods of understanding the alien, and of translating the languages of so-called primitives into European language-systems—all under the aegis of political and strategic goals. In this historical context, knowledge of the alien became—as Foucault has shown in his genealogical studies—a question of sheer authority and power, in which identity is created through the forceful reduction and levelling of everything that is different and heterogeneous.[18]

But it is also possible to look at *Bildung* from a different perspective—one that emphasizes the limits of integrating knowledge and reducing others to the terms of the self. In this sense, *Bildung* appears not so much as a process of "becoming oneself" as one of becoming alien and other through the encounter with the other. *Bildung* in this sense is not a process of centering consciousness, but of de-centering it. It is only when students experience the inevitable limits of knowledge of that which is alien and other that they are able to remain truly open and curious. In this sense, the experience of coming to terms with a foreign language and culture is marked by the awareness that one cannot simply appropriate it as a whole, and that one cannot become familiar with it in the same way that one is familiar with one's mother tongue and own culture. Among other things, such an awareness is necessitated by the pre-reflexive and pre-predicative roots in which the student has been born and raised, before he or she can even identify "language" as an explicit theme. Put paradoxically, children can speak before they are conscious of language itself. If later, through conscious processes, children learn a foreign language, they are then confronted, through means both methodological and didactic in nature, with a linguistic system which remains in a certain sense "artificial," and in no way shares the self-evidence and fluid expressivity of one's own mother tongue. In learning a new language, the learner is also in a certain way also dispossessed of it.

This is not unusual and applies to many processes of learning and *Bildung* in complex societies. One can see this in all its intricacy and systematic interconnection not directly through the senses, but through theoretically abstract, didactic and methodological knowledge. Such knowledge is not simply a reflection of reality. It is something else, since it can be "knowledge" only in an "artificial way"—a knowledge which refers to a reality which itself cannot be wholly absorbed into knowledge. Remaining outside of and in many ways alienated from this reality, knowledge in this modern and post-Hegelian sense is principally perspectival. This means that other knowledge is always a possibility, but not a matter of necessity. Such knowledge is an integral part of the contingent, historical mode of experience in critical modernity. Knowledge in this sense is always "critical" knowledge, a knowledge of differences, indexed according to degrees of otherness, alienness and uncertainty.

The Problem of Pedagogical Understanding of the Other and the Alien

Thus far, this brief, recuperative recasting of *Bildung* has made it clear that experiences associated with *Bildung* cannot complete themselves. They necessarily come up against internal limits in the form of the alien and other that cannot be integrated. To consider this further, I now turn to the pedagogical understanding of the child and adolescent. The citation from Langeveld provided at the outset of this paper offers an important point of entry to such an understanding. Adults, as Langeveld describes, see children in a manner that is only abstract or schematic. Professional pedagogues especially are subject to this kind of dangerous blindness, since they work with a multiplicity of models and theories—for example, with psychological models of development, or with concepts of socialization and sociology generally.[19] The results of such schematization and systematization are not necessarily immediately obvious. These systems operate in a realm of the general that is beyond the individuality of the child, and they often reveal a deterministic picture of humankind, one in which there is little room for childhood creativity, inventiveness and spontaneity. The child then is and remains that which is alien, that which is other and which is not thematized in analytical terms. In this sense, as an object of theoretical-reflexive thought, the child eludes the practice of identification and therefore also of ready theoretical access. Experienced practitioners and theoreticians observe the absence of such means of access and lament the misunderstandings that result. But how could such access be gained?

The traditional human science pedagogies in Germany[20] readily make one aware of the limits of pedagogical understanding and action. These pedagogies and theories extend well beyond the "proto"-humanism of Comenius and the neo-humanism of von Humboldt. They are strongly influenced, for example, by understandings of ethics and individuality articulated by Kant, by the hermeneutics of Schleiermacher[21] and Gadamer,[22] and include approaches ranging from second-wave cybernetics to phenomenology. The limits of pedagogical understanding and action are articulated in many of the theories and approaches using different arguments and models of understanding, and these betray different degrees of radicalism. Here are two examples, with brief discussions of how each sheds different light on the child as other or alien:

- Theories of pedagogy and of the subject in the Kantian transcendental philosophical tradition emphasize the indissoluble pedagogical antimony between education and freedom.[23] These theories are based on the model of the individual as a citizen of two worlds. On the one hand, the individual is a natural, animalistic being, driven by need. Child and adult alike are servant to causal-deterministic processes such as feelings, motivations and requirements—determined as if by something alien within them. The business of education is to counteract, control and tame these animal determinations through discipline, breeding and cultivation. On the other hand, humans are also intelligent and free beings, and thus capable of practical and reasonable self-determination. Of logical necessity, this rationality, and the ethical autonomy associated with it, are both absolute and *a priori*. This means that these characteristics actually cannot be affected through education, which always is to some extent an exercise in coercion, and therefore a form of determination-through-others (rather than determination through one's self). Pedagogical thought and action in the Kantian tradition is intrinsically paradoxical: The beginning of education marks the end of the freedom of the subject. But such education is also the precondition for regaining this freedom. From the viewpoint of those engaged in pedagogical activity, such activity is limited to exercising its influence over human nature, over the realm of human wants and needs. Understood as a means of becoming human, pedagogy is necessarily deterministic and quasi-technological. But this is precisely what pedagogy does *not* want to be. To again invoke Hegel, the pedagogue can be said to suffer from an unhappy consciousness: she wants to act, even though such activity is impossible. She wants to reach a goal that by its very definition must elude her.[24]

- Another limitation of human science approaches to pedagogy, which they have in common with traditional metaphysical and Christian conceptions of the individual is the idea that the individual is created in God's likeness.[25] From this follows the corollary that the ethical and moral relationship between the individual and their God is to be free from others' influence. Not only is this relationship exempt from external influence, but in some senses, it is beyond even the internal influence of the individual him or herself. For "*Bildung*" in this sense is a "gift" from God, an act of grace on the part of humanity's divine "other."[26] From the perspective of the development of personal morality and conscience, this gift is a particular kind of external determination, which "calls" the self in its true selfhood. We still say we are "called" to a profession or role, as if our development toward it were ordained by some higher power. What emerges from this line of thought is a model of *Bildung* that is, in effect, dis-integrative: Being and becoming one's self is, in the depths of the person, a process of becoming other. The Judeo-Christian edict against idols or graven images underscores this: The "becoming other" of the person, whose soul has been created in the image of God, cannot itself be presented imagistically. The pre-figuration, the goal of human development, in other words, must not be specified. The movement of human *Bildung* thus remains a search without a final known goal. In the sense of a simple unambiguous determination, pedagogy never reaches its goal. The last and authentic goal of pedagogy, of the work of *Bildung*, is the self-determination and self-becoming of the individual—a goal that remains a sacred secret. As such, this final purpose ultimately remains at a distance from the efforts of the most earnest pedagogue. Again, this leads to a paradox: Pedagogy is most effective precisely when it has least effect.

Is *Bildung* and education therefore ultimately and unavoidably limited to just what individuals themselves can achieve? Is *Bildung* necessarily limited to self-*Bildung* and self-education? Even further, is education robbed of its goal-oriented, instrumental or even technological character—so readily expressed through terms like "objectives" and "outcomes?" Alienness, as articulated by the likes of Langeveld could not confirm such conclusions more forcefully. They find further confirmation in the general pedagogical tradition of the human sciences. Like the Judeo-Christian interdiction against graven images, this pedagogical tradition does not subscribe to an objective ideal of *Bildung* or concept of culture. As a result, it does not seek to act directly upon the student in a direct, causal sense—unlike, for example, empirical-scientific theories of education. In this pedagogical tradition, the teacher or adult generally serves as an example, the representative of the dominant culture for the child. But this exemplification and representation works through an appeal to morality, rather than through practical manipulation. Furthermore, this tradition underscores that the child is a being who, in the future, will be self-determining. Consequently, the child undergoing *Bildung* should take learning, and those tasks associated with it, into his or her own hands. A non-empirical, axiological model of the Kantian duty to one's self then takes the place of a causal model of pedagogical effects. This duty to one's self can be introduced through "diluted" empirical models of cause and effect (such as pre-personal processes of habituation) or even through coercion. Either path can be taken to address the aforementioned Kantian paradox between freedom and necessity.

Whatever way related pedagogical understandings are refined empirically and whatever way expectations for education are coordinated using ever increasing developmental understandings of moral, cognitive and social competencies—at least in the development of leading models of pedagogical understanding—the difference between children and adults remains.[27] In the context of this pedagogical orientation, this set of concerns is often expressed in the notion that education requires a balance of risk and trust [see Chapter Eight]. Risk and trust need to be balanced by the educator, who does not know what the child will ultimately make of his or her pedagogical efforts. Risk and trust refer to the uncertainty and danger inherent in educational engagement. These are not contingent, but necessary modes of educational action and behavior. Since the autobiographical processes of *Bildung* does not reflect direct causal relations, the pedagogue must *risk* action that will have unknown effects and must *trust* that its effects are ultimately positive.

Such understandings from the human sciences end up emphasizing the difference between the generations [see Chapter Three]. But in the final end such a pedagogy of the human sciences is based on an optimistic view of the relationship between the generations. Alienness is an important theme in this pedagogy, of which Langeveld is a prominent proponent. But alienness is not amplified dramatically when the goal of education is taken to be the integration of the young into the continuities and traditions of earlier generations. The aforementioned optimism emphasizes the *resolution* of any difference and alienness that might separate the generations. It assumes that this is overcome through the integrative work performed on or by the young.

Alienness is given still more dramatic expression in other variations of German pedagogy. It is an important factor not only in the process of building understanding between generations, it is often a virulent driving force in an individual's life-history. It is a part of one's relationship to oneself. At certain moments, individuals encounter themselves as alien; everyone is in important aspects of his or her existence an unknown being. Siegfried Bernfeld, one of the first German psychoanalysts and Marxist educational theorists to gain prominence after the First World War,[28] provides a powerful description of how intergenerational alienness emerges in the relationship between educator and child: Regardless of their professionalized status, the roles of the educator and teacher have something to do with a peculiar professional deformation, with an unavoidable incompetence. When encountering any one child, the educator actually has a mostly unnoticed and little considered relationship with *two* children: with the concrete child before her, and with the recollection of the child she once was—the repressed and damaged "inner child," so to speak. Of course, Bernfeld developed this diagnosis in the context the repressive and neurotic suffering of the child in the authoritarian-bourgeois patriarchal families and society in turn-of-the-century Vienna. Such a society was thoroughly repressive. The psychological dynamic with which it is associated is at once powerfully effective, yet ultimately inaccessible to rationality. It renders impotent all moral and professional-ethical attempts to engender respect for the individuality of the child—or it makes such attempts appear only as ideological euphemisms for what is actually a coercive relationship. The concrete interaction between the educator and the child leads the educator, against her will, to undertake some form of revenge or compensation for that which she, as a child, had suffered at the hands of her parents and then herself repressed.

A psychological projection of the child inserts itself in front of the concrete child as he or she is encountered by the teacher or educator. This image is, in a sense, alien in different ways to both child and teacher. The pedagogue actually has nothing to do with the concrete child; the child as such remains foreign to the pedagogue. At the same time, when the child acts impulsively or unconsciously, they also remain alien to the unenlightened pedagogue. A pedagogy of good intentions and good will is, in this sense, made suspect and fundamentally de-legitimated. Anti-authoritarian and anti-pedagogical thought[29] find in such a psychoanalytic construct of alienness their subversive well-spring. But regardless of how they are phrased, there still are no answers to a number of questions that follow from the insights of Bernfeld and others: How much are normalizing or idealizing constructions of psychoanalysis themselves to blame for the desultory projections and compulsions of the pedagogical act? And how does psychoanalysis exempt not only pedagogy, but *itself* from this fatal involvement with childhood—an involvement which is so important in its "diagnosis" of pedagogy as a kind of symptom? And does such a diagnosis of compulsive alienness of the educator not also mean that this alienness is only due to insufficient psychoanalytic knowledge—which means that it can also be fundamentally undone?

Limits of Pedagogical Understanding—the Child as Alien

By way of a conclusion, it is worth looking at a much more radical pedagogical version of alienness. It also has to do with the generative relationship between adult and child invoked by Langeveld. This is given rich expression in a literary description written by someone in the process of becoming a father:

> These eyes should never be your measure, and when you experience me through such a judging glance, then I beg you …to forget me. You should penetrate behind such eyes, which are fixed on the past, which would reduce your being as a child to a mere developmental phase, to a mere preparatory moment in order to achieve a more comprehensive view of the world….[30]

Here, a father effectively radicalizes the statement of Langeveld cited above. He promises *not* to assimilate his child to what is already systematized, known, familiar or clichéd. In a sense, the father imposes upon himself the Biblical command against graven images, against prefigurations of the ideal. But in more contemporary terms, this idealization, reduction and normalization are nearly impossible to avoid in a society where there are forms of expertise, expert diagnoses and expert knowledge for nearly every event and sphere of life. But is it not the case that every item of knowledge which has been established by experts has not already effectively expired by the time it is applied? Does not the fixed character of such knowledge lie precisely in robbing events in the present of their open horizon, of their character as real, unfolding events? A child is born, and in the judging or measuring eyes of every "well-informed" adult, it is no longer just *that* "concrete child there," but an absolutely new beginning in the world, a new human and an alien in relation to the existing order. Instead, from the perspective of such an adult, the child is integrated into a pre-existing frame of reference for normal development, of family traditions, of scientific knowledge and of everyday knowledge. That which is new is ordered according to pre-existing "knowledge-bases" and "recipes," to use the terminology of Alfred Schütz, a theorist of everyday ways of knowing. The child is thus made understandable and treatable. In this way, the child, before it can even attempt to engage in self-determination as an independent social actor, is already determined, and has had many of its unforeseeable possibilities eliminated. The child is already "old" before it has a chance to be young.

All of this leads to some important, general questions: Does the interrelationship of successive generations follow a measure of continuity, or is the intergenerational process principally one of *dis*continuity? Does not each new generation, as something radically new, have the chance to live its own life, a life that remains inescapably alien for the parents' generation—even though it has its origins in the parents and their generation? Is it not the insuperable limit of all pedagogical action and planning that it never really has the future at its disposal?

The French philosopher Emmanuel Levinas (1969) developed a corresponding model of discontinuous generational procession under the rubric "fecundity."[31] As Levinas explains, the future of the son is not the future of the father. Discontinuity in the generations ensures that history does not forcibly repeat itself. Instead, it ensures that the unpredictable occurs. "My child is a stranger…but a stranger who is not only mine, for he *is* me. He is me a stranger to myself [sic]" (p. 267). The son continues the time of the father, which the father, as a mortal, does not himself actually have. But the son achieves this continuation in his own way, in that he breaks with the time of the father. In this sense, the being of the father is not a being that is indivisible and unchanging in its substance. Instead, through a strange kind of intergenerational "transubstantiation," it remains open to change in its essence. The father is continued through the child. He is, through the child, an other which continues the father's time as a future that is unavailable to him. "In existing itself there is a multiplicity and a transcendence. In this transcendence the 'I' is not swept away, since the son is not me; and yet I *am* my son. The fecundity of the 'I' is its very transcendence."[32] The fecundity involved in the production of children brings about a discontinuous unity of the many. As a result, the responsibility of the parents for the future of their children suffers a radical break. How can they answer for their children if they do not also have at their disposal the time that belongs to their children? Fecundity has a particular structure: Fundamental to it is an inability that is individual, and a possibility that is dispersed, that cannot be the initiative of a single self. In this sense, children are destiny for their parents, but the destiny of a given child is not that of the parent. In a radical sense, parents cannot take *any* responsibility for their children, since they do not have the future of the child available to them. Should they attempt to appropriate this responsibility without a view to the difference that separates the generations, then they lose their ethical justification and grounding. In other words, in this structure, parents lose respect for the otherness of the other, which expresses itself in the generative alienness of their own children.

From the perspective of Levinas' philosophy of the human other, alienness in pedagogy acquires a new and productive meaning. It is not merely the boundary or limit of pedagogical understanding and action, but much more. It is a discontinuity and breach between the generations which virtually holds open the relationship between children and their parents, between educators and students. Not determining, and not being able to decide that which children themselves are, this alienness opens up the actual possibility of pedagogy. It is as a result of this possibility that parents, those who are ostensibly closest to their children, are rendered alien to themselves through their children. And children are rendered alien in the eyes of their parents. It is only in this way that generativity and plurality is to be thought of in the context of pedagogy, which otherwise so easily shuts itself off in adult perspectives on action and meaning.

Notes

1. Husserl, E. (1960). *Cartesian meditations: An introduction to phenomenology*. Martinus Nijhoff, pp. 92–98.
2. Translated by N. Friesen.
3. Langeveld, M. J. (1966). *Die Schule als Weg des Kindes*. Westermann, p. 31.
4. "Lifeworld" refers to the taken-for-granted "intersubjective background understandings" that are a part of our everyday engagement in the world and with each other. From: Harrington, A. (2006). Lifeworld. *Theory Culture Society 23*, 341–343. [Trans.]
5. The fundamental considerations regarding the theme of alienness as presented from a phenomenological perspective are addressed in Waldenfels, B. (2011). *Phenomenology of the alien: Basic concepts*. Northwestern University Press. [Trans.]
6. This theme is also explored in: Waldenfels, B. (1996). *Order in the twilight*. Ohio University Press.

7   "Pre-reflexive" and "pre-predicative" refer to those forms of awareness that are most immediate and least affected by thought and reflection. [Trans.]
8   In some parts of Germany, the first day of school for a child is a celebration in which the family, even the extended family, partakes. [Trans.]
9   Lippitz, W., & Levering, B. (2002). And now you are getting a teacher with such a long name. *Research and Theory in Education, 18*, 205–213.
10 Langeveld, M. J. (1966). *Die Schule*. Westermann.
11 See: von Humboldt, W. (1793/1999). Theory of Bildung. In: Hopmann, S., Westbury, I., & Riquarts, K. *Teaching as a reflective practice: The German didaktik tradition* (pp. 57–61). Routledge. [Trans.]
12 Elias, N. (2000). *The civilizing process*. Blackwell, p. 72.
13 Scheibe, W. (1969). *Die reformpädagogische Bewegung*. Beltz. See also the concrete studies of life-world experience of children and of scholastic-artistic worlds of experience in Rumpf, H. (1986). For more about the model of dialectical experience as self-*Bildung* and its criticism, see Buck, 1984, pp. 155–230.
14 von Humboldt, W. (1999). Theory of *Bildung*. In S. Hopmann, I. Westbury, & K. Riquarts (Eds.), *Teaching as a reflective practice: The German didaktik tradition* (pp. 57–61). Routledge. p. 58. [Trans.]
15 The master-servant or master-slave dialectic refers to "a kind of primal, historical scene" based on Hegel's assumption that our self-consciousness is fulfilled only when we "are recognized and affirmed" by others. In this primal dialectic, two individuals "fight to *compel* recognition from each other:" the "servant" is the one who "loses," who chooses his life over honor and recognition from the other. The master, on the other hand, attains a higher consciousness, having "triumphed over his 'instinct for self-preservation.'" (Hegel goes on to explain that it is the master, though, who ultimately loses in his isolation from the world, and that the servant achieves superior self-consciousness through his engagement with it. Magee, G. A. [2010]. *The Hegel dictionary*. Continuum, pp. 140–141.) [Trans.]
16 Objective spirit is the expression of those things that are "within" us (i.e. "subjective spirit") in the outer world, especially in areas such as morality and politics. [Trans.]
17 Litt, T. (1965). *Führen oder Wachsenlassen*. Klett.
18 Foucault, M. (1983). The subject and power. In: H.L. Dreyfus. *Michel Foucault: Beyond structuralism and power*. (2nd ed; pp. 208-226). University of Chicago Press; Todorov, T. (1999). *The conquest of America: The question of the other*. Oklahoma University Press.
19 Gstettner, P. (1979). *Die Eroberung des Kindes durch die Wissenschaft. Aus der Geschichte der Disziplinierung*. Reinbek bei Hamburg: Rowohlt.
20 Nohl (Chapters Four and Five) is one of, if not *the* primary representatives of this tradition, with Bollnow (Chapter Eight) frequently being included as well. See: Friesen, N. (2020). "Education as a *Geisteswissenschaft*:" An Introduction to Human Science Pedagogy. *Journal of Curriculum Studies. 52*(3), 307–322. https://doi.org/10.1080/00220272.2019.1705917 [Trans.]
21 See Chapter Three in this book. [Trans.]
22 See: Gadamer, H. G. (2006). *Truth and method 2nd ed.*. Continuum.
23 Lippitz is referring to the following passage in Kant's Lectures on Pedagogy, well known in German pedagogy:
    One of the biggest problems of education is how one can unite submission under lawful constraint with the capacity to use one's freedom. For constraint is necessary. How do I cultivate

freedom under constraint? I shall accustom my pupil to tolerate a constraint of his freedom, and I shall at the same time lead him to make good use of his freedom. (p. 447)

See: Kant, I. (1803/2007). Lectures on Pedagogy. In G. Zöller, & R. B. Louden (Eds.), *Anthropology, history and education* (pp. 434–485). Cambridge University Press. For pedagogical interpretations of this aspect of Kant's theory, see also Ricken, N. (1999). *Subjektivität und Kontingenz*. Königshausen & Neumann, pp. 61–104. [Trans.]

24 Hegel describes the "unhappy consciousness" as being the result of the human desire for recognition by others. It arises when humans try to meet this desire by defining themselves in relation to "an empty, abstract ideal which they have projected into the heavens." Magee, G. A. (2010). *The Hegel dictionary*. Continuum, pp. 234. [Trans.]

25 Meyer-Drawe, K. (1999). Die Not der Lebenskunst. Phänomenologische Überlegungen zur Bildung als Gestaltung exzentrische Lebensverhältnisse. Fünf Überlegungen. In C. Dietrich & H.-R. Müller (Eds.), *Bildung und Emanzipation*, (pp. 147–154). Juventa.

26 *Bildung* has as its root "Bild" the German word for image, as in "made in God's image." [Trans.]

27 Lippitz, W. (2003). Selbständige Kinder im Kontext ihrer Lebenswelt. In W. Lippitz, (Ed.), *Differenz und Fremdheit* (pp. 129–164). Peter Lang.

28 Bernfeld, S. (1973). *Sisyphus or the Limits of Education*. University of California Press.

29 These two terms refer to a movement in West Germany in the 1970s and 1980s which rejected all forms of formal education as manipulative and oppressive, as an affront to children's rights. For an English-language example, see Bereiter, C. (1973). Must We Educate? *The Phi Delta Kappan, 55*(4), 233–236. [Trans.]

30 Kolleritsch, A. (1986). Lieber Sohn Julian! In: H. Haidler (Ed.), An mein Kind. Briefe von Vätern. DTV.

31 Levinas, E. (1969). *Totality and infinity: An essay on exteriority*. Duquesne University Press.

32 Levinas. *Totality and infinity*, p. 277.

CHAPTER TEN

J. Zirfas: Pedagogical Tact: Ten Theses

Editor's Introduction

Jörg Zirfas (1961–) has done as much as any contemporary German scholar to renew interest in the pedagogical phenomenon of tact. Not only did he publish the text translated here in 2012, he also produced an edited collection on *Tact and Tactlessness* in the same year. He has since co-authored a book-length study of pedagogical tact (together with Daniel Burghardt) titled *Pedagogical Tact: A Formula for Educational Studies* (2019),[1] the first book-length study on pedagogical tact in German since Jakob Muth's *Pedagogical Tact: Study of a Contemporary Form of Educational and Instructional Engagement* (see: Chapter Six).

Zirfas' "Pedagogical tact: Ten Theses" presents a contemporary reexamination and "re-grounding" of the phenomenon of pedagogical tact—one that takes J.F. Herbart's seminal account of tact (Chapter Two) as its basis. Like Lippitz before him, Zirfas takes a critical perspective and provides a historical reconstruction of tact in Western thought. In doing so, his essay serves as both a refresh and a recap of the many names and sources featured (especially earlier) in this volume, including Herbart, Schleiermacher, Nohl and Muth.

For example, unlike Muth (Chapter Six), who in discussing tact speculates that "educators of earlier centuries" may well have "acted in an 'unreflected' pedagogically tactful way" (p. 88), the entire possibility of being tactful for Zirfas is historically and culturally specific. The possibility of "tact" does not stretch back countless centuries but began only some 200 years ago: It is only "at the end of the 18th century," Zirfas explains, that "the well-being of the individual in society became increasingly dependent on the tact of the other person" (p. 179). The end of the 1800s brought with it the end of the remnants of Europe's feudal order; it ushered in a time that we can recognize as broadly contemporary with our own: One in which an individual's fate, their habitual ways of interacting, speaking and thinking were no longer predetermined by an inflexible, centuries-old social order. Whether born a peasant or an aristocrat, individuals were no longer destined simply to recapitulate the lives of their parents and grandparents. Making one's way in a world of new and changing social configurations required a new sensitivity and reserve. Zirfas argues that similar circumstances applied in education as well, making a particularly *pedagogical* form of tact necessary: The "specific question of pedagogical tact," as Zirfas says, "could only play a role in an age in which certain social and pedagogical conceptions of order were in decline and other forms of sensitivity were being developed" (p. 179).

Zirfas finds the "*locus classicus* for the theme of tact in pedagogy… in Herbart's first lectures on pedagogy from 1802"—a lecture which also happened to fall early in the decisively modern European era just mentioned. According to Zirfas, the "essential meaning" to be taken from this introductory lecture is its designation of tact specifically as "a medium" or a "principle of mediation" (p. 181). Tact is, in Herbart's own words, a "link intermediate between theory and practice… a quick judgment and decision that is not habitual and eternally uniform" (p. 32). Nonetheless, Zirfas qualifies some of the characteristics Herbart ascribes to tact: Tact is time-sensitive (involving "quick judgment"), Zirfas agrees, but it can also proceed with the slowness and patience that children often require; tact is not to be understood "only in terms of rationality" (i.e. Herbart's "judgment and decision"), Zirfas emphasizes, for it is "characterized not only by cognitive" aspects but also by ones "of sense, emotion and will." Zirfas also points out that tact is not just a matter of the "true demands of the individual case," but that it is also an attempt to reconcile these "with theoretical or normative requirements as well as with social expectations" (p. 182). Finally, Zirfas agrees with Herbart that there is "a preparation for the [tactful] art of education by way of [the] science [of education]:" "An educator who has not been formally educated cannot be tactful," Zirfas concludes (p. 188). For experience with both the theory and practice of education are needed in order to gain insight into "the emotional states of children, into child-oriented, curricular and instructional 'structurings' of time, [to acquire] capacities for sensual awareness, and a capacity for sensing subjective perceptions" (p. 188).

Zirfas goes on to explore the question of tact in general and pedagogical tact in particular by addressing a range of theoretical concerns. The most important of these have already been considered in various ways in earlier chapters of this volume. For example, Zirfas echoes Wilfried Lippitz (Chapter Nine, pp. 166–167), in considering the significance of Kant's pedagogical paradox: *"How can freedom be cultivated through constraint?"* Zirfas' point is not to respond directly to Kant's question, but to see the paradox to which it gives expression as a part of the paradoxical nature of pedagogical tact itself: "Pedagogical tact remains embedded in this pedagogical paradox: of needing to encourage people to behave in a way that is self-determined, and of their simultaneous inability to achieve this on their own" (p. 184).

But the paradox of freedom and constraint is only the start of the multiple paradoxes and contradictions which Zirfas sees as converging around pedagogical tact. His "Ten Theses"—and more explicitly in his book on tact with Burghardt—take the reader back to Schleiermacher (Chapter Three) and his own irresolvable pedagogical paradoxes and tensions. (Examples of these familiar from Schleiermacher include the tension between older and younger generations, between theory and practice and between the present and the future in the life of the child). "Pedagogical professionalism," Zirfas asserts, "can be understood as the subjective ability and willingness to tactfully balance pedagogical paradoxes" (p. 192; see also Friesen & Osguthorpe, 2018). And Zirfas includes in these paradoxes and contradictions "the promotion of personality and collectivity," the "transmission and innovation (of contents, methods and attitudes), the tension between general norms and individual people and situations" (p. 191).

The idea of a relation that is "pedagogical"—what Zirfas simply refers to as "the pedagogical relationship of the educator to the one being educated"—finally returns as an explicit theme in this article: The 9th out of Zirfas' 10 theses simply states: "The determining moments of pedagogical tact are principles of relation" (p. 189). This is followed by a listing of characteristics that contains some items that come very close to those outlined by Herman Nohl in 1933. Zirfas refers, for example, to the idea of "restraint," of "limiting oneself for the sake of the other" (echoing Nohl's definition of tact as the "most refined expression" of the educator's "singular distance to [the] …student;" Chapter Five, p. 81). Zirfas also includes the "observance of developmental and temporal structures" (p. 189)—which surely connects to what both Schleiermacher and Nohl say about the tension between present and future, between the child "as he is" and "his educational goal, the child's ideal" (p. 80).

Finally, Zirfas closes this chapter—and thus also this volume itself—by returning to the question of alterity: of otherness, and also (by extension) the alien itself. This occurs when he defines pedagogical tact as nothing less than "the response to the riddle of the other" (p. 192). Zirfas then hastens to add that tact in this sense "is not the *solution* to the riddle, but merely an educational response in which a specific responsibility for the protection and promotion of the other and of oneself is expressed" (p. 192; emphasis added). It is difficult to imagine a more fitting conclusion for this volume. For in defining tact in this way, Zirfas returns full circle to Pestalozzi's founding pedagogical concern with the otherness of the child, with their minutest feelings and joys, and with the question of how these might serve as the basis for an inspiring educative relation with the adult.

References/Recommended Reading

Friesen, N. & Osguthorpe, R. (2018). Tact and the pedagogical triangle: The authenticity of teachers in relation. *Teaching and Teacher Education, 70,* 255–264. http://dx.doi.org/10.1016/j.tate.2017.11.023

Herbart, J.F. (1802/2022). Introductory Lecture to Students in Pedagogy. (Chapter Two).

J. Zirfas: Pedagogical Tact. Ten Theses[2]

Preliminary Observations

[...]

This text assumes that pedagogical tact is required by the educator, but not by the child or student, i.e. that the question of pedagogical tact is a question of a tactful upbringing and *education*.[3] The term "education," in turn, designates those practices that provide the conditions for enabling people to develop towards a certain desired action and disposition. Such practices, it should be noted, may be more personal, intentional and direct or they may be more broadly and socially functional and indirect. Education is an influence or intervention for the purpose of promoting development. The goal of education in the modern age[4] is the independence of the individual in all practices of human life (economic, political, social, aesthetic, etc.). In short: In modernity, education is the *audacious demand* (*Zumutung;* or the request, requirement) for *maturity*.

This article attempts to present and discuss aspects of the historical and theoretical background of pedagogical tact, the dimensions of its meaning, and its forms and functions. And it does so in a perhaps exaggeratedly pointed manner through 10 theses.

The discussion of pedagogical tact is a modern one. It goes hand in hand with a change in the pedagogical relation between teacher and student that started in the 18th century.

To exaggerate, as long as it was assumed that the child had to be oriented completely to the authority of the educator, who in turn embodied the one true and correct order, tactlessness in education was, strictly speaking, not possible.

This first thesis does not claim that until the 18th century there were no norms for and debates regarding the correct behavior of educators. Indeed, there is a long history of discussion and debate concerning their moral qualities. This thesis claims, however, that the specific question of pedagogical tact could only play a role in an age in which certain social and pedagogical conceptions of order were in decline and other forms of sensitivity were being developed. So it is perhaps no coincidence that it was Voltaire who seems to have used the term "tact" (*"un autre tact"*[5]) for the first time in 1776. It is at the end of the 18th century when the well-being of the individual in society became increasingly dependent on the tact of the *other* person—i.e. "on the protection of the more vulnerable, which the stronger of the two imposes on himself voluntarily."[6] And it is at the same time that the question of tact becomes increasingly pressing, not only in society but also in pedagogy.

In this sense, it seems quite plausible that the development of the concept of pedagogical tact occurred during the time of the educational Enlightenment.[7] This was a time when a wide range of pedagogical questions emerged—including ones about the happiness of the child (which could certainly still be instrumentalized for the interests of society), about social utility, about the development of the independence and the autonomy of all people, about what the most non-violent and reasonable education might be, about the promotion of interests and learning capabilities, and also about an amelioratory education for the poor. Theodor W. Adorno sums this up:

> For tact has its precise historical hour. It is the one in which the bourgeois individual [*Individuum*] rids itself of absolutist compulsion. Free and solitary, it stood for itself, while the forms of hierarchical respect and devotion developed by absolutism, divested of their economic foundation and their threatening force, are still extant enough to make living together inside privileged groups bearable.[8]

It would be a worthwhile project to trace what Adorno is describing within the incipient emancipatory impulses of Enlightenment education. For this education aimed at promoting the autonomy of the individual and thus also the autonomy of broad, underprivileged strata of the population; but at the same time, Enlightenment education was also aimed at disciplining and channeling individual and collective self-development within the confines of existing social hierarchies.[9]

In the Early Modern Period, with the Renaissance and Humanism, New Standards of Cultivation and Thresholds of Pain and Suffering were Established. And According to Everything we Know from the History of Education, Educators Did Not Always Do Justice to these

Pedagogical tact could have implicitly played a role in related debates; however, to my knowledge this form of tact in this sense is not explicitly addressed until the early 19th century.

During the Reformation and Humanism (1500–1650), the problem of bodily conduct and comportment became so important that even humanists of the rank of Erasmus of Rotterdam (1469–1536) took up the topic. His short book "*De civilitate morum puerilium*" is important not only for the history of education but also for the history of the civilizing process as a whole.[10] For after its initial appearance in early in the 16th century, no fewer than 30 new editions quickly entered circulation. These eventually totaled about 130, signaling the effect of this text throughout Europe.

According to Norbert Elias,[11] it is precisely this work by Erasmus that brought the long-familiar notion of *civilité*—in the form of modest and respectable (physical) behavior—to society in a form that was both specific and far-reaching.[12] For in the historical shift in social hierarchies from a knightly feudal to one that was courtly and absolutist, and in the associated establishment of a new upper class, new forms of living together were needed. Behavior that is more restricted and that gave greater consideration to others was increasingly required of the individual. As a result, the question of good behavior overall becomes increasingly urgent.[13] In view of the political and religious turbulence of the time, Erasmus and other humanists believed that a reconciliation of people with each other could only be achieved through an education of the spirit and the heart, through a more personal tone, through growing social sensitivity, and through more careful observation of people and a greater understanding of one's fellow human beings.

Although these discourses are related to tact, they are not included in this discussion of specifically *pedagogical* tact for two reasons. Firstly, debates about politeness, decency, etiquette, civility, etc.—as well as the behavioral demands associated with them—have a much stronger relationship to morality, i.e. to lived and required socio-ethical behaviors, than does tact itself. Pedagogical tact, meanwhile focuses on the (direct) interpersonal relationship of one or more people with each other.[14] Secondly, as is paradigmatic for Erasmus, but also of the pedagogy of the Renaissance and the Baroque, education towards *politesse* is often understood as a kind of education of oneself in becoming a polite person. But our concern here is not with such education or cultivation of the self by itself.

The Concept of "Pedagogical Tact" in Its Essential Meaning for Pedagogy Goes Back to Johann Friedrich Herbart (1776–1841)[15]

Since Herbart, tact has received more intensive theoretical treatment in pedagogy. The *locus classicus* for the theme of tact in pedagogy can be found in Herbart's first lectures on pedagogy from 1802:

> But for every theorist who puts his theory into practice in particular cases—and who does not proceed with pedantic slowness ... a link intermediate between theory and practice involuntarily inserts itself. By this I mean a certain tact, a quick judgment and decision that is not habitual and eternally uniform. But this tact is unable to boast, as a fully developed theory should, that while remaining deliberately consistent with the rule, it can at the same time answer the true requirements of the individual case.[16]

Pedagogical tact, in other words, is above all a principle of *mediation*. As such, it is marked by (1) its quickness; (2) its rationality (involving "judgment and decision"); (3) its flexibility ("not habitual and eternally uniform"); and (4) its sensitivity to individuality (to "the individual case"). Each of these four qualities assigned to tact by Herbart can be elaborated further.

First, for example, one can emphasize together with Jean-Jacques Rousseau that it is not the *speed* of educational actions that is most important in pedagogy but giving the child *time*.[17] In this sense, a tactful pedagogical judgement or action could be one that does *not* proceed quickly, but slowly and deliberately—in a leisurely way, so to speak. When Herbart speaks of a quick decision above, he is probably looking at pedagogical situations in which a determination has to be made immediately or an action taken in which the pedagogue sees themselves as under pressure to make a decision—a decision that cannot be postponed. Here pedagogical tact comes to their aid, which suggests an immediate choice of goals, methods and attitudes. In her summary of Lazarus' theory of tact from his work on the "Life of the Soul" (1882),[18] Birgit Ofenbach, for example, also refers to the important temporal dimension of tact—to "the speed of one's perception and the speed of one's thought."[19]

Secondly, the relevant literature shows that it is quite controversial to understand (pedagogical) tact only in terms of rationality. Terms that are often used synonymously with "tact," such as sensitivity, sensibility, attention, taste, intimation, (un)adroitness, intuition, etc. indicate that tact can be understood above all as emotional engagement. Hans-George Gadamer sees tact as a taste for the special case, a feeling for the singular.[20] It should be considered to what extent emotional qualities have always been included in rational considerations or to what extent tact is characterized not only by cognitive elements but also by aspects of sense, emotion and will.

Thirdly, again in the tradition of Herbart, an involuntary tact is anathema to educators.[21] For many, tact which does not know how to commit itself to morality, which is not integrated into the "conscious recognition of a binding order"[22] degenerates into mere subjectivism and arbitrariness. Does pedagogical tact therefore need to be socio-ethical, normatively bound to pedagogical standards or does it actually rather constitute a form of compensation for these standards? In the pedagogy of the successors of Herbart, tact has been understood above all as pragmatic compensation for a never complete "theory" and for missing technique.[23]

Fourthly and finally, pedagogical tact, as adumbrated in the historical context above and discussed further below, owes its existence to the (pedagogical) "discovery" of individuality in the 18th and 19th centuries. In other words, pedagogical tact is an attempt to do justice to the individual. But that's only half the truth. This is because the "true demands of the individual case" can collide with theoretical or normative requirements as well as with social expectations.

Pedagogical Tact is Simultaneously Independent from Thoughts of the Individuality and Sociality of the Child

The idea of individuality and the radical otherness of the subject did not become significant in education until the 18th century. Above all with neo-humanism[24] *and Romanticism it became the determining element of educational thought. On the one hand the individual should retain his or her distinctiveness, on the other hand he or she should be made socially and morally accessible and compatible.*

Anthropologically understood,[25] behind these considerations stands the figure of a singular, completely unique being. And although this unique being can be compared with other people, they are at the same time radically different and incomparable: *individuum est ineffabile*.[26] Because every human being finds his radical destiny in determining himself individually, pedagogy must react tactfully to individuality in order not to destroy it: "That which is directed towards the individual is what we call tact, a feeling for that which is unbecoming in each of us."[27]

The indeterminacy of the individual can be encountered pedagogically in very different, sometimes contradictory ways: Rousseau, for example, sees the child's nature as originally good, and combines his vision for education with a view of society as being essentially corrupted and corrupting. Immanuel Kant on the other hand sees education as a disciplining of the human being's inherently wild nature. In both cases, though, the indeterminacy of the individual corresponds with education's ultimate goal, the individual's ability for self-determination. In this sense, the rise of the concept of *Bildung*,[28] which owes its current significance to its emergence in the late 18th and early 19th centuries, emphasizes the tactful withdrawal of the educator from the pedagogical process, for it conceives of *Bildung* as above all as self-*Bildung*. The tactful educator, as it were, is the only one who provides the pedagogical framework in which people can educate themselves. Pedagogical tact is a form of indirection that provides the conditions of the possibility of the *Bildung* of oneself.

But modernity is not only an era of the individual; it is a social era as well. This is already suggested by Kant and Enlightenment pedagogy more broadly which demands that the child should not only be disciplined, but also cultivated, civilized and moralized.

That one must do justice both to the individual and to society indicates that pedagogical tact is to be dealt with through paradoxes—an important problematic in and of itself. The other, and perhaps more profound problem is that it seems impossible to actually do justice to the individual within the paradox of individual and society. This problem is expressed, for example, by Helmuth Plessner in outlining the meaning of tact in social situations:

> Tact is the ability to perceive incalculable differences, the ability to comprehend that untranslatable language of appearances which situations and persons in their constellation, in their behavior, and in their physiognomy speak worldlessly according to unfathomable symbols of life.[29]

Tactful pedagogical behavior cannot be specified either on the part of general social theory nor on the part of concrete individuality. As Adorno says: "Tact is the determination of difference. It consists of knowing deviations."[30]

A Decisive Question for Modern Pedagogy is Raised by Kant: "How can freedom be cultivated through constraint?"[31]

Since Kant originally formulated this question, pedagogy has been left with a guilty conscience inasmuch as, on the one hand, it has to intervene in what the child wants and, on the other, it risks hurting the child to achieve its own purposes. In order to guarantee the pedagogical goal of modernity, namely self-determination, one must understand pedagogical tact as a renunciation of the will to implement a specific world view or method of practice: Pedagogical tact is a plea for plurality and heterogeneity.

Modern pedagogy is called upon to act in accordance with the imperative of understanding the human being (more precisely: humankind) "at all times also as an end, and never merely as a means."[32] Here one can first detect an exoneration for education, for a person's instrumentalization seems to be norm, whereas their recognition as an end in themselves is something that is achieved only afterwards—and something that pedagogical action has as its aim. As a result, a required (pedagogical) action is always characterized by two tendencies, a (tactless) instrumentalization and a (tactful) respect of the other. If one connects this with Kant's previous question—how freedom is to be cultivated through coercion—it can be said that Kant does not speak of education in the sense of maintenance (food, entertainment), discipline (child rearing), civilization and moralization, but specifically in the sense of *cultivation*, that is, teaching and instruction—"establishing correct principles, and leading children to understand and accept them."[33] According to Kant, coercion does not result from education, but rather from submission to the *law* of public education, that is to say from the fact that children and the young are required to be educated to independence at all. Thus it is not submission to restraint *per se* that educates man, but the reasoning and making comprehensible of this restraint. For only when one "feels" the coercion of society, according to Kant, can one learn self-preservation and independence. Behind this is the thesis that people can only recognize their freedom in the light of the law: If there were no law as the *ratio cognoscendi*[34] of freedom, one would not accept freedom at all; if there were only laws, there would also be no freedom, but only determinism.

The aim of education in modernity is a paradoxical "symmetrification:" the child should become that which he always has been, namely a free, independent human being. The educator thus has the task of recognizing the child or young person as someone they are not yet and of asking them to do something they cannot yet do.[35]

> Pedagogical tact turns the personal relationship between child and educator into a kind of experimental field in which one can test the potential of the child's autonomy without danger, and the other can test and verify the correctness of their own actions and the validity of their own knowledge in attentive self-reflection.[36]

Pedagogical tact remains embedded in this pedagogical paradox: of needing to encourage people to behave in a way that is self-determined, and of their simultaneous inability to achieve this on their own. This paradox also plays into the flexibility of pedagogical tact. The pedagogue must therefore be tactful in order to promote independence and to not form in the child or student a submissive character. The pedagogue must also be tactful in order to aim at the goal of education, which is the pedagogue's own superfluity.[37] But this also means limiting the sometimes audacious demands that are placed on the maturity of the other and—if necessary—also releasing them from the requirement of such maturity.

Pedagogical Tact is Dependent on the Idea of Education as a Self-negating Relationship of Violence

The history of violence against children is long and sobering: child killings, abuse, exploitation and punishments of all kinds have been the constant companion of education over the centuries. Since the 18th century, education has progressed on the basis of various reform movements. Social, child-centered and other developments increasingly recognize that children have a right to a non-violent upbringing. Compared to other European countries (e.g. Sweden), Germany has taken a relatively long time to codify the child's right to a non-violent education and upbringing. German law now says: "Children have a right to a non-violent upbringing. Physical punishment, mental injury and other degrading measures are inadmissible."

Whether and to what extent there can actually be an education that is non-violent has been debated since then, given that the boundary between violent and non-violent education cannot be clearly drawn. To what extent are bans on television, withholding allowances or other forms of admonition—or even the simple request of an educator—not expressions of pedagogical violence? When such violence takes the form of a restriction of freedom, however, it can be justified within the pedagogical tradition in those cases when the child threatens not only their own independence, but also that of others. On the other hand, if they can assume responsibility for themselves and for others, the person being educated is then regarded as independent and the educational relationship is dissolved. Generally, it can be stated here that in the modern age, educators are required to be at all times as non-violent, respectful, empathic—in short, as tactful—towards students as possible: Pedagogical tact is, as it were, the implicit imperative for the educator in the modern age.

> Above all he who has the power is in danger of losing the measure upon which all nobility and all the beauty of life rests. The discriminating feeling for the right measure is what we call tact. Tact is the real, intrinsic educational tool.[38]

In general, today, tact—even in the broadest social sense—is not associated with striking outwards, but instead with restraint and sensitivity towards the other and also with the protection of the other. These two moments, sensitive restraint and protection, are emphasized by Jacob Muth:

> That sensitivity which characterizes tactfulness is a feeling for the "you" (or thou), for one's fellow human beings, for the singularity and singular rights of the other human being; it is a respect for the final remoteness of the other. [...] And reserve, which the tactful person exercises in engagement with others—as paradoxical as it

may sound—involves an encompassing congruence, since that which is tactful reserves itself for the sake of the other.[39]

Humiliations, insults, intimidation and disrespect for children should be avoided as far as possible in education. Pedagogical tact is a practice of friendliness.

Helmuth Plessner has summed up this connection intersubjectively: "The wisdom of tact: protection of the other for my own sake, protection of myself for the other's sake, is the justification—as paradoxical as it sounds—for the ungrounded interludes of our social life."[40] Although pedagogical discussions about tact refer without exception to the educator, there is a hint here that educators not only have to treat the child tactfully and gently, but that they also protect themselves through their tactful engagement. Indeed, there is a hint that tact represents an intersubjective medium of mutual protection. Niklas Luhmann also touches on this connection in his definition of tact: "Tact is not simply the fulfillment of other people's expectations, but a way of acting, in which A presents himself as the one whom B needs as a partner in order to be the one [that B] wants to present himself to A as."[41]

If one translates these sociological observations into a pedagogical context, it becomes clear that a type of mediation is being addressed in pedagogical tact. This is one, namely, that serves to protect both sides in communicative relationships—in terms of both of their self-presentations, emotionality and individual developmental possibilities. It is also important to point out the difference between the ethos of a lived (unconscious, habitualized) pedagogical tact and a conscious, intentional one—with the latter deliberately set into motion as a result of the unique pedagogical situations that deviate from previous ones.

There are No Rules (Either Theoretical or Practical) for Pedagogical Tact, since Tact Itself Generates (Theoretical) Rules that Make Sense in Practice. How the educator acts or should act in a specific situation cannot be determined in advance.

Does pedagogical tact have specific criteria for its orientation? What does the "appropriateness" of tact mean, or can one speak of an *in*appropriate tact? Is pedagogical tact dependent on certain manners in society and/or on pedagogical or situational requirements? As a rule, (pedagogical) tact is not defined in a very precise sense, and it is precisely the fact that it remains indefinite and indefinable that distinguishes it. One can say that the "essence" of tact is its indeterminability and its openness. Tact is therefore to be understood negatively in a dialectical sense: as restraint or unwillingness to act; or vaguely: a taste for the special case as Gadamer has suggested, a feeling for the singular.

> Being ungrounded is an essential moment of tact. How else does it form the guiding principle of our behavior in situations encountered in everyday life that are effectively "value-equivalent?" In all situations for which there are no reasons to act in an alternative manner, no other moral maxim remains to us.[42]

Tact denotes the fact that we are unable to state any readily available reasons for a particular action.

But even more accurately, tact appears as an irregular or spontaneous ordering principle or as a system for an order that is to intervene in concrete pedagogical situations: Tact cannot be planned; it represents the irregular in the regular.

> Tact is Not Subsumed to the Planning Intention of the Teacher, and Therefore Tactful Action Cannot be Realized in a Pre-planned Educational Operation but it is always only in the unforeseeable situation in which the educator is engaged. […] it appears as dynamic irregularity within static regularity.[43]

The fact that tact is ultimately described as a result of feeling is therefore less a sign of the circumstances of an empathetic or sympathetic relationship than it is of the fact that the judgments and actions expressed via tact cannot be subsumed to completely logical, rational structures—or to those determinable through research.

> *Takt* is dependent on the situation of each moment […]. *Takt* also acts to generate the next situations as it works. […] *Takt* is a motion that continues to form itself and it also forms a boundary by itself. *Takt* is always forming itself by means forming a boundary. Indeed, *Takt* is comparable to skill, because it is polished as it is used.[44]

In this sense, tact must be related to *art*, which is based neither on a technique, nor on *poiesis*,[45] but on concrete practice.[46]

Pedagogical Tact is Not without Prerequisites, since According to Herbart It Can Be Acquired through Engagement with Theory and through Reflection and Experience

Is it possible to train tact, is there a kind of training-in-tact or a pedagogical professionalization of tact—for example, training to develop an awareness of or thoughtfulness for the other? Herbart once again speaks to this:

> There is then—and this is my conclusion—a preparation for the art of education by way of science, a preparation of both one's understanding and one's heart before

beginning one's duties. In other words, there is a way in which the experience that we can obtain only by engaging in our work itself becomes instructive to us. Only in action do we learn the art; only in this way do we acquire tact, aptitude, quickness and dexterity. But even in action, one learns this art only if one has earlier thoughtfully learned the science, made it one's own, attuned oneself through it, and is able to make sense of future experiences through it.[47]

Indeed, according to Herbart, the art of pedagogical tact requires knowledge and forms of judgment that open up possibilities of tactful interaction to the pedagogue. An educator who has not been formally educated cannot be tactful:

> The development of tact depends on the fact that the eye of the practitioner, supported by a formal education, processes the impressions of experience meaningfully for themselves [so that they] can make the right decisions in individual actions and promote structures of learning through experience as one progresses from the past via the present to the future.[48]

In this process, various aspects of tact (including those related to theories of practice, psychology and of tact itself) can play a role in training.[49] These aspects include the mediation of theory and practice and the evaluation and decision of the educator; they also include insights into the emotional states of children, into child-oriented, curricular and instructional "structurings" of time, capacities for sensual awareness, and a capacity for sensing subjective perceptions of time. According to Herbart, it is decisive that the pedagogical practitioner not only prepare the objects or content of their mediating activity, but that above all that they prepare themselves, so that in their guidance of student exercises and their reflection on pedagogical practice, tact can develop as a "a coping-mechanism for their professional practice."[50] In this context, it makes sense to speak of pedagogical tact as theorizing practice *and* practicing theory.[51]

According to Herbart, pedagogical tact forms a mediating figure insofar as it establishes a connection between theory and practice. Anyone who wants to do justice to the individual or the singular pedagogical situation must not apply rules and norms of theory without reflection but must instead apply them in practice on a case-by-case basis. Pedagogical tact mediates theory and practice in the form of a quick assessment and decision and in a form that is not only cognitive but above all (unconsciously) sensitive.

> *Takt*, which encompasses the idea of tact, tactfulness and tacit knowing, is an innate ability that can at the same time be polished and refined into a skill. Moreover, in the sense that it functions as an instinct or intuition on the borderline between consciousness and the unconscious, it is neither purely rational nor is it purely affective.[52]

The Determining Moments of Pedagogical Tact are Principles of Relation

If one were to summarize the definitions, frameworks and contexts of the relevant pedagogical discussion of tact, the following characteristics—connected to the pedagogical relationship of the educator to the one being educated—would emerge:

- *Sensitivity, empathy*: a feeling for each other's individuality and rights;
- *Compassion, taking on others' perspectives*: to put oneself in the shoes of others; to think from others' perspectives; to expect and take into account expectations of others;
- *Restraint*: "with the negative idea of not giving out"[53] especially in relation to (physical) violence; limiting oneself for the sake of the other; self-control;
- *Consideration*: regard for the individual; or rather, forbearance;
- *Veneration*: "to excuse an inappropriate expression. Then especially reverent, fearful timidity;"[54]
- *Appropriateness*: "to contain the quality of the concept, no more, no less, than the object requires;"[55] balanced acting and reacting;
- *Comprehensive attention*: mobile (free-floating) perception, contextual awareness, focusing;
- *Con-Tact*: Taking up relation; striking a balance between proximity and distance;
- *Speed of grasping the situation*; speed of judgement;
- *Balanced weighing of paradoxes and contradictions* (see below): dissolving, accepting or dealing with them;
- *Improvisational skill, creativity*: playful moments, ease of action, happy coincidence;
- *Freedom or openness for the unpredictable*: Granting free space to those being educated; openness for variability.
- *Observance of developmental and temporal structures*;
- *Forms of the expression of pedagogical tact can be considered, according to Muth, as follows*:
    i. Language: communication, contact, understanding, commitment;
    ii. Action: naturalness; absence of artificiality and bias, authenticity; feeling of security;
    iii. The avoidance of injury to the child: In (family, school) life, in the classroom, in teaching methods; non-stigmatizing;

iv. Maintaining distance: no violation of privacy;
v. Successful handling of contingencies: disturbances, mistakes and that which is unpredictable;
vi. Performative competence: appropriate self-presentation.
vii. And finally it can be stated that on the part of pedagogy, it is not clear whether pedagogical tact is a theoretical object-construct, or whether is a form of knowledge, of action, a type of competence or a psychological construct.

Pedagogical Tact is Engagement with Pedagogical Aporia

In contrast to the traditional discourses surrounding pedagogical tact, this document seeks to develop an understanding of pedagogical tact which allows it to be recognized as dealing with its own intangibility or inaccessibility.[56] One can understand tact, following Derrida, in this sense as a relationship to a unique situation or to the singularity of the other in their irrepresentability and intangibility.[57] Moreover, if one further assumes at the same time that there *is no* socio-ethical and/or pedagogical model for dealing with the other in this situation, neither as a principle nor as a criterion, neither as an ideal nor as a regulative idea, then tact can be said to mark an aporia: One must act in a situation in which there is no prescription for action. But doesn't it amount exactly to this? What if the pedagogical process does not "go" specifically as it should—i.e. in such a way that one, for the sake of another, can, indeed *must*, detach oneself from particular normative positions?

One could say that in pedagogy, tact denotes (successful) engagement with that which is paradoxical and also intangible. Such an approach addresses a variety of dimensions:

- Tact does not arise as a result of us willing it; it cannot be planned but requires an unpredictable situation in which it can show itself.
- Tact depends on the (intangible, unconscious) reactions of the other as well as on one's own (inscrutable, unconscious) reactions.
- Tact occurs because educational reasoning can never be comprehensive given that it never includes all the factors and criteria that are significant for practice. Pedagogical tact is creative tact in relation to the creative life as a whole.
- The form of adequacy proper to tact is the measure of an appropriate (or just) contact with the other, without this appropriateness being fixed in any form.

In contrast to Heinz-Jürgen Ipfling,[58] for example, who understands tact as a kind of sensitive, regulative measure that is capable of dissolving aporias (such as the aporia of theory and practice), tact can be understood as precisely that which keeps these paradoxes and aporia alive, that sustains them and keeps them going. Thus, for example, in tactful thinking and acting it becomes more or less clear to us that a just and appropriate decision implies the necessity of a pedagogical rule that will have to be overridden in relation to the singularity of the other.[59] Educators must therefore proceed from fundamental undecidability. One has to decide (pedagogically) in a situation that represents the impossibility of such a just decision.[60] Only where one can assume a radical undecidability can one do justice to the uniqueness of the other, otherwise we would merely follow the requirements of a law, a norm or a rule which must necessarily fails the other's singularity.

> On the other hand, Plessner speaks of the paradox of a safe tact that knows how to deal with each person in an individual way and to find its way in the dark, so to speak. [...] Tact is the capacity to perceive imponderable differences, the capacity to comprehend that untranslatable language of appearances.[61]

For Plessner, tact is security in the dark, the perception of the imponderable, the comprehension of the untranslatable. But isn't tact also—and perhaps even more—the darkness within one's sense of security, the imponderable within perception, the untranslatable within comprehension, the "irregularity within static regularity"?[62] Tact itself forms a paradoxical figure of engagement, since it implies moments of contingency and intangibility as well as necessities, rules and structures of meaning.

In pedagogical discussions, one's engagement with the aporias, ambivalences and paradoxes proper to modernity are a familiar theme. In particular, the following tension(s) and contradictions in pedagogical practice should be kept in mind (some of which have already been discussed): the gap between theory and practice, education for autonomy within heteronomy, leading or letting grow (of the one to be educated),[63] transmission *and* innovation (of contents, methods and attitudes), the promotion of personality *and* collectivity, the tension between general norms and individual people and situations, between guidelines requiring both selectivity *and* support, demands for proximity *and* distance (of the educator), doing justice to both the individual *and* society, standardization *and* individualization (of pedagogical and instructional efforts), evaluation based on factual, personal *or* broader social norms, and similarly, the factual, personal or goal-related appropriateness of basic teaching principles. And finally, one must keep in mind the tension between independence as both a *prerequisite* and a *goal* of pedagogy.[64]

In professional engagement with these dilemmas and paradoxes, there are various strategies that work with models of mediation, compensation, balance and oscillation. Pedagogical tact is the name for the fact that even under conditions of effective equivalence, a given working sequence, a cyclical type of reflection, a counterfactual testing, even a suspension of the mediation of differing points of view—none of these things nullify the basic contradictions underlying the paradoxes outlined above. Instead, these contradictions are preserved in and through practice. Pedagogical professionalism can be understood as the subjective ability and willingness to tactfully balance pedagogical paradoxes—"to endure the uncertainty of engagement, to reflect again and again on the implications for action in uncertainty and to assume responsibility for action on the basis of one's own abilities."[65]

Proper to pedagogical tact are both indeterminacy and indeterminability, since it is difficult to determine which action is appropriate and professionally correct in every specific case. If pedagogy is obliged to do justice to the singularity of the other under the conditions of the impossibility of a programmatic tactfulness, then all that tact turns out to be is a (pedagogical) attitude of openness towards the irreducibility of the other—or more precisely, towards that which this irreducibility owes itself. Tact can win this openness through "free-floating attention" in Freud's sense.[66] The experience of the singularity of the other exists only in the experience of an aporia. The recognition of aporia means being able to respond in any way at all to the singular other—in which any answer must be so open that it does not endanger their development or pedagogical support. In pedagogically tactful thinking and acting we become aware that acting appropriately in relation to another takes the form of the impossible possibility of encountering the singular. In pedagogical tact, one takes responsibility for or answers to the relationship with another and to oneself, i.e. for something for which one cannot actually answer to or be responsible for. For tact creates the intangible grounds on which an action is based, a grounding that is not given in the situation that requires tact in the first place.

Pedagogical tact is resonance with the openness, dynamics, variability and unfathomability of the other; to put it more lyrically: tact is the response to the riddle of the other. However, pedagogical tact is not the solution to the riddle, but merely an educational response in which a specific responsibility for the protection and promotion of the other and of oneself is expressed.

Additional Sources

Blochmann, E. (1950). Der pädagogische Takt. *Die Sammlung: Zeitung für Kultur und Erziehung* 5, 712–720.
Bourdieu, P. (1990). *The logic of Practice: Critique of the theoretical reason.* Palo Alto: Stanford University Press.
Luhmann, N. (2004). *Law as a social system.* Oxford: Oxford University Press.
Müssener, B. (1977). Begriff und Funktion des pädagogischen Taktes in Herbarts System der Pädagogik *Zeitschrift für Pädagogik. 14th supplement,* 259–269.
Zirfas, J. (2001). „Dem anderen gerecht werden. Das Performative und die Dekonstruktion bei Jacques Derrida." In: C. Wulf, M. Göhlich, & J. Zirfas (Ed.), *Grundlagen des Performativen. Eine Einführung in die Zusammenhänge von Sprache, Macht und Handeln* (pp. 75–100). Weinheim/ München: Juventa.

Notes

1. Burghardt, D., & Zirfas, J. (2019). *Der pädagogische Takt. Eine erziehungswissenschaftliche Problemformel.* Beltz Juventa; Gödde, G., & Zirfas, J. (2012). *Takt und Taktlosigkeit: Über Ordnungen und Unordnungen in Kunst, Kultur und Therapie.* Transcript.
2. Translated by N. Friesen. Originally: Zirfas, J. (2015). Pädagogischer Takt: Zehn Thesen. In: G. Gödde, & J. Zirfas (Eds.), *Takt und Taktlosigkeit: Über Ordnungen und Unordnungen in Kunst, Kultur und Therapie.* Transcript.
3. Tact is thus *not* seen as a kind of formation (*Bildung*) undertaken by and for the self towards a general tactfulness.
4. "Modern" here does not equate to "contemporary," but instead refers to the post-medieval and more specifically the post-revolutionary age (i.e. in terms of the French and American revolutions). [Trans.]
5. Voltaire is believed to have been the first to use tact to describe a broad sensitivity or sensibility: "The man of taste has other eyes, other ears, and another tact from the uncultivated man." (*"L'homme de goût a d'autres yeux, d'autres oreilles, un autre tact que l'homme grossier."* Voltaire, 1764/1879, p. 172. Trans.)
6. Blochmann, E. (1951). Die Sitte und der pädagogische Takt. *Die Sammlung: Zeitung für Kultur und Erziehung 6,* 590.
7. Enlightenment education refers to the educational thought of figures such as Immanuel Kant and John Locke. It is also influenced by others such as Francis Bacon, Gottfried Wilhelm Leibnitz and Voltaire himself. [Trans.].
8. Adorno, T. (1984). *Minima moralia: Reflections from a damaged life.* Verso. p. 36, with minor revisions.
9. See Herrmann, U. (1981): *"Das pädagogische Jahrhundert." Volksaufklärung und Erziehung zur Armut im 18. Jahrhundert.* Beltz.
10. Erasmus. (1530/2008). *A handbook on good manners for children.* Preface.

11 Norbert Elias is a German/British sociologist who wrote historical studies of the "civilizing process" in the West; e.g. Elias, N. (1978). *The history of manners: The civilizing process Vol. 1*. Pantheon. [Trans.]
12 Elias, N. (1978). *The history of manners*, pp. 53–59.
13 Elias, N. (1978). *The history of manners*, pp. 70–89.
14 See: Felderer, B., & Macho, T. (2002). *Höflichkeit: Aktualität und Genese von Umgangsformen*. Wilhelm Fink.
15 See Chapter Two in this volume. [Trans.]
16 Herbart, Introductory Lecture (Chapter Two), p. 32.
17 Rousseau, J.-J. (1762/1979). *Emile, or on education*. Norton.
18 Moritz Lazarus was an early German psychologist who developed a "psychology of the people" (*Völkerpsychologie*) on the basis of Herbart's work [Trans].
19 In addition, three further elements of tact are mentioned by Ofenbach: "a comprehensive perception, a subtle balancing of manifold and conflicting relationships, and a creative (or artistic) application in life." Ofenbach, B. (1988). "Wenn das Allgemeine praktisch wird …" *Pädagogische Rundschau 42*, p. 574.
20 Gadamer, H.-G. (2004). *Truth and method 2nd ed*. Continuum, especially pp. 5–15.
21 As noted elsewhere in this volume, the tradition of Herbart is strongly associated with careful instructional and lesson planning [Trans.].
22 Ipfling, H-J. (1973). Über den Takt im pädagogischen Bezug. In N. Kluge (Ed.), *Das pädagogische Verhältnis* (pp. 378–394). Wissenschaftliche Buchgesellschaft, p. 391.
23 Treml, A. K. (2000). Pädagogischer Takt. In: A. K. Treml (Ed.), *Allgemeine Pädagogik. Grundlagen, Handlungsfelder und Perspektiven der Erziehung* (pp. 201–206), Kohlhammer, p. 204.
24 Neo-humanism refers to a German cultural and intellectual movement in the last half of the 18th century. It sought to continue Renaissance humanism, linking ideals of Antiquity to a humanistic idea of knowledge under the aegis of *Bildung*. *Bildung* was understood in this context as the intellectual, physical and moral formation of the individual and humanity as a whole [Trans.].
25 Anthropology here refers to the philosophical study (-logy) of "human nature," or more broadly, of "what it means to be human" (anthropo-) [Trans.].
26 The individual is ineffable. This is a thought that can be traced back to Greek antiquity, including in the writings of Plato and Aristotle [Trans.].
27 Schleiermacher, F. D. E. (1981). *Brouillon zur Ethik*. Felix Meiner, p. 147.
28 *Bildung* refers to refers to one's overall individual, biographical development, and especially one's own active, reflective engagement in this development. [Trans.]
29 Plessner, H. (1924). Die Logik der Diplomatie. Die Hygiene des Taktes. In H. Plessner. *Grenzen der Gemeinschaft 2nd Ed*. (pp. 87–102). Bouvier, p. 107.
30 Adorno, *Minima Moralia*, p. 38.
31 As quoted in Chapter Nine, Kant asks: "How do I cultivate freedom under constraint? …For constraint is necessary." Kant, I. (1803/2007). Lectures on pedagogy. In G. Zöller, & R.B. Louden (Eds.), *Anthropology, history and education*. Cambridge University Press, p. 447. [Trans.]
32 Kant stated this as follows: "Act in such a way that you treat humanity, whether in your own person or in the person of another, always at the same time as an end and never simply as a means" another, always at the same time as an end and never simply as a means." Kant, I. (1996). *Groundwork of the metaphysics of morals in Immanuel Kant: Practical Philosophy*. Cambridge: Cambridge University Press. [Trans.]

33 Kant, (1803/2007). Lectures on Pedagogy, p. 447.
34 "the ground of knowledge; something through or by means of which a thing is known" (Merriam-Webster) [Trans.]
35 Benner, D. (1991). *Allgemeine Pädagogik: Eine systematisch-problemgeschichtliche Einführung in die Grundstruktur pädagogischen Denkens und Handelns* (2nd ed.) Juventa.
36 Parmentier, M. (1991). "Self-activity, pedagogical rhythm and relative autonomy." *Vierteljahrsschrift für wissenschaftliche Pädagogik 67*, p. 130.
37 Insofar as the teacher's purpose is to have the child become capable of self-determination, the teacher's work is effectively to make *their own* determinations unnecessary for the child. The teacher's task is in this sense to make themselves superfluous, to dissolve the relationship as one that is specifically *pedagogical*. See also Chapter Five [Trans.].
38 Nohl, H. (1962). *Schuld und Aufgabe der Pädagogik*. Karl Hofmann, p. 33.
39 From: Chapter Six, p. 92; See also Merleau Ponty, M. (1973). *The prose of the world*. Northwestern University Press, p. 19: "If I have any tact, my words are both a means of action and feeling; there are eyes at the tips of my fingers."
40 Plessner, H. (1924). Die Logik der Diplomatie, p. 99.
41 Luhmannn, N. (1987). *Rechtssoziologie. 3. Ed.* Leske & Budrich, p. 34; see also: Goffman. E. (1982). *Interaction ritual: Essays on face-to-face behavior*. Pantheon.
42 Plessner, H. (1924). Die Logik der Diplomatie, p. 102.
43 From: Chapter Six, p. 89.
44 Suzuki, S. (2010). *Takt in Modern Education*. Waxmann, p. 167. Suzuki uses the German spelling and capitalization of the word "tact" in this text [Trans.]
45 *Poesis* refers to a "bringing into being" or a "bringing forth" of something that is new, that did not exist before. *Art* here and below refers back to its origin in the Greek word *techne*: a practical knowing and doing that is variable and context-dependent and that involves craft and technique. [Trans.]
46 See: Sünkel, Wolfgang (1998). "Takt." In: Ritter, J. *Historisches Worterbuch der Philosophie* (pp. 882–883). Wissenschaftliche Buchgesellschaft.
47 From: Chapter Two, p. 33.
48 Suzuki, S. (2008). Takt als Medium: Überlegungen zum Takt-Begriff von J. F. Herbart. *Paragrana. Internationale Zeitschrift für Historische Anthropologie*, 17, pp. 156, 161.
49 Suzuki 2008, Takt als Medium, p. 152.
50 Dewe, B. (1996). Das Professionswissen von Weiterbilden: Klientenbezug – Fachbezug. In: A. Combe, & W. Helsper (Eds.), *Pädagogische Professionalität: Untersuchungen zum Typus pädagogischen Handelns* (pp. 714–757). Suhrkamp, p. 735.
51 If one compares the training model suggested by Herbart with Pierre Bourdieu, it becomes clear that Bourdieu expressed skepticism regarding any formal education for successful practice, and that he understood any academic implementation of rules rather as a compromise of the pedagogical art of practice (Bourdieu 1997: 188ff). I owe this insight to Astrid Baltruschat.
52 Suzuki S. (2010). *Takt in modern education*, p. 169.
53 This characterization comes from the etymology of the German verb for restraint, *zurückhalten*. It and all other definitions attributed to Grimm and Grimm 2006 come from this same etymological reference source. See: http://dwb.uni-trier.de/de/ [Trans.]
54 Grimm & Grimm 2006.
55 Grimm & Grimm 2006.

56 The original German term here is *Unverfügbarkeit*, which strongly suggests something that is not capable of being placed at one's disposal for use and manipulation. [Trans.]
57 Derrida asks questions in this text such as the following: "How are we to reconcile the act of justice that must always concern singularity, individuals, irreplaceable groups and lives, the other or myself as other, in a unique situation, with rule, norm, value or the imperative of justice which necessarily have a general form, even if this generality prescribes a singular application in each case?" [Trans.] Derrida, J. (1992). Force of law: The "mystical foundation of authority." In M. Rosenfeld & D. Cornell (Eds.), *Deconstruction and the possibility of justice*. Routledge, pp. 17–18.
58 Ipfling, H-J. (1973). Über den Takt im pädagogischen Bezug, p. 387.
59 Derrida, J. (2018). *Before the law: The complete text of Préjugés*. University of Minnesota Press, p. 18.
60 Derrida, J. (1992). Force of law, pp. 24–26.
61 Plessner, H. (1924). Die Logik der Diplomatie, p. 95.
62 From Chapter Six, p. 92. Muth vacillates in his assessment of the contingency of tact, insofar as he understands tact as freedom or exception to the rule, but also as the amplification or distortion of the rule. This ambivalence can be seen, among other places, in the four manifestations of tact identified by Muth: Two of these emphasize one's certainty and dramaturgical ability in indeterminate situations—rather than coping with contingencies—while the other two emphasize a capacity for improvisation and above all the risk that inheres in "free forms" of pedagogical engagement—rather than the moments of intangibility and inaccessibility associated with tact.
63 "Leading and Letting Grow: a consideration of a fundamental pedagogical problem" is the title of a famous 1965 study by German pedagogue Theodor Litt (Ernst Klett Verlag). See also Bollnow's opposition of these terms in Chapter Eight, p. 140. [Trans.]
64 See: Wimmer, M. (2006). *Dekonstruktion und Erziehung: Studien zum Paradoxieproblem in der Pädagogik*. Bielefed: Transcript; Bräu, K. (2008). Die Betreuung selbstständigen Lernens—vom Umgang mit Antinomien und Dilemmata. In: Breidenstein, D., & Schütze, F. (Ed.), *Paradoxien in der Reform der Schule: Ergebnisse qualitativer Sozialforschung* (pp. 1791–1799). Wiesbaden: VS Verlag.
65 Rabe-Kleherg, U. (1996). Professionalität und Geschlechterverhältnis. Oder: Was ist "semi" an traditionellen Frauenberufen? in: Combe, A. & Helsper, W. (Eds.), *Pädagogische Professionalität: Untersuchungen zum Typus pädagogischen Handelns* (pp. 276–302). Suhrkamp, p. 295.
66 Freud describes this attention as necessary on the part of the analyst, saying that in it, one "listens and does not care whether one remembers something." Freud, S. (1912). *Ratschläge für den Arzt bei der psychoanalytischen Behandlung. Studienausgabe, Ergänzungsband*. Fischer. [Trans.] See also: Gödde, G., & Zirfas, J. (2007). Von der Muße zur "gleichschwebenden Aufmerksamkeit"—Therapeutische Erfahrungen zwischen Gelassenheit und Engagement. *Psychologik. Jahrbuch für Psychotherapie, Philosophie und Kultur, 2*, 135–153.

Index

Adorno, T. 179, 183, 193f.
alien (also: alienness, foreignness, alterity) 2, 6, 138, 154–155, 156–172, 177
alienation, from nature 120
    education as 162
    Bildung and 152, 163–164, 165
anthropology (as the study of the human, philosophical anthropology) 123 passim 128–129, 132
    defined 194 (n25)
aporia (*see also*: paradox, riddle) 190–192
art (pedagogical practice as; *see also* science) 9, 26, 27, 28–31, 33–34, 36(n10), 45, 46–50, 57(n11, 12), 81, 128, 176, 187–188, 195(n45, 51)
authenticity 87, 101, 190
    of speech 95–98, 110(n 25)
autonomy
    of pedagogy as discipline 45, 62, 64, 65
    individual, as pedagogical goal 26, 128, 163, 179, 184, 191

Bernfeld, S. 169–170
Bildsamkeit (also: educatability, plasticity) 35, 110(n21–23), 123 (passim) 140, 152(n4)
    defined 36–37(n15)
Bildung (also: formation, self-cultivation) 8, 34, 57(n14, definition), 79, 81, 84(n11, definition), 93–94, 125–126, 162–169
    formative community 76–78, 82
Blochmann, E. 85–86, 88, 92, 109(n5, 6), 193(n6)
Bollnow, O.F. 5–6, 112(n41), 137–139, 139–152(passim)
Buber, M. 102, 104

civilization (also: civilizing process, civility) 127–128, 159–160, 180, 182–184 passim

Derrida, J. 190, 196(n57)
Dewey, J. 16, 42, 153

dialectics
  of Schleiermacher 40
  of *Bildung* 162–163, 173(n 13)
  of master-servant 163, 173(n 15)
  and negativity 186–187
didactics (i.e. instruction, *Didaktik*) 45, 90 (n7, 9), 159, 165
didactic triangle 101, 109, 111(n40)
dignity
  of education 32, 139
  of pedagogy/practice 3, 42–43, 48, 50
  human 51, 122, 135, 140
Dilthey, W. vi, 65, 73(n 10), 79, 84(n 10)

educatability, (*see*: *Bildsamkeit*)
Elias, N. 159–160, 173(n12), 180, 194(n11)
Enlightenment 39, 56(n2), 138(n6), 179, 183, 193(n7)
ethics (and pedagogy) 8, 10, 35, 48–53, 67, 68, 78, 143, 166, 167
existentialism 5, 112(n41), 118, 130, 131–132, 137, 141

failure (in pedagogy) 27, 31, 32–33, 72, 98, 106–107, 138, 139–141, 142–148, 154, 191
fascism (*see*: Nazism)
Fink, E. 5, 8, 117–119, 119–136(passim)
freedom (of the one being educated) 5, 33, 81, 123, 128–129, 131, 135, 137, 138, 140–141, 166–167, 173–174(n 23), 177, 183–184, 185
Freud, S. 66–67, 69, 72(n 9), 73(n 18), 192, 196(n66)

Gadamer, H.G. 166, 181, 187
Geist (i.e. spirit) 46, 56(n8), 62, 67
generations (pedagogy as occurring between) 4, 7, 8, 41–42, 46–50, 57(n13), 62, 77–78, 106, 121, 132–133, 154, 157, 169, 171–172, 177

Hegel, G.W. 82, 163, 164, 167, 172(n15), 174(n24)

Heidegger, M. 117, 118, 136(n8), 137
Herbart, J.F. 2, 3–4, 6, 9, 10(n6), 25–27, 28–37(passim), 39, 42–43, 67–68, 80, 86, 90, 91, 93–94, 110(n21), 138, 175, 176, 181–182, 194(n21), 195(n51)
Herbartianism/Herbartians 96, 101, 111(n28), 112(n45), 194(n21)
hermeneutics 39, 57(n 12), 166
human science pedagogy (*geisteswissenschaftliche Pädagogik*) 154, 166–169, 173(n20)
Humboldt W. von 39, 158, 162, 166
Husserl, E. 117, 118, 154

influence, influencing (*see*: pedagogical influence)
instrumentalization (pedagogy as) 117, 122–124, 125–127, 168, 183–184

Kant, I. 25, 39, 56(n2), 82–83, 136(n6), 166–167, 168, 173(n23), 177, 182–184, 194(n31, 32)

Langeveld, M. 104, 154, 155, 166, 168, 169, 170
Levinas, E. 154, 171, 172
Lippitz, W. 6, 138–139, 153–155, 155–174(passim), 175, 177
love (pedagogical) 17, 21, 22, 30, 33, 66–68, 76, 79–83, 84(n19), 112(n 44), 121, 133

maturity (also: immaturity, *[Un]Mündigkeit*) 4, 39, 76, 78–80, 84(n 8), 94, 128, 135, 135(n 6), 138, 178, 184
metaphysics 129–130, 131, 159, 163, 167
Mollenhauer, K. 8, 16, 72(n4), 109(n1)
morality (*see*: ethics)
Muth, J. 5, 6, 27, 64, 76, 85–87, 88–113, 152(n9), 154, 175, 185–186, 189–190, 196(n62)

Nazism (also: National Socialism, fascism, Hitler) 4, 63–64, 85, 86, 88, 117, 118, 137–138, 153

Nohl, H. 2–3, 4–5, 7, 8, 42, 43, 62–64, 65–73, 75–76, 77–84, 87, 108, 109(n5), 112(n50), 137–138, 154, 173(n20), 177

other, otherness (*see*: alien)
ownness (*see*: alien)

paradox (*see also*: aporia, riddle) 30, 92, 121, 132, 167, 168, 177, 183–184, 185–187, 189, 190–192
parents (role in pedagogy) 3, 8, 9, 16, 30, 36(n12), 41–42, 44, 62, 127, 130, 157, 171–172, 176
pedagogical influence 4, 5, 7–9, 10(n7), 41–43, 47–54, 57(n13), 78, 82, 83(n4, 7, 9), 86, 89, 92, 127, 134, 167, 178
pedagogy (*Pädagogik*)
 defined 7–10, 10(n7), 178
 as art 9, 26, 27, 28–31, 33–34, 36(n10), 45, 46–50, 57(n11, 12), 81, 128, 176, 187–188, 195(n45, 51)
 as science (*Wissenschaft*) 9, 26–27, 28–30, 32–35(passim), 36(n9), 45, 49, 56(n10)
 as an autonomous discipline 45, 62, 64, 65
phenomenology 86–87, 89, 109(n11)
Plato (also Platonism) 45, 47, 71, 129–130, 131, 135, 194(n26)
Plessner, H. 183, 186, 191
poetry, poetic 30, 78, 79, 100, 141, 150, 180
politics, the political, political studies 7, 10(n7), 45, 49, 62, 63, 65, 81, 123, 134–135, 178
psychoanalysis (*see also*: Freud) 67–72, 72(n9), 73(n13), 169–170, 196(n66)
psychology 22, 23(n8), 27, 35, 37(n16), 63, 73(n20), 140, 166, 169–170, 194(n18), 196(66n)

rationality, rationalism 67, 89, 127, 129, 159, 167, 176, 181, 187
reason 22, 31, 32, 33, 34

recognition 80, 95, 96, 151, 163, 173(n15), 174(n24), 183
reform, educational 15, 16, 25, 31–32, 65, 73(n10), 85, 101, 134, 162, 185
riddle (*see also*: aporia, paradox) 17, 129, 177–178, 192
Romanticism 39–40, 182
Rousseau, J.J. 16, 34, 66, 103, 127, 128, 181, 182

Schleiermacher, F.D.E. 3–4, 7, 25, 39–43, 44–57, 62, 78, 81, 82, 83(n4), 84(n7, 9, 20), 154, 166, 177
science (*Wissenschaft*) 56(n10) 119, 154, 176, 188
 human 154, 166–169, 173(n20)
 natural 23(n8), 67, 120, 122, 125, 128, 142
 in relation to art (practice) 9, 26–27, 28–30, 32–35(passim), 36(n9), 45, 49, 56(n10)
subjectivity 16–17, 65, 67, 68, 125, 136, 164, 176, 177, 182, 188, 192

temporality (of pedagogy, of tact) 32, 50–6, 49, 76, 80, 91, 131, 133, 171–172, 176, 177, 181, 188, 189
theory (in pedagogy) 3–4, 6, 9, 26–27, 31–32, 37(n15), 41–43, 44–50, 56(n6), 57(n12), 86, 176, 177, 181, 182, 188, 191
tone 91, 96, 105, 150
totality (also: totalizing) 131, 159, 164–165
touch (sense of) 17, 91, 107, 135
triangle, didactic 101, 198(figure 6.1), 111(n40)

violence 68, 127, 164–165, 179, 185, 189
Voltaire 90, 179, 193(n5)

Waldenfels, B. 154, 172(n5)

Zirfas, J. 6–7, 10(n7), 17, 27, 139, 175–178, 178–196

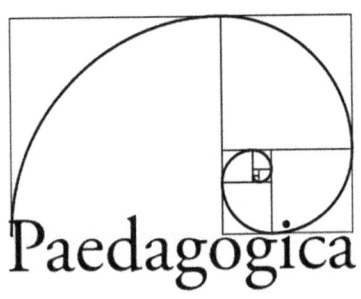

Norm Friesen and Karsten Kenklies
General Editors

Paedagogica publishes original monographs, translations, and collections reflecting the thought and practice long known, for example, as *le pédagogie* in French, *pedagogía* in Spanish, and *Pädagogik* in German. Pedagogy in this sense starts with the influence of one person or group on another—often an older generation on a younger. Pedagogy is not just about school or college, but interpenetrates many spheres of human activity, forming a domain of practice and study in its own right—one that is ethical in its implications and relational in its substance. This pedagogical tradition has been developed over hundreds of years, for example, by John Amos Comenius (Komenský), Jean-Jacques Rousseau, Johann Friedrich Herbart, Maria Montessori, and Janusz Korczak.

For additional information about this series or for the submission of manuscripts, please contact:

> NormFriesen@boisestate.edu or
> Karsten.Kenklies@strath.ac.uk

To order books, please contact our Customer Service Department:

> peterlang@presswarehouse.com (within the U.S.)
> orders@peterlang.com (outside the U.S.)

Or browse online by series:

> www.peterlang.com

www.ingramcontent.com/pod-product-compliance
Lightning Source LLC
Chambersburg PA
CBHW061714300426
44115CB00014B/2678